Dear Sally

Pleasure meeting you.

Warm regards

27 Nov 18

BE A LION

Dare to dream and live fearlessly

Rakesh Wahi

PENGUIN BOOKS

Published by Penguin Books
an imprint of Penguin Random House South Africa (Pty) Ltd
Reg. No. 1953/000441/07
The Estuaries No. 4, Oxbow Crescent, Century Avenue, Century City, 7441
PO Box 1144, Cape Town, 8000, South Africa
www.penguinrandomhouse.co.za

Penguin
Random House
South Africa

First published 2016

1 3 5 7 9 10 8 6 4 2

Publication © Penguin Random House 2016
Text © Rakesh Wahi 2016

Cover photograph by Motlabana Monnakgotla

PUBLISHER: Marlene Fryer
MANAGING EDITOR: Bronwen Maynier
COVER AND TEXT DESIGN: Ryan Africa
PROOFREADER: Dane Wallace

Set in 11.5 pt on 16 pt Adobe Caslon

Printed by Emirates Printing Press LLC, Dubai

ISBN 978 1 7760 9136 2 (print)
ISBN 978 1 7760 9175 1 (ePub)
ISBN 978 1 7760 9176 8 (PDF)

DEDICATION

I dedicate this book to the three most important people in my life; without their love and support, I would not be where I am today.

The first two are my parents, Satya Pal and Shobhana Wahi, both of whom, from the time I was born until this day, have given me nothing but unconditional love and boundless support; I owe them the gift of life. They gave me my identity and my courage, and ingrained in me a value system to stay on the right path. Above all, they taught me the importance of being kind and thoughtful towards others.

The third is my wife, Saloni. We have been married for 31 years and she is my best friend, my greatest strength and my North Star. She embraced my dreams as her own and sacrificed endlessly, so that I could relentlessly pursue them. She has been with me through life's tumultuous journey, weathering each storm with a smile and nudging me forward, contributing silently and seeking no recognition.

CONTENTS

ABBREVIATIONS

ABN: Africa Business News
BEE: black economic empowerment
CCMA: Commission for Conciliation, Mediation and Arbitration
CDC: Communications Development Corporation
CEA: Communications Equity Associates
CMA: Capital Management Advisors Limited
CME: College of Military Engineering
GCC: Gulf Cooperation Council
GEDA: Gauteng Economic Development Agency
GFC: Gauteng Film Commission
GFH: Gulf Finance House
GPG: Gauteng Provincial Government
ICASA: Independent Communications Authority of South Africa
IDC: Industrial Development Corporation
JSE: Johannesburg Stock Exchange
MIS: management information system
NDA: National Defence Academy
NSE: Nigerian Stock Exchange
SMEs: small and medium-sized enterprises
TMT: technology, media and telecommunications
TNE: Trans National Education Limited
UAE: United Arab Emirates
YLP: Young Leaders Programme

PREFACE

No matter your age, one of the most enlightening journeys of self-realisation in life begins inadvertently when visiting the zoo. As you reach the information desk to ask for directions, even as you enquire about the enclosures that house the most exotic animals and birds, there is an unconscious impulse at work. There are certain animals that you feel you must see. Some find the magnificence of the elephant absolutely enchanting; others are drawn to the aura of the rhino, the complexity of the hippo, the agility of the cheetah, or even the simplicity of the *chinkara* deer.

For me the animal that always stood out was the undisputed king of the jungle: the lion.

From my early childhood, the enclosure that I was most impatient to get to was the lion's den. Nothing changed as I grew up. Through visits to zoos around the world – from Delhi, Kuala Lumpur, Singapore and Dubai to London, Zurich, Prague and Johannesburg – my fascination and respect for this beast remained unwavering. I would stand for hours watching the alpha male laze in the sun, oblivious to everything around him.

What fascinates me most is that this animal is so revered and feared, yet he is seldom seen at the forefront when the pride hunts. Whether it is the protocol within the pride; the ability to merely watch the pack hunt and then demand the privilege of being the first to share in the spoils; or, above all, the dignity that allows him to choose his battles, all animals recognise his place in the food chain, making the lion an undisputed leader.

This aura imparts great responsibility: to protect his family, procreate and continue his bloodline. There is an unconscious desire for immortality that spurs the lion on.

My fascination with the lion is not unique. Lions have been revered for as long as humankind has existed. From the Sphinx in Egypt, the Nemean lion in ancient Greece and Rome, Narasimha in India and Simha in Sri Lanka to the historic lion dance in China, irrespective of culture, there is a very deep respect for the royal qualities that the lion embodies. Singapore derives its name from the animal, and famous leaders, like Richard the Lionheart, consciously identify with this awe-inspiring creature.

So where does this innate recognition of supremacy come from? If you extrapolate this discussion from the animal kingdom into the context of leadership among humans, there are some compelling lessons.

Our imperative to lead and to inspire others through leadership is the manifestation of a DNA that compels each one of us to look into an invisible mirror every day. This mirror reflects not only who we are, but also who we want to be. It is a desire to be the king of our own jungle. To be fearless; to protect that with which we are entrusted; to build something that will stand the test of time. This genetic predisposition to pass on that of which we are proud, to ensure a succession of strong, resilient leaders who will give their lives to protect the honour and legacy of what we set out to establish, this is the credo of the leader. From one *simha* to another passes the mantle of succession and a legacy of immortality.

The inspiration for this book came in 2012 when I visited the Johannesburg Zoo with my wife, Saloni. We did the usual pilgrimage to the lion's enclosure, and as Saloni and I stood there and talked about our journey together, something told me that I had found the central theme for the story that I have always wanted to tell. A story that began in the Indian Armed Forces in June 1976, when I joined the National Defence Academy (NDA), in Khadakwasla, and continued on the battlefields of the corporate world after I left the army in September 1988.

I was commissioned into the Corps of Engineers (Bombay Sappers) in June 1980 and served with 113 Engineers, which was then a part of the 12th Infantry Division, and later with 114 Armoured Engineers, supporting the 1st Armoured Division. In 1984, I completed an engineering degree at the College of Military Engineering (CME) in Pune. In 1986, I was decorated by the president of India with the Vishisht Seva Medal; I was perhaps one of the youngest soldiers to receive this decoration in peacetime. I went to the Antarctic in 1987 as part of India's 7th Scientific Expedition. In September 1988, I finally decided to hang up my boots and took early retirement from the army. Perhaps the greatest lessons I learnt came to me from there: lessons that no textbook can teach and which I will enumerate throughout this book. The most important one was that caring for people, and fearlessly protecting them, is at the core of our existence. No battle can be won without the involvement, loyalty and commitment of the very people we are called upon to lead.

These lessons are no different from what a young lion learns as he grows up and leaves the pack as a young adult to form and lead his own pride and create his own legacy.

Perhaps this journey of self-actualisation revolved around defining at every step what I wanted to stand for and what was important to me. Throughout this period, my father's reminder that there is no absolute truth in this world constantly reverberated in my head. This has a deeper meaning than I realised at the time. It means there is always another point of view, making everything in life open to interpretation, and we have to fight against justifications that favour what does not seem right.

The lionhearted will always live by an honourable code of conduct no matter how difficult it may be. This code rests on the basic values of consistency, continuity and honour. These qualities, in the long term, build credibility and trust: two words that sound simple, but that become the stamp of your existence. People must know how you will react, both within the value system to which you conform, as well as when your values are breached. Trust is not triggered by the toggling on of a switch. Trust is built through consistent actions over a period of time. No matter how onerous the path, your reactions should always be in accordance with what you believe, in good conscience, to be right.

The journey of building a reputation like that of a lion is filled with challenges that will test your existence at every stage. You will have to make unpopular decisions that will draw resentment from a small cross-section of people. But, if you are consistent, people will soon realise that you have a higher purpose than what is apparent from the decisions being made. The challenging part is that most of these decisions have to be made on your way to the top. The fear of being unpopular is daunting. Yet you have to make tough decisions in the best interests of the cause that you serve.

My parents taught me an important lesson. Material things will come and go and are as inconsistent as the weather; there will be good days and there will be bad days. However, what will stay with you, and what you will leave behind, is your reputation. Building your name, your reputation and consequently your legacy is what life is all about. I have tried my best through all my trials and tribulations to keep this lesson at the forefront of all that I have done. I have not always been right, but I have learnt and never faltered from this path of self-improvement.

My first boss in the army, Colonel Jagannathan, taught me an important lesson: you do not have to win an election, like a politician, to retain your place in the armed forces or the corporate world. No one will re-elect you to your position year after year. What will keep you there is your unfaltering belief in your mission and the value system by which you choose to live. Always remember that it's lonely at the top and, irrespective of the decisions you make, you cannot be in agreement with everyone. Since there is no absolute truth, our decisions will always find detractors. By definition, therefore, as a leader you need to be fearless and move relentlessly along the path that you have chosen.

Your path in life, whatever it may be, is never going to be defined from the get-go. It will be derived from opportunities and challenges that you face and from which you learn. During your journey, you will be unsure at times and you will need reassurance and sometimes validation. You will fall and then stand up again, stronger than before. When you finally achieve success in whatever you do, a clear pattern will emerge, defining the stamp of your legacy.

With these words I lead you into the story of my journey. I hope that you will enjoy reading it and draw lessons that may perhaps simply reinforce the beliefs that you already have.

1

THE IMPORTANCE
OF PEOPLE

As we grow, some of the greatest influences come from our family; then, perhaps a close second, from people who come into our life, sometimes randomly; and, finally, from books.

I would like to reflect first on the impact that books have had on me; more specifically, those of Ayn Rand. Rand means different things to different people: she is loved as much as she is reviled. I first read *The Fountainhead* and *Atlas Shrugged* when I was still at school. They had a strong effect on me, but I must admit that much of her philosophy was lost on my teenage self.

It didn't end there. My real love affair with her work began in 1982 when I was in a hospital bed in Rajasthan fighting for my life. Life prevailed and Ayn Rand's philosophies stayed with me forever, particularly the question regarding the importance of people in shaping one's life. I have battled with this and Rand's argument that an individual is the centre of his or her own universe and lives solely for his or her own reasons.

When I look back at my life, I would never have achieved what I have without the influence of the various people whom I encountered along the way, yet we often tend to disregard the importance of chance meetings and interactions with others. There are some who help and influence us as we grow, a few who teach us life's bitter lessons, and then finally those whom we lead and help to achieve their own dreams.

But it is Rand's philosophy of reason that particularly resonates with me. In *Philosophy: Who Needs It*, Rand states that, "Reason integrates man's perceptions by means of forming abstractions or conceptions, thus raising man's knowledge from the *perceptual* level, which he shares with animals, to the *conceptual* level, which he alone can reach."* It is this ability to reason that allows man the freedom to rise to the top of the food chain. Those who rise above others in the pack become the kings of the jungle.

Books aside, my greatest influencers growing up were my parents. I was privileged to be born into relative comfort in Delhi, India. Consequently, growing up did not involve any of the pressures of day-to-day responsibilities and chores. Support staff were always available to deal with all our routine needs, which was very convenient but had its disadvantages. My wife, who had a conservative and sheltered upbringing, was curious about and amazed at my inability to come to terms with even the most basic functionality of a home. Through this unintended ignorance, and free from contributing to the everyday management of the household during both my childhood and my married life, I benefited by being able to focus on developing myself. I was able to visit coal mines and steel plants at the age of eleven; by sixteen I had completed projects on turbine and cement manufacturing; and by the age of twenty I had a working knowledge of oil exploration. This practical knowledge, in conjunction with some intense lessons from my parents – my father on leadership, and my mother on the

---

* Ayn Rand, *Philosophy: Who Needs It*, New York: Signet, 1984, p. 62.

importance of spirituality – helped form my basic value system. Between them, my parents gave me a sense of balance and I imbibed the best of their traits. A point of convergence for them was their shared belief that all people are inherently good. From them I learnt that good fortune comes from hard work, and that once we have achieved fortune, big or small, we must give back. Throughout my life I witnessed their contribution to society, both tangible and intangible, including an enviable association with Mother Teresa.

What I found remarkable in their empathy with people was that they continued to give more and more, with no expectation of anything in return. In some cases, people let them down, but my parents stayed their course. As they neared retirement, I witnessed the long lines of people at various farewells at my father's place of work and at the schools and institutes that my mother set up. There was a consistent reverence for them. But it was only after their retirement from public life that my opinion of Ayn Rand's philosophy of individualism began to change. As my parents aged, people began to show up to visit them. When my father was diagnosed with cancer, they were there to offer support. It did not matter who they were or what their station, in my parents' hour of need, people repaid their gratitude with their time, that priceless commodity that we all seem to have in short supply these days. This touching emotional bond between my parents and the people with whom they associated over the years, this interdependence, seemed to me to contradict Rand's radical individualism theory.

Through my own life's journey, I have come to conclude that a person does indeed exist as the centre of his or her own universe. However, where I depart from Rand's philosophy is in my belief that people cannot live in a vacuum. I have come to recognise that there is a strong interdependence between humans. Those relationships where this interdependence is absent eventually diminish in value. But for the rest, this interdependence increases over time. I now see this as a gospel truth. Without exception, people come into our life for a reason and become entwined in our destiny. Some may disagree, but for me, interdependence is at the core of our growth and is therefore as important as our own existence.

* * *

As I mentioned previously, my life has been greatly influenced by the various people who came into my orbit. I advocate that it is difficult to achieve anything without the involvement, commitment, loyalty and assistance of others. When you come across a person with whom you can see a future, you must grasp the opportunity and mutually make the most of it.

I was posted to 113 Engineer Regiment as a young second lieutenant in January 1981 and was dispatched to 358 Field Company led by Colonel (then Major) Jagannathan. He was my first mentor on leadership. Though physically short in stature and medically on the borderline for combat duties, this man was nevertheless a soldier par excellence.

Jagannathan was a veteran of two wars and prided himself on his achievements as a soldier on the battlefield. The troops loved him, despite his foul language and rough exterior, and would do anything for him. My first question was, what is the genesis of such loyalty? What drives people to give up their lives for a cause that they probably don't understand and follow a man seemingly so coarse? This was not just a question for the soldiers in our regiment, but for soldiers all around the world; Vietnam, Iraq and Bosnia are just some theatres of war that come to mind. People have different callings, but the central theme of all conquests is good leadership. Combat soldiers may have strong beliefs about patriotism, but when it comes to the crunch, they follow their leaders. They follow men and women who have established their credibility through consistent actions and who can therefore be trusted implicitly. As I was to realise over the next three years, Jagannathan personified these ideals.

We were on a classified defence works project in the Rajasthan desert on India's western front. The task was Herculean and required us to be at a location from where, for security reasons, we could not take leave for an indefinite period of time. The camp did not have electricity or flowing water and I was given a standard-issue 112-pound tent as my shelter and home. The temperatures varied from close to fifty degrees Celsius in the summer to sub-zero in winter. We worked seven days a week and fourteen hours a day. For my induction, I was ordered to stay with the troops for the first month with no officer privileges. During this period I was invisible to the other officers.

This grand tradition in the Indian Army went a long way towards informing my understanding of the challenges faced by people under my charge. Unless one lives in the barracks with the troops, eats from the same mess tins, drinks insipid tea and coffee from the same chipped enamel mugs and uses the toilets shared by 200 men, it is difficult to understand how hard it is for soldiers to get up in time for morning muster. This exercise in humility, however, also had a deeper rationale. It allowed the troops that I was to lead to get a better understanding of the man that I was. Could I share their lives with empathy and a smile? Could I join them in their evening banter without allowing the weight of the stars on my shoulders to create a superfluous divide? By the end of the month, I knew each man by name, background and trade, and in most cases where they came from and the number of children they had.

Right through this induction phase, Jagannathan was relentless in taking what appeared to be a sadistic delight in making my life miserable. In addition to all the operational duties and reconnaissance missions, I was appointed officer-in-charge of the officers' mess and given all the administrative assignments that the other officers shunned. When all the work was done, I was expected to lead the troops to drive out cattle and dogs from the campsite. On completion of the designated task, I then had thirty minutes to get ready and present myself in the officers' mess.

Jagannathan was a soldier to the core and enjoyed his rum. Each night I patiently listened to his war stories. After a while, I learnt the art of switching off and listening for key words from which to take my cue. I even mastered the art of sleeping with my eyes open. Leave of any kind was taboo, particularly sick leave. Officers were never to fall ill; Jagannathan's motto was, "You get sick leave when you die." He was not an easy man to please. Perhaps this rigour tempered me and over time made me unduly wary of people who stayed home for minor ailments. It was ingrained in me that "wimps" don't make good leaders.

Jagannathan was ruthless when it came to any administrative gaps where the troops were concerned. He made sure they were served food on time, slept on time, went to prayer every Sunday, communicated regularly via letters with their families and enjoyed a movie screening on Saturday nights. Showing exceptional conviction, he was at constant loggerheads with our commanding officer in making sure that the supply chains were properly managed. Once he had taken care of the needs of his people, he ensured they delivered results and pushed them to the edge in the pursuit of excellence. He drilled one important lesson into my DNA: even if there is a single man on duty under your command, you have to be there to make sure that he is all right. I was deployed many times on overnight duties to make sure that this value was never violated. Much as I silently complained, over time I saw his rationale. To be effective, you cannot lead from behind.

This maxim was proven right time and again. His expectations were brutal, but each time we had a major catastrophe, I was at the scene and could provide him with accurate feedback. It took time to build trust and fine-tune what he needed at times of crisis, but it was this effective chain of command that enabled Jagannathan to make informed decisions. It became one of the factors that made our unit far more effective than others.

Over the years that I served under him, I formed a bond with Jagannathan, and despite his tough and often ruthless exterior I began to understand what he stood for. There was no agenda other than excellence. I was injured twice during my stint with the regiment. On one occasion I was taken to our command hospital where I was declared clinically dead. The doctors who eventually resuscitated me advised a month's rest. Despite this order, I returned to operations within seventy-two hours to be with the regiment and my troops. Jagannathan simply looked at me when I returned and smiled. He didn't have to say anything; I just knew that he was proud of me. This was evidenced when he was nominated for the Vishisht Seva Medal. He told his colleagues at army headquarters that he would not accept this honour unless I was also decorated. A year later, I was awarded the Vishisht Seva Medal, for outstanding service and dedication to the country beyond the call of duty.

Jagannathan taught me many things, but the most important were these: tireless persistence in the pursuit of perfection; leading from the front; humility; conviction; the ability to always stand up for what was right; and giving due credit to the people you lead. While I never saw him again after 1988, he has never left my thoughts and prayers. He was a soldier who honoured and served his country and the people under his command, before focusing on his own needs.

I left the Indian Army in September 1988 and moved to Dubai in the United Arab Emirates (UAE) in 1989 to seek my fortune. I spent five years between Dubai and Russia, and during one of my social exchanges came across another very interesting man who has perhaps shaped my destiny more than anyone else. American entrepreneur Rick Michaels was travelling through Dubai in December 1993 and a business associate suggested that I meet him. It was one of Rick's first trips to the Middle East and he was looking to establish a foothold for his boutique investment bank, Communications Equity Associates (CEA).

My first meeting with Rick was, from my perspective, a mismatch like no other I have experienced. Here was a sophisticated investment banker who had built a boutique investment bank and who specialised in the media, communications and technology sectors. Rick spoke a language foreign to me. I was at this time a trader operating in Russia and dealing in just about anything that the Russians were ready to pay for.

To put it in context, at this point the market for satellite television had virtually exploded after the first Gulf War. CNN had provided live coverage of the war and people had suddenly woken up to the impact of satellite TV. Arabic TV stations like MBC, LBC and Future TV were mushrooming all over the Middle East. With no revenue models in sight, they were all bleeding financially but were supported by the deep pockets of sheikhs from Saudi Arabia. This was at a time when pagers were still in use, emails were non-existent, internet was just becoming a reality and cellphones resembling bricks were still a novelty. In 1993, Rick spoke of convergence and the importance of building infrastructure for the seamless delivery of voice, data and video. As an engineer, I had an interest in the subject but had no clue about the business.

As we finished dinner, Rick asked if I would be interested in representing him in the Middle East. At first I didn't know what to say, but I was more inclined to decline. The only thing that had stood out for me throughout the dinner was complete respect for a man who started out in his garage in 1973 with US$2 000 and a dream, yet built a sizeable business spanning twenty countries. I asked Rick why he would want to work with someone who didn't understand his business. He said he had a good feeling about me. We left things for a few days and then, true to his word, Rick sent me an invitation and a ticket to visit him in Tampa, Florida, to see his operations. This was my first lesson in instinct and following my gut. It's a lesson that I have never forgotten. When you get a good feeling about people, don't let them go. I have made some of the best hires over time because of my great reliance on gut feeling.

Meeting Rick at his Tampa offices was an enlightening experience. He extended his hospitality by asking me to stay at his house. Culturally, as an Indian, this was a great honour. This more than anything else made a huge impression on me and kindled a respect that would last a lifetime. CEA's headquarters in Tampa were plush, with the most remarkable collection of furnishings. Rick's philosophy was that you had to live the life you wanted and cultivate a lifestyle that people would aspire to. These frills were just the early pickings of a destiny far greater than was visible to anyone else. Rick could see clearly ahead. He knew where he wanted to be in terms of both industry and geography.

I joined CEA in 1994. Over the years, I found Rick's perspective to be distinctly different from that of his employees. He was a born entrepreneur who would take risks and chances. He wasn't swayed by financial models and valuations. For him these were benchmarks and not solutions. He believed in the philosophy of following one's clients. As United States media and communications companies began moving East, Rick grew with them, providing the same services to clients but in different geographies.

An opportune and important decision that Rick made, not uncommon for small boutique brokerage firms, particularly in the start-up phase, was to take sweat equity in companies that he was advising. Sometimes he put in small amounts of capital from his own pocket. In other instances he injected capital through a special purpose vehicle that facilitated participation from other senior CEA executives. Between 1973 and 1991, CEA demonstrated an 80 per cent internal rate of return on investments made on their own balance sheet.

Rick later used this track record to set up a successful private equity business, which at its peak managed over US$1.2 billion.

Between 1994 and 2002, I remained dedicated to CEA and its business in the Middle East and Asia. I decided to study finance, as the people at CEA spoke a language I just didn't understand. There was no way I could take time off during working hours to study, and so began my intense grappling with Finance 101 at home, from 4 a.m. to 9 a.m. every day, until I was able to grasp all the fundamentals needed to be ahead of the game. You cannot lead through ignorance. I had to work doubly hard, not having the formal education in finance that was essential for the work we did as investment bankers.

This period was a steep learning curve for me on the flow of money. Business, in its final analysis, is not just about products and services and their distribution. Business is mainly about money: its sources, its arbitrage and its judicious use. I learnt during this period that the ability to raise capital was the integral part of setting up a project. You could have the greatest idea, but without capital it would never see the light of day.

My association with CEA and Rick unquestionably opened the door to everything that I have achieved today. Rick exhibited qualities that were dramatically different from those of Colonel Jagannathan. Yet both were great leaders. Jagannathan was simple, cautious, hands-on and painfully detail-oriented. Rick was sophisticated, a financial wizard, someone who delegated responsibilities and was the ultimate dealmaker. He never came back from a meeting feeling that there was no opportunity. A born optimist, Rick always saw the metaphorical cup as full. If it appeared to be a quarter, a third or half full, he felt that, whatever the gap, he could fill it with ideas and good people and thus create value where most saw none. People at times joked about his instincts, but his record of accomplishment spoke for itself and even his detractors had abundant respect for his judgement. This was another great lesson: never listen to the views of people who do nothing but criticise those who are trying to build something. Rick taught me how to have unwavering faith in the people with whom you work, and he persevered in this, despite at times being let down by some of those closest to him. This was a lesson that I also sadly learnt through experience. True leaders, like lions, move on their chosen paths, irrespective of obstacles that come their way.

* * *

Besides Rick, Carsten Philipson significantly influenced me at CEA on a day-to-day basis. I met Carsten soon after my first trip to Tampa in 1994. He was leading CEA's efforts in raising its third private equity fund in partnership with Barings Bank and came to Dubai to meet with some of my contacts. The first few meetings were spent getting to know each other, as we came from very different ends of a spectrum on which we were trying to converge. Carsten had grown up in Denmark and, during a posting in New York with the Danish Foreign Service, had applied and been accepted to Harvard Business School. With his exceptional intelligence and knowledge, I believe he could have joined just about any institution he wanted. His joining CEA intrigued me and was perhaps one of the reasons behind my own decision to work with the company. Rick had surrounded himself with some great people; Carsten was a noteworthy example.

A lot of my understanding of CEA and its business came through my interactions with Carsten. His greatest quality was his exceptional knowledge, both about work and things in general. He was exceedingly well informed about changing global trends and the impact they would have on the technology, media and telecommunications (TMT) sectors. What also made him a great ally, and a formidable adversary, was his ability to negotiate; an art form that I picked up during our years together as colleagues and later as partners. Carsten would leave nothing on the table; if there was any juice in a deal, it would flow into our corner. However, the most distinctive part of Carsten's personality was his attention to detail. I have never met a more analytical mind. He would spend hours and even days pondering over solutions before he arrived at a decision. He had trained his mind never to be in a hurry, something that always paid him handsome dividends. He taught me about the opportunity cost of time, and the importance of focusing on the right opportunity and of not spreading resources too thinly.

While the opportunity to enter the investment banking business came from Rick, the real driver for the implementation of this phase in my life was Carsten. I considered him to be my guru, as he seamlessly introduced me to a world that can be quite intimidating for someone only getting into it at the age of thirty-five. To excel, you need the support of someone who prods you along and boosts your confidence; Carsten was this person for me, and it is something that I will never forget. We built a great relationship over the years, not just at work but also personally, and while we are no longer doing business together, we often try to map our diaries so that we can meet for a beer and dinner. In 2002, when CEA pulled out of the Middle East, Carsten returned to a different position with Rick and eventually moved to the International Finance Corporation in Washington, DC.

* * *

In 2002, I met Zafar Siddiqi with whom my destiny is now inextricably entwined. We met on an occasion when I was introduced to a former cabinet minister from Pakistan who was passing through Dubai. The meeting was to discuss the launch of a new TV station in Pakistan and to determine whether CEA would be able to help. The meeting was held in the offices of Telebiz, a production company owned by Zafar (and which later evolved into CNBC Arabia). While

I did not make any progress with the former minister, Zafar and I struck a chord and began talking about opportunities in the Middle East. Thus began an association, and then a partnership, that neither of us had planned for nor thought would develop.

Zafar's story was intriguing. He was a qualified chartered accountant who had been with KPMG for most of his professional life when he found his calling in media. In 1995, he gave up his successful accounting career to establish a TV production company in Pakistan. I always compare his story with the stage production and movie *The Producers*, and often use this analogy when I talk about Zafar. He built his business bottom-up as an entrepreneur and perhaps took greater risks than most people I know. He had the tenacity and perseverance of a survivor, and took every opportunity to continue on the path that he had charted for himself.

My relationship with Zafar is unique and based largely on a strong interdependence. In 2002, when I founded my own investment banking business, Capital Management Advisors Limited (CMA), I became Zafar's advisor. Subsequently, we co-founded CNBC Africa and Murdoch University Dubai and became partners. Being older than me, he chose to remain strategic in our relationship, leaving the actual operational oversight to me. This works well for both of us and we have a very comfortable working relationship.

As an entrepreneur, I have shared more with Zafar than with anyone else. We faced the shattering recession in 2008 and built our two fledgling businesses one day and one dollar at a time. Both of us risked a lot and financially contributed equally to keeping our businesses afloat. Our endurance was put to the test during the period when one of our shareholders pulled out and we had to stabilise an educational start-up business that needed more than US$350 000 per month and a media company that was burning more than US$1 million a month. It required tremendous hard work, patience and faith in what we were doing, but we finally managed to pull through because of an unwavering belief in each other and what we had set out to do. He remains strategic as chairman of the companies and provides invaluable guidance whenever I need it.

* * *

While my identity was built by my parents and my character by two strong mentors (Colonel Jagannathan and Rick Michaels), the person who gave me confidence and self-belief was undoubtedly my wife, Saloni. I was blessed to meet her as we were growing up and our introduction was the greatest gift my younger sister, Shalini, has ever given me. Through life's trials and tribulations, Saloni has stood by me, my proverbial Rock of Gibraltar. Coming from an affluent business family, Saloni recognised early on in my transition to an entrepreneur that the task I had undertaken was not going to be an easy one.

We decided very early in our life together on our individual roles, particularly after I left the army. So while I was seeking our fortune by experimenting with opportunities, she undertook the role of homemaker, almost single-handedly raising our two children, as well as providing me with unconditional support.

The responsibility she took on was so significant that never in our thirty-one years of marriage have I had to look at any domestic or personal matter. Since Saloni has a strong background in commerce and economics, she took complete charge of all our personal finances and investments; I have never had to meet our bankers and some of our private bankers have even questioned whether I actually exist.

I recall an incident when I attended my daughter Shweta's parent–teacher meeting one year when Saloni couldn't make it. I was totally at a loss and a complete embarrassment to Shweta. The teachers and my daughter were unanimous in their feedback that I was simply excess baggage. In my defence, they had not prepared me enough for what I needed to do! The partnership with my wife has perhaps been one of the integral parts of my ability to focus and succeed at my work.

* * *

Just as I found spirituality in my parents, mentorship in two great men and strength in my wife, I have spent the last twenty years building great teams and mentoring people to achieve their dreams and, in some cases, contribute to my own vision and dreams. I have been able to build interdependence with other individuals who play an equally important role in my life.

As an entrepreneur, I have taken an inordinate interest in two facets of my businesses: human resources and finance. It is my belief that if you get the right people, and if the finances, particularly cash flow, are properly managed, you have a better chance of success. Start-ups fail for many reasons, but the most common are incompatible teams and ineptly managed financial resources.

Building start-ups in emerging markets is a gigantic task. There are complexities of every kind, including political volatility, currency fluctuations, unfamiliar and inconsistent regulations, and language and cultural barriers. The greatest challenge, however, is finding the right people and making them believe in your vision and ability to fulfil a dream. My father aptly described leadership as "an ability to influence and inspire people to work willingly and enthusiastically to achieve group goals".

All successful businesspeople will acknowledge that the real secret to success is finding good people with complementary skills. There is, however, no absolute definition of good people. All people are inherently good. It is the recognition of each other's value proposition, at the right time and space, which builds a relationship of interdependence.

There is profound logic in finding people to share your vision. This logic is not dependent on what you are offering, but on the state of mind and the personal situations of the people who are around when you are seeking certain skills. If the stars are properly aligned, you will find through trial and error the person whose needs at that time fit exactly with what you are offering. Despite this, there is inevitably a period of courtship where you get to know the person and work towards building a relationship of consistency and trust.

In my experience, there is a distinct pattern in the career life cycle of most people. This holds mainly for professionals and not entrepreneurs, and is largely dependent on the circumstances of individuals. In general, I find that people in their twenties tend to experiment in their career. They are sometimes unsure of the sector or the path they wish to pursue. There is a need to experiment with diverse experiences and travel the world. There is rightfully an arrogant belief that the world is their oyster, and then there is the need to enjoy the spoils of early success.

There is a level of stability that comes around thirty, when people tend to settle down and make commitments to family. The period around thirty-five is the most critical, as most professionals are getting to where they want to be, and are eyeing that all-important position. By this time, most people have made up their minds on their career path and work hard to get to the top. By the time individuals get to forty, they are on the top of their game and should be leading their field, whatever it may be. These age groups evolve with generations and indicate trends rather than absolute answers.

Though not always accurate, by simply examining their career life cycle, you can determine very early whether a person is likely to fit into your long-term vision from his or her own perspective. An understanding of where a person is in their life cycle is crucial. In my view, therefore, straightforward capability is not the quality that may qualify a person for the position you are offering. You need to factor in the possibility of mismatched needs or that it may be the wrong space and/or time. So you keep looking until you find the right person for the job. Similarly, by the same logic, people leave for a variety of reasons. They may want to experiment when they are young and look for stability as they get older.

By setting high expectations and goals, I have never been an easy man to work with. People who have worked with me have at times recognised their inability to keep up with the sheer pace at which I expect things to be done. The important attributes I seek in people are a belief in what we are doing and a can-do attitude. I took away the word "jobs" from my businesses. If people merely want jobs, they can find them anywhere. I ask people to take on responsibility. Responsibility is not time-bound. When you take on the respons-ibility of bringing up a child, you can't do it in a single shift. Similarly, you cannot build a start-up by going home and forgetting about the needs of the business. You have to find the balance between your various responsibilities – one cannot be traded for the other; to try is a recipe for disaster – because you have to fulfil *all* your responsibilities to achieve goals. People will take their cue from you and make you their benchmark.

In 2007, Zafar and I started laying the foundation for our educa-tion business, Global Institute Middle East. The business model was to academically partner Murdoch University from Australia in setting up a core campus (to be called Murdoch University International Study Centre Dubai) in Dubai. We established the campus in 2008 but were hit by the recession almost as soon as we opened our doors. The business needed a dynamic academic who could also understand the nuances of a start-up business, take on a full teaching load and bring together a complex organisational structure to fit with the legislation in Dubai. The skills we were looking for were scarce. After an initial error in hiring a dean, I approached the head of our Murdoch Dubai Business School, Dr John Grainger, to lead the team. John had a strong entrepreneurial and teaching background, had spent considerable time in the Middle East, and understood the nuances of the local culture and values. Most importantly, he recognised that for a start-up to be successful there had to be a 24-7 work culture and optimisation of resources. John readily accepted this leadership challenge because he shared my vision and enjoyed working in the UAE. Despite the recession, the business broke even in five years and grew from 39 students in the first year to 600 students in the fifth. My strategy was to give John the freedom to operate and to build an excellent team of professionals around him. In 2013, when a significant new opportunity arose, John agreed to move to Ghana as president of Trans National Education Limited (TNE) and provost of our second university in academic collaboration with the highly ranked Lancaster University based in the United Kingdom.

Dan Adkins joined Murdoch University Dubai in 2009 to lead our foundation programme, and in 2012 started the transition to take over from John as head of the business in Dubai. Dan had been responsible for the successful launch of the foundation programme that eventually became the lifeline of the business, but John, through his interaction with Dan, had a feeling that Dan was only interested in teaching. I was not convinced and made Dan the offer, which he accepted without hesitation. None of us looked back from there. Dan was most un-American in his demeanour and we realised over the years that despite his calm exterior he was not someone to take lightly, as a lot of people found out to their detriment. He was an able successor on the Dubai campus and continued to grow the operations from where John left off, bringing in his own stamp of authority and competence. Dan was driven by an inordinate passion for excellence and, with the able team of Chris Pilgrim, Sanjay Rodrigues, Biju Veetil, Sudeep Sachin and Gary Fernandes, he was able to grow the campus from strength to strength. Dan put in long hours and had such a diversity of skills that if there was more time in the day, he could probably have taken on almost all the academic positions at the university single-handedly. Dan is a man of few words but someone whose actions speak louder than anything he may have wanted to say.

* * *

CNBC Africa has been the greatest challenge of all the start-up businesses that I have founded over the years. The sheer magnitude of the project was overwhelming. To set up an advertising-driven business in 2007 in a fragmented pan-African market was groundbreaking and unprecedented. The key challenge was finding the right people to run and manage a state-of-the-art TV station. At the time, there was no server-based television network in Africa and all competitors were focused on regional and terrestrial television. Leadership was a challenge and I struggled with the commitment of some of the senior staff on the team, which meant a lot of time was spent overseeing the work of people who, under normal circumstances, would be expected to be independently firing on all cylinders.

In 2008, Roberta Naidoo joined the company in a temporary capacity to complete our audit, which had been delayed by a year. She finished the task in the stipulated time and when I made her an offer for a full-time role, she agreed to stay on as CNBC Africa's head of finance. She was a hard worker and brought discipline into our policies and governance. She was a stickler for detail, and with finances under her watchful eye I knew I had nothing to worry about. In two years she had got to grips with the entire business, provided oversight to HR, oversaw all our corporate set-ups across Africa, and in 2010 took over as general manager. Finally, in 2013, when the opportunity arose, I made her managing director of Africa Business News (ABN) Group, the holding platform I founded in 2006 and which includes CNBC Africa and *Forbes Africa*. She kept pace with what I was trying to do and patiently and diligently worked with me to set up additional companies in the ABN Group. Over time we established a relationship of implicit trust.

When my son, Sidharth, joined the business, Roberta took on the role of his mentor and helped him establish himself within the group. There was nothing that crossed her desk that she thought was outside the scope of her responsibility. As she continued to learn and grow in her role, her accomplishments were recognised by the industry. She has been nominated for Business Woman of the Year by several forums, as well as CEO of the Year for the media category, and she featured in the Top 100 CEOs in South Africa in 2013. Nothing gave me more pride than to see her win all these accolades.

Nigeria is one of the more difficult markets in Africa. There are challenges in anything and everything that one wishes to do, beginning with a lack of basic amenities, poor infrastructure, bureaucracy and the age-old malady of supplementing incomes. Yet as Africa's largest economy, it is a sleeping giant that cannot be ignored. I had been travelling there since 2005 and right through the setting-up process of a CNBC Africa bureau in Nigeria I had struggled with hiring the right person. In 2008 we were introduced to Frederic VandeVyver, a Belgian who was heading up another media company's interest in Lagos. It was a friendship made in heaven. Despite Fred's thick accent, he took to our culture like a duck to water and bought into our vision. We expanded in Nigeria from an eighteen-member team to a fifty-member team in eight years, with operations in three cities. Fred exhibited some of the greatest qualities of leadership by demanding the highest standards of performance, achieving all the short-term goals, building great relationships, contributing to long-term strategy and, most importantly, being there for me whenever I needed his advice. He endeared himself to his team and it was not surprising that Nigeria had the lowest churn rates of all our operations.

One of the people at CNBC Africa who stayed in the shadows for a long time was Bronwyn Nielsen. She was around through every phase of the company's growth, chipping in from a distance, but she was going through her own self-realisation and was not ready to take on a significant role within the company. She turned down the offer to head our programming department in 2008 and later declined to lead *Forbes Africa*. Perhaps through her own ambitions of being an entrepreneur, she was undecided about what she wanted. Things changed in 2012 when she joined the ABN Group as executive director of strategy and moved a year later to head of programming of CNBC Africa. Bronwyn is not only one of the best financial journalists on the continent but is also an inspiration for other journalists, exemplifying the fact that with hard work and commitment you can achieve pretty much anything.

Mainly because of connectivity, the technical infrastructure at CNBC Africa was a significant challenge. The infrastructure required a complex blend of fibre, microwave and satellite connectivity, not just within South Africa but also in connecting fifteen cities across twelve countries. We had exceptional technical heads, starting with Anton de Wit, then Marisa Meyer and finally Jean Landsberg. When Marisa decided to move on in 2011, we asked Jean to consider the position. Since he had no formal management experience, he at first declined. However, after re-examining the opportunity, he asked a few days later if he could still be considered. Jean overcame his qualms and, with Roberta's help and guidance, we have produced one of the finest heads of broadcast operations, not just in South Africa but on the continent.

* * *

When I was setting up *Forbes Africa* I went through yet another bout of recruitment. Business magazines are not scarce in Africa, so I could choose from a large pool of qualified and well-respected journalists. I met several potential candidates who had the experience, but I was looking for something unique. *Forbes* is unlike any other magazine title. It is sexy and aspirational. The character of the editor had to be unique, to ensure the magazine did not replicate an existing format.

This decision again was a tough one, but I followed my gut and appointed Chris Bishop as managing editor of *Forbes Africa* in 2011. Chris had worked with us at CNBC Africa and had done me proud by putting together a documentary on Liliesleaf (the farm where Nelson Mandela was finally arrested) and the Rivonia Trial in 2008, a historic initiative to which I had committed. The documentary was a tremendous success and he delivered it in his usual low-key style with absolutely no fanfare. Appointing Chris as managing editor was perhaps one of the best decisions I have made. He gave the magazine the character, uniqueness and integrity that I was looking for and it was not surprising when we broke even in the first year of operations. Chris was awarded the 2013 PICA Award for Editor of the Year by the Magazine Publishers' Association of South Africa, an honour that recognised his competence and leadership. Backed by the success of the magazine, we launched *Forbes Woman Africa* and *Forbes Life Africa* with Chris eventually overseeing all three magazines with a team of strong editors supporting him.

* * *

What impressed me about all these individuals was that none of them ever discussed compensation. There was complete alignment of individual goals with those of the company, and a focus on long-term wealth creation. They all took a short-term risk in their pursuit of a larger purpose. They are what I call organisation builders and value creators. I knew I could count on them and each exhibited personal acts of loyalty and commitment.

I always single out one of Roberta's acts of empathy. In 2009, when we were going through a tumultuous cycle during the global financial crisis, Roberta walked into my office and said, "I am aware of the difficulties that we are facing in the business. I am happy not to take a salary until we pass through this period." I never took her up on the offer, but this was commitment beyond what anyone had ever shown to the organisation, and I knew then that as long as she was at the helm of the ship, I had nothing to worry about, as she was prepared to make personal sacrifices in the interests of the business.

As with most exceptionally passionate and talented people, all these individuals had very strong minds of their own. Their skills complemented my own, and each had a deep understanding of our mission and goals. We would spend hours discussing strategy and putting together action and resource plans. We would differ on many issues, but once a path was agreed, they would implement it relentlessly. It was not always smooth sailing. We had severe differences from time to time. In most instances, I gave in to their point of view and, regrettably, on a lot of occasions I was proved right. Some of these errors in judgement were expensive, but the school fees needed to be paid for them to learn. My only requirement was for mistakes not to be repeated. I knew at all times that their intentions were right, and in most instances the mistake they made was trusting others whose interests were not aligned with our business. The intuitive aspect of knowing whom to trust comes with experience, and in most cases through bitter lessons.

When I look at all of these people, I see common qualities. These include an exceptional work ethic; loyalty and commitment to the organisation; a can-do attitude where nothing is deemed to be impossible; the ability to take on responsibilities and see them through consistently; the strength to understand their own weaknesses and overcome them by bringing complementary skills to their teams; and, finally, the ability to look after people in the organisation, to mentor them, reprimand them, encourage them and fight for them where necessary.

The greatest joy for an entrepreneur is when you realise that you are no longer essential to the everyday running of the business. John Grainger once said to me, "Leadership is tested, not on how your team performs when you are present, but on how your team performs when you are away from the office." This resonates well with all the individuals I have mentioned, as I seldom needed to look over my shoulder to see how they were doing.

As part of our long-term strategy, I convinced other shareholders to give equity to senior management in the various businesses. Through this, we have managed to integrate the future of the group with that of the senior teams. They can no longer take decisions thinking that they are not going to be affected by the execution, as all our long-term interests are now completely aligned.

*   *   *

In a modern organisation, youth should be integrated into management structures in decision-making as well as in implementation. Technology is enabling but also potentially disruptive to the future. We cannot predict how we will do business in the future, and unless there is a comprehensive understanding of technology and its applications, organisations will become irrelevant. Kodak's reliance on chemically processed film is a classic example of obsolescence. The younger generation is representative of our future consumers. Related to our business, they more than anyone else understand how people will buy software, educate themselves, read magazines or watch television in the future. It is therefore imperative to identify the bright sparks in the younger generation and integrate their brain power into the organisational think tank.

With this in mind, I started the Young Leaders Programme (YLP) in the ABN Group. The idea was to put young leaders through the complete business processes of the group and give them a taste for strategy, operational parameters and performance benchmarks, and in return tap their minds for innovative and out-of-the-box thinking. Initially the HR manager structured the programme with a local business school, but when I attended one of the sessions I realised the complete futility of the exercise and took the curriculum development in-house to make it relevant. Heads of department became the faculty deans for their respective sessions and suddenly people were interested in attending classes. The exercise culminated in a written exam, a difficult oral interview and a presentation of case studies.

As we progressed, I made a commitment to the members of the YLP that they could question every decision made by the management of the company. This was done not to forfeit the accountability of the senior team, but to ensure that the young leaders clearly understood why decisions were made in a particular manner and that they had the ability to question, comment and contribute towards these decisions. I asked Sidharth to chair a separate monthly meeting with the young leaders, so that they could set up a formal interface with the senior team.

On 12 July 2014 the first batch of eight members graduated from our first YLP. I wasn't surprised when Natascha Jacobsz, executive producer of special projects, came out on top. She was followed closely by Svetlana Doneva and Kudzai Kanyangarara. All three had climbed Mount Kilimanjaro with me and had the tenacity to succeed. In my opinion, they are budding stars who will do well wherever they go and in whatever they do. All three have since moved on to pursue their own dreams, but they remain our greatest brand ambassadors.

Another youth initiative, undertaken in March 2013, involved fifteen members of the ABN Group and Murdoch University Dubai summiting Mount Kilimanjaro. Kilimanjaro is the tallest freestanding mountain in the world and the highest point in Africa. Statistically only 41 per cent of people attempting the climb succeed, and more have perished climbing Kilimanjaro than ascending Mount Everest. These are some very daunting statistics. I gave the team one mission:

everyone had to make it to the top. Failure was not an option. When we finished the climb, I had achieved two objectives: integrating my middle management into one fighting unit, and ensuring each member of the team reached the objective – the top of Kilimanjaro.

I had appointed our head of sales, Quinton Scholes, as team leader. He was physically the strongest member of the team, but he also proved himself mentally tough. During training exercises in the military, we were put under extreme physical stress to test our endurance and capacity to think and lead despite personal fatigue and discomfort. Many people would crack under the physical pressure. However, to qualify to be an officer, you had to pull through. In my eyes, Quinton earned his stripes on Kilimanjaro, as he led from the front and made sure that every member of the team made it to the top. He is a man I know I can trust to be there when the chips are down; a good soldier capable of compassionately leading his team forward.

* * *

While I have managed to talk about some of the people that I have been able to mentor into leadership roles, there are so many others in the various organisations who are doing wonders each day. It brings me to the interdependence that I spoke about at the beginning of this chapter. A relationship between an organisation and its people is like a marriage; it has to work for both. Compromises need to be made equally on both sides, so that the relationship can be sustained through day-to-day challenges. It is not a blood relationship and the bonds can be easily broken if there is a clash of values.

I have always worked on the "rule of 51". If a relationship provides 51 per cent of what you are looking for, then the odds are in your favour. You can improve this to 60, 70 or even 90 per cent and the opportunity cost of doing this is far lower than if you were to end the relationship and start all over again with someone else.

There are times when you will lose good people for the wrong reasons. It may be painful, but do not give up on the people you want around you, except if they fail to uphold a key value. Pursue them relentlessly, keeping in mind that the future of your organisation depends on the people who voluntarily follow you. As a leader, you do not have the luxury of an ego. You have a mission and it has to be achieved at any cost, provided you stay true to your ethics. If this requires humility on your part, then so be it. The bigger picture is far greater than its individual parts. On the one hand, I have never hesitated to metaphorically get on my knees to bring back people who I believe are valuable to my long-term success. On the other hand, I have shown equal disdain for disloyalty and where necessary have managed to clinically excise people from my orbit.

In tribute to everyone who has either influenced my life or has placed their trust in me, I say this: Every now and then in your life, there will come another human being who will touch your heart, soul and destiny. He or she will be the messenger of an opportunity and, consequently, your destiny.

Through the years, I have, as a human lion, rationalised that the immortality of my organisations will only be realised if there is succession in the DNA of my tribe. I can pay no greater homage to the people around me than to acknowledge their readiness, through their dedication and competence, to succeed me.

2

MAKING CHOICES

Life, as it turns out, is eventually a sum of all the choices we make. From the subjects we choose at school, the friends and company we keep, how we spend our free time, the university we attend and the career we pursue, to the values we set for ourselves, the code of conduct by which we live, the compromises we make and the battles that we fight. And ultimately, we are responsible for the choices we make, so we may as well make them ourselves, with minimum outside influence and keeping in mind that our decisions must reflect our broader goal.

The former CEO of the Johannesburg Stock Exchange (JSE), Russell Loubser, and I were playing golf one morning at the River Club in Johannesburg. Russell raised a subject that has become embedded in my memory. He asked, "What are the two most important decisions that every person has to make in their lifetime?" After going back and forth, we concurred that the two most important decisions in each of our lives were the courses we took at university and our choice of life partner. Russell had a 100 per cent strike rate as he hit the jackpot with both. While I had got my choice of life partner right, as evidenced by my thirty-one-year-and-counting marriage, I had struck out on the university side. Having graduated with a science degree with physics and mathematics as my majors, and later civil engineering, nothing in my initial education had prepared me for the world of business or finance. (Over the years, I did, however, on anecdotal evidence, conclude that engineers made better business-people because of their inherently logical minds.)

Subconsciously we all believe that if our vocation or profession matches our hobbies, we can achieve the dual objective of making money while having fun. And it comes down to making the right choices. In 1975, when I was at this juncture, my options were limited to becoming an engineer, a doctor or an accountant, or following in my father's footsteps and joining the army. I had always been enamoured by the idea of a career in the military and so enrolled in the NDA, graduating with a Bachelor of Science degree in 1979. In 1986 I earned my Bachelor of Technology degree in civil engineering from the CME. Interestingly, the army was not my first choice. I had wanted to join the air force. I ranked near the top in the Pilot's Aptitude Test in my Services Selection Board, and the commanding officer actually recommended the air force, but parental pressure got the better of my decision and I applied to the army instead. In 1978, I applied to the navy with a view to joining the Fleet Air Arm. If it wasn't going to be MiGs, I would settle for Harriers. But once again, my father's invisible hand prevailed and I was asked to withdraw my application. Sometimes when I hear jet engines above, I wonder whether I would have left the military if I had become a fighter pilot.

I spent a little over twelve years in uniform, including four years of training. It was not until I was posted to 114 Armoured Engineers in Patiala that the first signs of boredom began to set in. I could sense that a change was needed and, after contemplating leaving the forces, I decided to give it one more chance. Hoping that a change in scenery would bring me clarity, I volunteered and was selected for the 7th

Indian Scientific Expedition to Antarctica in October 1987. It was one of the most spectacular adventures of my life. The enormity of the frozen continent, with its savage conditions, brought home to me how helpless we are before Mother Nature. While building India's second base at the Antarctic, I started to think about the universe outside the armed forces and finally made up my mind to leave. Perhaps I needed this solitude to peer deep into my soul and determine what I really wanted. I cannot say with any conviction that I knew what I wanted then, but I was certain that I did not want to continue in the military.

The decision would not have been an easy one had it not been for that near-fatal accident during my first field tenure in Rajasthan. It was while I was in hospital reading and re-reading Ayn Rand that the importance of making choices began to resonate with me. I think at some point after the accident, I changed my way of thinking. It was a deep realisation that life was not a given and that every moment had to be savoured. No one can understand and satisfy your needs except you. You need to make the ethical choices in the pursuit of your own perception of happiness.

My father was opposed to my decision to leave and did what he could to advise me against it. He felt that given my track record I would make general by my fifties. I wasn't convinced that I wanted to be a general. My rationale was simple. The Indian Army was a great life and an exceptionally noble career, but each day I spent there, I grew more frustrated with my own inactivity and lack of personal stimulation. The army was not going to change in any way to meet the needs of one confused soldier. I would have to change. And in order to change, I would have to move out of the ecosystem of implicit obedience and protection, and into a world full of mystery that was completely foreign to me.

My son was born on 13 April 1988, a week after I returned from the Antarctic. I resigned from the army on 28 April, after consulting

Saloni. Faced with the prospect of an unemployed husband and a newborn baby, my wife turned out to be a lot more solid than I had imagined. She was only twenty-two years old at the time, but she looked at me and said, "It does not matter what you end up doing, you must do what makes you happy and I will take this journey with you for better or worse." Saloni would become the greatest constant in my life, giving me the freedom and support to do what I wanted. This freedom, however, was tied to great responsibility; it was an inevitable dichotomy.

We make choices based on circumstances. I joined the Indian Army when I knew no better. Did I regret joining? Never! It provided the best experience and training for a young man. My life's code of conduct is based on the honour code that I learnt as a soldier. I chose to leave because I had outgrown the life, and not because the army did not keep its commitments to me. The whole experience taught me that if you feel stifled in what you do, it is not necessarily because the workplace is lacking, but rather because you have grown and your needs have changed, and so you must respectfully move on. However painful it may seem at first, it will be beneficial for both sides.

When I left the armed forces in September 1988, I had 17 000 rupees in my bank account, at that time little more than US$500. I remember going to my father's office in October to ask his advice. He was then the chairman of ONGC, India's largest conglomerate in oil and natural gas exploration. He gave me perhaps one of the greatest lessons of my life, which was not very palatable at the time, but over the years I have come to recognise its value. He said, "Son, a lot of people are going to want to meet you today; don't mistake that interest as any value you bring to them. You will only be a means for them to get to me and that is never going to happen. So go out there and make it on your own. If you are in trouble, let me know. But never make the mistake of discussing my business with anyone."

In my entire business career, I have never touched a single industry with which my father was associated. This has been a conscious choice and it has not made my journey an easy one. On the contrary, I had to restart my life with absolutely no connection with my heritage, professionally or personally. I realised that as long as I stayed in India, I would not be able to escape the shackles of a very well-recognised family name. When my older sister, Sunanda, and her husband, Rajeev, gave me the chance to move to Dubai to gain some experience in their business, Frontline, I embraced it and never looked back. It was the best opportunity I could have been given and the best decision I made. It formed the foundation of my destiny and is something for which I have remained forever grateful.

* * *

After leaving India, I was twice faced with a fundamental choice relating to my work life. The first came when I met Rick Michaels in 1993 and he suggested that I represent CEA in the Middle East. Having moved on from my sister and brother-in-law's business, I was running a small but relatively successful trading operation from Dubai at the time. After my humble beginnings in the army, the returns from trading were gratifying. I could afford what I wanted for my young family and enjoyed the challenges in Russia, Bulgaria and Ukraine, the three markets I had entered into. However, something about Rick's offer was intriguing. The media and communications sector was creating a lot of buzz and I reflected long and hard on the challenges and opportunities that this presented. The sector was a complete unknown to me, but the thought of specialising in something relatively new was compelling, as it psychologically brought down some of the barriers of ignorance. The trip to Tampa clinched it for me, but I still had to go back to my sounding board. I discussed the implications with Saloni, who, true to her style, encouraged me to follow my heart. Sidharth was six years old and our daughter, Shweta, was three when I chose to gamble again.

Every lateral move sets you back as it takes time to learn the ropes. You have to work harder each time to stay ahead of the curve. If the move involves a sector or industry change, you invariably have to go back and study. The greatest change for me at that point was to my routine. I engaged in self-study, which required that I get up at 4 a.m. and study until 9 a.m. every day before leaving for work. In one year I had picked up the basics of media and communications, and the related world of finance. There is no greater mistake than to step into battle unprepared. Carsten Philipson, though younger than me, in many ways became my guru, teaching me the ropes of private equity and corporate finance. In turn, he was fascinated with my experiences in Russia. Perhaps Harvard Business School didn't acknowledge that the wild frontiers of business still existed. He laughed uncontrollably when I told him about some of the outrageous deals I had concluded in Russia. Notwithstanding our differences, as a team we became a formidable force thanks to our common values, complementary skills and diverse experiences.

Carsten and I travelled together extensively across the Middle East, from Jordan, Syria and Lebanon in the Levant to all the Gulf Cooperation Council (GCC) countries and Yemen. We met just about everyone we possibly could and introduced them all to the fascinating world of media and technology. From punting TV stations and cable networks to call centres, we did it all. Towards the end, I remember one of our clients telling us at a meeting, "I have seen you boys for eight years; your story hasn't changed, you have just become a lot slicker." In turn, we called him a bandit, as he always got the better of us. This period was my renaissance, and I got to grips with the communications industry and the world of investment banking. After reading one of my speeches at a convergence conference, Carsten smiled and said, "In the land of the blind you are the one-eyed king!" I took that as a compliment. Today Carsten runs around doing the same work for the International Finance Corporation, "just a lot slicker".

These endeavours shaped my destiny, and I ended up spending the next eight years with CEA gaining invaluable experience and meeting with almost every financial institution and major institutional investor in the GCC. During this time, the media and communications industry in the Middle East and the Indian subcontinent exploded, and I was able to leverage CEA's success in the US into opportunities in the Middle East and India. As part of CEA's private equity business, we started raising capital for various private equity funds around the world. The icing on the cake was when I was able to develop an opportunity to set up the Middle East's first Islamic private equity fund, focused on the technology sector. This was an exciting project and one of the most rewarding experiences of my life.

In 2000, the inevitable happened and the world went into a tailspin as the internet bubble burst. Although CEA had consciously decided not to invest in internet companies, the impact of the industry's decline forced Rick to consolidate the business back into the US. In 2002, CEA decided to exit the joint venture in the Middle East. I had the option of staying with the joint venture and continuing to build the business with a large balance sheet, but to my mind it would have been disloyal to CEA, Rick and particularly Carsten. While the offer was personally extremely attractive, I could not ethically commit to the proposition. My exit saw the initiative collapse. As I walked away from an eight-year journey, I once again found myself at a crossroads and faced with the second material choice relating to my work life.

Carsten and I spent hours contemplating what to do next. We came up with many ideas, including raising another fund. The timing, however, was all wrong. It was then that I decided that I would go back to basics and start developing projects from the ground up. Once again, it was a complete lateral shift. Having achieved distinction in investment banking and becoming one of the leading media consultants, and having helped raise and advise an Islamic private equity business, the time had come to do something different. This time around, I decided to remain totally entrepreneurial, just as I had during my stint in Russia. The only difference was that I was now better prepared – both financially and in terms of experience.

After doing a SWOT analysis (SWOT being the acronym for strengths, weaknesses, opportunities and threats), I concluded that I had to find investment opportunities in emerging markets and set up projects bottom-up. It was a model aimed at leveraging industry experience, a known investor base and relatively virgin markets. It was perhaps the most entrepreneurial thing I had ever done, as the opportunity cost of developing projects was extremely high. Each opportunity had to be properly researched, planned, financed, staffed and executed. It was going to be a journey with no breaks or rest.

This phase in my career turned out to be as volatile, painstaking and risky as predicted. However, in the last fourteen years I have been able to establish some of the most prestigious projects in a variety of territories, including CNBC Africa, *Forbes Africa*, ABN Training Institute, ABN Productions, ABN Pictures, Murdoch University Dubai, Lancaster University Ghana and Tech One Global, and there are many more in the pipeline. The choice that I made in 2002 enabled me to set up small and medium-sized enterprises (SMEs) that now cumulatively employ over a thousand people. At the age of fifty-seven, I finally feel that I have achieved what I set out to do in 1988.

* * *

The question I now ask myself is whether I would have been happier as a serving general commanding a sizeable military force, rather than at the helm of my own organisation overseeing 1 000 people working towards building long-term value for the organisation and for themselves. The easy answer is that there is no comparison, as each achieves a different objective. I would not change the path I took. At the end of the day, I think I have had a more wholesome experience because of it. But true to life's many contradictions, I would not be the man of business that I am today without my military background.

I am a great advocate for change and constantly tell the people who work with me to try new things. You only live once, and you must live each day according to your value system, doing what you want to do. Be transparent and ethical in everything you do. If you do not take chances and try different things when you are young, you will have regrets. And regrets should be avoided. Time is irreversible and finite; you must make each moment count and make whatever necessary changes to improve your life. There is no growth without change and change is an inevitable part of life. Not every change will work out for the better. They will, however, make you wiser and prepare you for the next challenge.

One of the integral parts of change is risk. Perhaps the reason why most people resist change is because they prefer to remain within the comfort zone of their existence. They continue to accept the status quo so long as it does not create conflict. This also means that they accept less from life; we fear taking a risk for something that may not come to be. But no one has made a fortune by standing still. You need to be out there testing and benchmarking yourself every day. Your benchmarks help you to progress, even in uncharted waters. You can always fall back to where you started, which may be lower but no worse than in the past.

Your choices will have an impact on others, some positively and others negatively. There will be a constant turmoil within you when you make choices. They may not be as radical as those taken by a soldier on a battlefield, who has to live by the dictum "kill or be killed". But if life is indeed a jungle and only the strong survive, then it is incumbent on you to make ethically sound choices that are in your best personal interest. Extrapolated to a business, you must always do what is ethically in the best interest of your business. Not all your decisions will be right, but you will learn from experience.

The guiding force, particularly if the decision concerns others, must be your conscience.

I often talk about ethics: your ethical behaviour should be derived from your conscience. If the choice you make conflicts with your ethics, then you should not proceed on that path, irrespective of the desired result. The end does not always justify the means. Be a path setter and not a follower. Set high standards for yourself and let others benchmark themselves against your standards. Popular choices are not necessarily the best ones. You need to make the right choices, even if they are unpopular, and stand by your decisions. Your opinion will often differ from others, including those closest to you. If you are proved wrong, acknowledge it and make amends. If you are right, be magnanimous and accept the failings of others. The greatest impediment in life is our ego. If you wish to achieve success, there can be no room for ego. Do not let your ego get the better of you when making choices. Remain humble and forgiving. That is the path to success.

Invariably, there will be someone in your life who acts as your sounding board. They play a crucial role in helping you make changes and decisions. More often than not, your life partner is the person who understands your circumstances better than anyone else and whose interests and fortunes are completely aligned with yours. The greatest gift is a partner who shares your value system, and who encourages and pushes you to do better and achieve more. For this interaction to be fruitful, your partner must be competent and content in what she or he does. Down life's mysterious and complex path, if there is one thing you need, it is that familiar face smiling at you irrespective of the outcomes. I am grateful to have such a partner. Saloni has made my journey possible, sacrificing much so that I could continue on my path.

3

EMERGING MARKETS

The choice of where you work and choose to establish yourself is dependent on many factors. These include the country in which you were raised and spent your formative years; the opportunities that come your way, particularly when you are starting out; the institutions with which you come to be associated; and the people who enter your life and with whom you cultivate interdependence.

I believe that everyone has a destiny independent of their beliefs; that our destiny is written in our stars. The opportunities that come our way are derived from our destiny. Our destiny therefore comprises myriad small opportunities, which come our way again and again; often we see them but do not act. You will hear people say, "He was in the right place at the right time." Well, there were a million other people in that place at that time, but it was that one individual who grasped the fleeting opportunity and made something of it. It is safe to say that life is a continuous flow of opportunities that arise from the depths of the bountiful ocean that we call our universe. Our universe consists of our individual spheres of influence of family, friends and circumstances. We must learn to train our minds to identify and seize opportunities as and when they arise.

As I have said before, some of the most important influences in life are the people who come into our orbit and with whom we form interdependences. I am a great believer in the idea that people come into our life for a reason. We must make every experience count, and when people, opportunity and geography align, we will find the road map to our destiny. The most important requirements, therefore, are to keep our antennae in receiving mode and to learn to distinguish messages from noise.

INDIA

I was born, raised and educated in India. It is a complex and diverse country with a dysfunctional and corrupt political system. With twenty-nine states, seven union territories, twenty-two official languages and 1600 dialects, India offers a genuine home to every faith in the world. In analysing the challenges in India, you wonder what holds this behemoth of 1.2 billion people together. This is a question I am still unable to answer. What I do know is that the people of India have exceptional tenacity. It is in our DNA to survive, irrespective of the odds.

While the availability of basic amenities is still largely inadequate, the situation in India has improved greatly in recent years. If I think back on my childhood and the experience of growing up in the 1960s and 1970s, we never took anything for granted. Not electricity, not water, not road infrastructure, not even Indian Standard Time, redefined by many as Indian Stretchable Time. Nothing ever happened on time. Yet, everything got done eventually and no one complained. Our DNA ensures high thresholds of pain and perseverance. India has moved forward in spite of its problems and despite its politicians, indicating that there is a spirit in the people that supersedes any impediment. Growing up in India was perhaps the greatest training ground for me personally. It lowered my expectations and allowed me to give a greater deal of latitude to some of the shortcomings that I faced as I built my businesses in emerging markets around the world. My yardstick when passing judgement has always been based on a realistic appreciation of the problems faced by emerging economies.

When I left the army, my first preference was to find employment related to my education. I was delighted when my uncle gave me a job in his construction company in India. The group had a project to build barracks for the army in Punjab and I enthusiastically joined as executive director for the project. It took four months for me to become completely disillusioned with both the industry and the questionable ethics associated with the enterprise. What I found on site was that the quality of all materials being used was far inferior to what had been tendered and quoted for. Instead of using Class A red bricks in the foundation as per specifications, our project engineer had approved Class C yellow bricks. A few weeks later, they started the anti-termite treatment using agricultural bentonite instead of industrial bentonite. In the pre-construction phase we were to drill holes two feet apart along the entire building perimeter and pump into them diluted aldrin or chlordane under pressure, to create a chemical barrier between the soil and masonry so that insects would not infest the building. As per the tender, the treatment was to be guaranteed for ten years. Instead, some of our workers went around with buckets and casually sprayed the foundation area with bentonite slurry.

I couldn't help but reflect on the leakages from barrack roofs and the termites in the buildings that I had lived in as a soldier. Now I realised that these were caused by differential settlement of the foundations because of poor-quality bricks and improper anti-termite treatments before and after construction. The officers in the Military Engineering Services who were responsible for overseeing the construction projects and for approving the monthly progress billings knew about these inadequacies. In exchange for turning a blind eye to the poor quality of construction, they received a percentage of each month's billings. When I respectfully raised this with my uncle, he justified it by saying that he could not pay the fees and maintain tender quality requirements without making a loss.

After just four months I packed my bags and returned to Delhi, and vowed never to go back to the construction business again. Having now chosen to move away from the field in which I was qualified, I realised that, while a world of opportunities had opened up, I had neither the qualifications nor the experience to apply for a job. Knowledge of explosives, landmines, bridging and anti-tank warfare are not skills that are in high demand in the new world economy.

THE UAE

This was a difficult time for me personally as I was unsure of what I was going to do. As my father had predicted, most conversations about prospective opportunities seemed to lead back to people wanting to do business with him. My real break came when Sunanda and Rajeev suggested that I move to Dubai to get some experience with their business before making a decision about my future. This was my introduction to the media business, as Rajeev was a pioneer in publishing in the UAE. Among other things, he published the UAE business directory.

In the year that I spent with Rajeev, I learnt how to sell niche publications and media in a very limited marketplace. Although the business was small, it was in the information industry and gave me a tremendous opportunity to get a sense of what was happening in the country. We had a pretty good run and some of my first lessons came from Rajeev. He operated a focused business and was an astute businessman. He kept a black book and did the most basic accounting on a daily basis. It was Cash Flow 101. He had a simple philosophy: don't spend what you don't have, and in all the years I have known him, he has stuck to this mantra and not once has he had any trouble with his business. This, as any businessman knows, is the basis of running a successful enterprise.

Another valuable lesson that he taught me was about the importance of travel as part of the educational process. After we concluded a publication project in mid-1990, he asked me to take a trip across Europe. I spent three weeks on the road and visited all the major European countries, ending at the CeBIT expo in Hanover, Germany. Even in 1991, CeBIT was perhaps one of the largest information-technology fairs in the world. It was also one of the greatest revelations for me, as I could see where things were heading. A number of what appeared to be incredible innovations at the time are a reality today. The exhibition was a great experience, as it put into perspective the role IT was going to play in every business going forward. It also taught me the importance of travelling and opening my eyes to the world.

The first Gulf War started with Iraq's invasion of Kuwait on 2 August 1990 and continued until 28 February 1991, and shook the foundation of the small but meaningful start that I had made. The Middle East was completely overtaken by hysteria, as no one really understood what Iraq planned to do beyond the invasion of Kuwait. Scud missiles were flying all over the place and a few found their way into Saudi Arabia and the Arabian Gulf. The GCC countries were worried about Saddam Hussein's intentions, as it was widely believed that the aggression would continue in a bid for complete domination of oil resources.

Shortly after the start of the invasion, Saudi Arabia asked the United States for help. The American and coalition forces launched Operation Desert Shield between 2 August 1990 and 16 January 1991, using bases in all the GCC countries. This was followed by Operation Desert Storm from 17 January to 11 April 1991. Throughout the war, Dubai as a trading centre was impacted significantly, but with the uncertainty came a plethora of opportunities, as people scrambled to provide support to the allied forces. Dubai businesses began to prosper.

This period also saw a change in leadership in the UAE. The Emirate's founding father, Sheikh Rashid bin Saeed Al Maktoum, died on 7 October 1990. It was a dark day for the UAE, as the country had lost the visionary leader responsible for transforming Dubai from a small trading port into one of the greatest trading centres in the world. The mantle was transferred to his oldest son, Sheikh Maktoum bin Rashid Al Maktoum. However, those in UAE business circles believed that the man who was really shaping the future of Dubai was the third of Sheikh Rashid's sons, Sheikh Mohammed bin Rashid Al Maktoum. And indeed, Sheikh Mohammed succeeded Sheikh Maktoum as leader of Dubai after the latter's untimely death on 4 January 2006. Sheikh Mohammed is undoubtedly the man whose vision has spearheaded Dubai into one of the most dynamic business and economic hubs in the world.

It was during all this turmoil that Saloni and I were blessed with our second child. Shweta was born on 27 January 1991, in the middle of the first Gulf War. Much to my own unhappiness and lifelong regret, I stayed in Dubai to complete some projects and so missed her birth in Delhi. Saloni remained supportive and in her usual way took it in her stride and forgave me. From my perspective, I had to make personal sacrifices as the Gulf War affected the state of the economy and I had to work harder to secure business. The advertising industry, for obvious reasons, took a serious hit and all the projects on which I was working were completely marginalised. After Shweta's birth, and with each passing day, it became more and more obvious to me that the business that I was in was unsustainable at that stage of my life. Armed with some practical experience, the time had come for me to make another change.

It was my first experience with recession. I knew that to make things work I had to seek opportunities outside the Middle East, as the local markets, particularly in the GCC, were too saturated and too small.

The UAE itself has a very small, and marginally growing, local population. The country had approximately two million people when I arrived, made up of roughly 80 per cent expatriates. Since then the expat population has grown significantly, while the local population, as a percentage of the total population, has diminished. The total population today exceeds nine million. While Dubai has historically been a trading hub with a large number of multinational businesses headquartered there, most of the economic activity is stimulated from outside the region. Dubai is uniquely positioned longitudinally in the centre of the globe, right in the middle between the East and the West. The immediate catchment area around the UAE includes the rich GCC countries, the Levant, North Africa and the Indian sub-continent comprising India, Pakistan, Sri Lanka and Bangladesh. The catchment area population is approximately two billion people.

In the 1980s, Sheikh Rashid had positioned Dubai as the greatest trading centre between Europe and Singapore. The two major ports grew in stature and the free zone in Jebel Ali gained a reputation as the only place in the GCC where a foreigner could own 100 per cent of their business and gain tax exemptions for 100 years. People from all over-regulated countries flocked to Dubai to establish their businesses and the city began to thrive. Despite the turmoil in the region, the invasion of Kuwait gave Dubai a huge investment boost, both through banking channels and in cash, as Kuwaiti families fled their homes in search of safety.

While Abu Dhabi continues to grow in prosperity on the back of oil income, Dubai has had to continuously reinvent itself, taking advantage of global changes and adapting to demand. What has always amazed me is the speed with which Dubai has adapted to circumstances. This is largely because of the Emirate's agile leadership compared to neighbouring countries. For example, Bahrain had an early-mover advantage as a banking centre, owing to its proximity to Saudi Arabia. However, Dubai's leadership reacted at lightning speed and instituted policies and concessions that attracted investors from all over the world.

While it was clear to me that I had to seek opportunities outside the Middle East, what was equally clear was that there was no better place to live than Dubai. It was ideal from every point of view: three hours from India, tax free, well regulated, safe to bring up a family, and well connected. There were some major impediments as well: an evolving legal system, ownership restrictions, and absolutely no long-term certainty surrounding residence status. However, the positives far outweighed the negatives and the business model I began developing used Dubai's strengths and sought opportunities in markets that were only just opening up.

I had two choices at that time: go to Iraq or explore the Russian market. I looked objectively at both and found that the reasons to be in Russia were more compelling. In addition, I had friends who graciously opened doors to me in this unknown territory.

RUSSIA AND UKRAINE

India was Russia's ally throughout the Cold War and the countries had a strong interdependence. India was perhaps the only real window to the outside world for countries belonging to the former Soviet Union. While India relied heavily on Soviet defence, oil, coal, space technology, steel, nuclear and other resources, the Soviet Union imported pharmaceuticals, engineering goods, textiles, food and other consumer products from India. It was, therefore, not surprising that a large number of Indian companies had set up operations across the former Soviet Union.

As war raged in the Middle East, the Soviet Union was collapsing. Mikhail Gorbachev was a reformist leader, who in 1985 wanted to make changes to the way the Soviet Union was administered. He came up with two principles of change: *perestroika*, to deal with economic reform, and *glasnost*, to ease social and media controls. While the principles were laudable, it became impossible for Gorbachev to control the outcomes. Media censorship ended in November 1988 and CNN was the first international TV station to be beamed into Russia, in 1989. The subsequent proliferation of media made it almost impossible to control the process of change. The Berlin Wall came down in November 1989 and Russia declared sovereignty on 12 June 1990. On 8 December 1991, the Commonwealth of Independent States was formed. At its conception it consisted of ten former Soviet republics, namely Armenia, Belarus, Kazakhstan, Kyrgyzstan, Moldova, Russia, Tajikistan, Turkmenistan, Ukraine and Uzbekistan. Gorbachev resigned as the last president of the Soviet Union on 25 December 1991 and on the following day the Union of Soviet Socialist Republics was dissolved.

The transition into the next phase of my life resulted from an interaction with another great human being. Ramapati Singhania represented the third generation of business leaders from the Singhania family, which ran the J.K. Organisation based in India. Ramapati was a mentor and a great supporter through this very constructive phase of my life. He was a visionary and someone with dreams that were far ahead of the Indian business and political environments. I attended a number of workshops with his senior management in India and saw the great divide between his vision and that of the people around him, all of whom showed a complete lack of commitment. Traditional families in India often reward misplaced and questionable loyalty over competence and reason. This was a great lesson for me on the importance of having the right people around me and ensuring that they possess all the attributes I require to implement my vision.

With Ramapati's support, I set foot in Russia soon after the country declared *perestroika*. Indians were always welcome and I went to Moscow courtesy of an old school friend, Jagdeep Rangar, who had business interests in Russia and had arranged for me to meet a few of his associates. Aeroflot was the only airline flying to Moscow at the time, and I remember landing at Domodedovo airport with a sense of unease. I still recall the stern look on the faces of the immigration officers; they sat in pairs and went through every page of my passport. On a lighter note, someone remarked mischievously that during the Soviet era Russian officials were not permitted to laugh or smile in public, and this behaviour was merely reminiscent of the old habits.

At first I stayed at the Cosmos Hotel on Prospekt Mira. This was perhaps the largest hotel, with over 1775 rooms, and I still remember getting the "Indian rate" of US$25, while other visitors paid over US$100 a night. That, for an opportunist, was by no means a bad start. The quality of hotels improved dramatically over the years and after a few stays at the Cosmos, I moved to the Slavyanskaya on Ploschad Evropy and then to the grand Metropol Hotel on Teatralny Proezd. All of these hotels were from the old Soviet era and, apart from the lethargic service, offered an absolutely delightful stay. When Lufthansa started the Baltschug Kempinski in Moscow it became my hotel of choice until I finally pulled out of Russia.

Communicating was a nightmare, as hardly anyone spoke English, and for every meeting we had to engage the services of an interpreter. This was an inefficient way of doing business, as often the essence of the discussion was lost in translation. At times it would appear that the Russians were having longer discussions with the interpreter than what was being conveyed to me. Nonetheless, I got by. A large number of Indian students who had been sent to Russia to study became interpreters and, in some cases, the entrepreneurial ones would "cut" themselves into the transactions. It was wheeling and dealing at its best.

Russians in the early 1990s were in a state of flux. Most of them did not know what was happening, but you could see that those who had been in government positions since 1985 were generally cognisant of the unfolding opportunities. I met senior people in the banks, in administration and in some of the larger state organisations, and I remained totally confused by everything that was happening. The pace at which things were moving was far too great and there was no system, process or logistics to support the volatility and speed of change. It was a breeding ground for chaos of astronomical proportions as the word "capitalist" began to take on a new meaning for the people of Russia.

This change, however, was not happening at the grassroots level. People on the street were still living in relative uncertainty, under the influence of misleading propaganda on radio and television. The elderly were affected the most. They could not hold on to the past and the future was evolving at too great a pace for them to adapt. My first observation when interacting with everyday Russians was that they were among the warmest, simplest and most sincere people that I had ever met. The simplicity of their existence was refreshing but scary, as one could feel the winds of change on the horizon.

From a business perspective, there was abundant opportunity. There was a need for every known consumer product, and in the case of basic commodities, the need was immediate. Those of us in Dubai were ideally positioned, as in-demand products were stocked by Dubai traders to service the entire Middle East and, in some cases, the Indian subcontinent. I got involved in the supply of consumer goods to various clients in Moscow. The only glitch was that Russians liked signing contracts for everything, but to get contracts drafted and signed was a nightmare, since everything was one-sided and in Russian. My only condition was that payments were to be made upfront. It worked for everyone, and I established relationships with several up-and-coming Russian procurement houses. As there was no internet in those days, research was limited, and I was able to make relatively good margins in the beginning. Dubai was the best place to be, as prices there were the lowest. We set up an excellent trading platform: Saloni managed all the purchases, paperwork and shipping, while I focused on bringing in the orders and all the customer interactions.

Doing business with Russians was a unique experience. I remember the story of an American business executive who spent a few days in Moscow, and after various abortive attempts to meet his business partners decided to return to the US. Apparently he told his company that it was impossible to do business in Russia. There was some merit in what he said. What he did not realise, however, was that not all markets are mature like the US and Europe. At the time, in places like China, India and parts of the Middle East and Asia, business depended on relationships as well as economic sense. Often the relationships were more important than the economics. The older generation of Russians especially conformed to a very conservative way of dealing with foreigners. One had to be patient and understand the people, before trying to drive commerce.

I learnt early on that, coming from the archaic traditions of the Soviet Union, Russians were unlikely to make snap decisions. I therefore allowed for deliberation and discussion between collaborators before any consensus was reached. In some cases, I was invited into these deliberations.

Owing to their fondness for vodka, there was no tradition of drinking only in the evening and one was expected to drink when invited to do so. The weather and mood dictated consumption. I remember being at a dinner one evening where champagne and vodka were flowing. I was thirsty and asked my host for water. He looked at me, smiled, and poured beer into my third glass. I was startled and repeated my request, but he just poured me more beer. He later told me that he did not have water because no one really drank it. Later still, I learnt that Perrier was more expensive than beer.

The Russians were also fond of visiting fancy saunas attached to tennis courts and swimming pools. I was occasionally invited to these saunas for business discussions, where we would drink to our countries, people and friendship. As one Russian stated in a cavalier manner, "We won't do business with people who don't drink; but we will never do business if you can't hold your drink." Luckily, over the years my Russian friends changed their habits. I think travelling outside Russia opened their eyes to other cultures and sensibilities. Certainly, their visits to our home in Dubai made them aware of the similarities in our family-based societies.

As Russians began travelling to places like Dubai, the UK, France, Hong Kong and Singapore, their business models changed quite rapidly, too. Like all good traders and businesspeople, they were fast learners and adapted quickly to differing styles of negotiation. Another noticeable shift was the importance they placed on material comforts. After years of a relatively frugal existence, the Russians now had the means to spend, and spend they did. Over the years, several delegations of senior executives from government and large organisations visited us in Dubai, and their travel budgets were always outrageous. The lid was off the pressure cooker, and years of pent-up desire were unleashed. While the men were busy in the boardroom, their wives were out buying the latest brands. One Russian businessman, who later became a good friend, complained to me that his wife had spent US$75 000 on hats alone during a visit to London. I suspect the impulse to spend was driven by an underlying fear that the party was going to end soon. And end it did, as the excesses were just not sustainable.

During the years that I travelled to Russia, the change in the consumption pattern was markedly visible. On my first visit, there were predominantly Lada (Jiguli) and Moskvich cars on the road; then the imports from Europe started arriving and within a year Moscow had more BMWs and Mercedes on the streets than most other cities in the world. Some of my newly acquired Russian friends came to Dubai and bought Range Rovers and other high-end four-wheel drives and took them back to Russia on cargo flights. I do not believe that any other place in the world experienced such rapid transformation as Russia between 1991 and 1994.

If there was ever a case for being at the right place at the right time, it was holding the post of director general of a company in the Soviet Union at the end of 1991. Most of the exports from the Soviet Union were transacted through state monopolies, specialised by sector, and financed through Vnesheconombank, the State Corporation Bank for Development and Foreign Economic Affairs. After the breakup of the Soviet Union, all exports were decentralised back to individual companies in their respective countries. With the complete disintegration of processes and structures, the directors general of the state enterprises suddenly found that they had complete autonomy and absolutely no accountability.

The senior management of companies that had high export quotas benefited the most. Products were being exported, but a large portion of the export earnings was retained overseas. The companies were slowly but systematically drained of working capital. The banking system had collapsed and there was no money available to finance the large state enterprises. During the same period, the government had privatised many companies by issuing shares to all workers in the enterprises. Senior management, with the help of politicians and overseas financial institutions, then purchased the shares from workers at discounted prices, injecting much-needed working capital into the very funds that had been siphoned off and retained overseas. This gave a few individuals complete control over large organisations in a relatively short period of time. The oligarchs of Russia were born through some crafty financial engineering with the necessary blessing from the state administration.

Given this landscape, the terrain was extremely hostile for both regulated industries and industries going through privatisation. Much has been written about the emergence of the Russian mafia, which essentially consisted of businesspeople and politicians who had formed alliances for control of licences, state assets, land and property. The stories of violence and corruption that emerged were nothing more than the initial battles over turf in which individuals and groups vied for control of banks, telecommunications, media, cable TV, ports, liquor licensing, hotels, restaurants, real estate, airlines, commodities, mining and all other big businesses. Once the pie was divided, every-thing began to settle down. Of course, this took many years, and throughout this period the influence of Russian business spread across Europe, while Cyprus became the banking tax haven for Russian money. It was a very interesting time to be in Russia, to see the com-plete turnaround from communism to capitalism.

Eventually the chaos receded in the former Soviet Union. As time went by, the nefarious activities of the few began to come to light. As their various indiscretions were discovered, the directors general and senior executives from the banks and government simply disappeared, never to be heard from again. This was not unexpected. Information was scarce in Russia, and the government prevented a lot of what was known from going public. The judicial system was quite centralised and evidently without recourse. Nevertheless, a clean-up had begun and it brought sanity back to the country.

With the passage of time, I evolved our business model and we began investing in real estate in Moscow. This included apartments on Kutuzovsky Prospekt, with a Russian partner who had established a company to refurbish and sell them. The real-estate boom was on the horizon and we caught the market just in time. We also invested in properties in the GUM shopping complex, just adjacent to the Kremlin. The GUM had been constructed as a trade centre by Catherine II of Russia. It was privatised in 1991 and turned out to be one of the opportunities we were able to leverage quickly. The investments were extremely risky, as there was no foreign ownership and no paperwork. Everything was done on trust and in cash. (In the early years, there was no easy way to transfer money from Russia. The banking requirements and bureaucracy was laborious. When I visited a Russian bank in 1991, they did not have computers and were using the abacus for calculations. It was like operating in a market that was fifty years behind the rest of the world.)

For a while our business took me to Perm in the Ural Mountains, about 1150 kilometres east of Moscow. The city was among the twenty largest cities in Russia and its economy depended on engineering, oil and gas, and the industrial sectors. The banks were largely cooperatives serving different sectors. We had a few clients in the city and I flew down periodically to meet with them. It was on an Aeroflot flight back from Perm to Moscow, on a Tupolev Tu-134, that I had one of my more harrowing Russian experiences. As we landed at Sheremetyevo airport in Moscow, the aircraft skidded on the runway. Some of the panic-stricken passengers started screaming, but calm returned once the aircraft came to a halt in the soft snow on the side of the runway. It took an hour for an old truck to reach the point where our aircraft was stuck. After an initial assessment of the situation, the truck driver spoke with the captain and then pulled the aircraft out of the snowdrift using the truck's winch. Without checking anything else, the pilot switched on the engines and took the aircraft under its own steam to the arrivals' apron. I could not believe the poor safety standards. If it were not for the lack of options and the need to travel, that would have been my last flight on Aeroflot.

That experience was illustrative of a far deeper problem. Russia had some of the largest manufacturing facilities at the time, but most of the plants needed overhaul in terms of processes, reporting and equipment. This period saw the most significant brain drain from the former Soviet Union as people left in droves, seeking a better life. Anyone who had the requisite skills (particularly qualified technicians, academics and scientists) was immediately snapped up by Western European, Israeli and US companies. To my mind, this brain drain was the most significant loss for Russia and other countries in the newly formed Commonwealth of Independent States during the period from 1990 to 1995.

When I first arrived on the scene in Russia, I approached two major cable manufacturers, a large bus manufacturer and the largest earth-moving equipment manufacturer in the country with offers to represent them in the Middle East. These opportunities would have resulted in a home run, if we had managed to tie them down. We participated in some large tenders, on behalf of the Russian manufacturers, with a few utilities and government departments in the Middle East, but the handicap was the track record, specifications, and lack of corresponding Western ratings, accreditation and standards. Most Middle Eastern countries followed British, American or German standards and did not want to take risks on Russian products, although the Russian products were equally robust and efficient. The other major problem was marketing and promotional material. The concept of marketing did not exist in the former Soviet Union. The brochures were substandard and in Russian, and the translations to English or Arabic were very poor. The meetings and presentations were equally unsatisfactory, as those in senior management did not speak English, making it difficult for them to form relationships with their counterparts in government. I watched with total helplessness as some great opportunities simply slipped by.

*   *   *

In 1992, as our network of business contacts expanded, I began looking at two other markets: Ukraine and Bulgaria. I started travelling to Ukraine in 1992 and used the flight connections from Moscow, as there were no daily direct flights from Dubai. Furthermore, Kiev's proximity to Moscow made that journey a lot more efficient. I visited Kiev, Odessa, Donetsk and Dnipropetrovsk to look at various opportunities. Ukraine was even more backward than Russia during this period, and the people were far simpler. So while we had a lot of conversations, there were absolutely no systems in place to execute investments.

Ukraine's economy was going through major turmoil in 1992, and after the break away from Russia the country did not even have its own currency. As a stopgap arrangement in 1992, the government of Ukraine issued karbovanets, or coupons, as its official currency. When I first visited, the official rate against the US dollar was 150 karbovanets. Between 1992 and 1994, the denominations of the currency moved from 100- and 200-karbovanet notes to denominations of 500 000 and then one million, indicating the hyperinflation in the country. In 1996, the government introduced hryvnia as the official currency and subtracted five zeroes from the denominations. These were truly difficult times in Ukraine.

It was not just the banking, the political uncertainty and the infrastructure, but all aspects of implementation that were serious constraints. Since I was partnering several companies from the region, I established a memorandum of understanding between a steel plant in Magnitogorsk, Russia, and a shipping company in Odessa, Ukraine, to supply reinforcement steel to clients in the Middle East. At the same time, we signed another contract to supply timber from Perm to the Middle East, using Odessa as the loading port. I travelled through the region, visiting the loading points on the Ural and Kama rivers and booking passage with transportation companies. I negotiated all the details, spoke to the buyers in the Middle East, and established the credit lines. But upon returning to the sellers, I found that the shipping companies had sold the barges intended for the inland transportation. The logistics of doing business were almost impossible during that period, as people were out to make a fast buck, any way they could. Values like personal credibility and integrity were clearly not "the order of the day".

I embarked on yet another adventure/experiment when I purchased a retail business and bar in Odessa through a lawyer who was visiting Dubai. Our partners were a dignified old couple, who were well connected with the local administration. I visited them several times in Odessa and had a great feeling about them. I invested the money and established the business, albeit through a proxy because, as a foreigner, I could not own land or buildings in Ukraine. Having had a great experience with my partner in Moscow through earlier real-estate transactions, I thought this experience would be no different. However, in the absence of proper control systems and banking procedures, we faced a lot of pilferage. The operations were doing exceedingly well, evidenced during my visits to Odessa, but there were no returns from my elderly partners. I realised during the course of the next year that to get a return on this investment I would need to move to Odessa. This was not an option, and as there was no legal recourse to make any claims, I finally decided at the end of 1993 to withdraw from Odessa and cut my losses.

Also in 1993, I put together a group of angel investors to invest in Donuglecom Bank in Donetsk. The bank was a cooperative, focused on the coal-mining industry. We spent a lot of time going back and forth, looking at the investment opportunity, but were limited by a statutory obstacle. The legislation would not allow us to hold more than 24 per cent and we did not want to put ourselves into a situation where we did not have adequate protection. We put our stake in the ground at 26 per cent and were ready to walk away if the legislation was not approved. In early 1994, our bid was finally turned down, and we had to decline the transaction. In many ways it turned out to be a blessing. If our bid had gone through, in mid-1993, the currency devaluation over the next year would have eroded our entire investment. Within one year, the currency devalued from 150 karbovanets to the US dollar to 150 000 karbovanets. We would have lost four zeroes from our investment within a year. It was an invaluable lesson that I have never forgotten. Without exception, I have faced this hurdle in every emerging market into which I have invested.

I had a few intense interactions with some influential people in Ukraine. In anticipation of the Women's Day celebrations in March 1992, one of our clients from Donetsk purchased tons of chocolates, which he flew back to Ukraine on a chartered Antonov An-32. For months he did not pay us, and while the amount was not very large, it was not small enough to be written off as a gift. Even after repeated requests, we seemed to be making no progress.

Around this time we had also concluded a transaction with another Ukrainian businessman who was visiting Dubai with his family. He was so overwhelmed by our hospitality and the success of our business transaction that after dinner he took me aside and made me an astounding offer. Through his interpreter he said, "I would like to thank you for all you have done, and Mr Wahi, if you ever need to kill anyone, please call me." I was amused at his choice of words, and I knew he did not mean it literally, but I told him very nonchalantly that there was a client from Donetsk who owed me some money. He suddenly became animated, and just as suddenly my problem became his problem. He collected a copy of the contract and left for Kiev the next day. I did not think anything would come of it and promptly forgot the matter.

Two days later, I got a call in the middle of the night from my non-paying client in Donetsk. He was frantic and needed my bank details. I asked him to call me back in the morning, when I would fax the details to him. He would not hear of any delay; he wanted the information immediately. From a client who generally dealt in cash and pretended ignorance about bank transfers, I got my money in forty-eight hours. He would not tell me the reason for his sudden change of heart, except to say that he was extremely sorry for the anguish he had caused me. It sometimes pays to have the right friends …

The most rewarding opportunities were those in the services and trading sectors. I partnered the Ukraine–America Trading House and Ramapati Singhania's PGR Group to host several exhibitions in the Middle East and India. One in particular stands out. Held at the Pragati Maidan in Delhi in March 1996, it was the largest trade exhibition hosted by the government of Ukraine in India. We flew in 300 guests representing 100 major corporates from Ukraine in a chartered aircraft. The most interesting aspect of the entire project was the daily allowance paid to each guest. Owing to restrictions, the payments could not be made in Ukraine and we could not remit the money to India, as there were tax implications for the receiver. We eventually got around this by landing the chartered Ilyushin Il-76 at Dubai airport to pick up one passenger, who carried 300 envelopes as hand luggage, which were then distributed to the eager delegates on the plane. It was a hero's welcome.

Overall, the logistics of this project were extremely challenging. Even getting the personal details of each individual delegate for visas was a nightmare, as there were changes to the delegation up to the eleventh hour. With 100 corporates exhibiting, we had a colossal amount of product, some of it high-tech equipment. When the two cargo-laden Il-76 aircraft finally landed in Delhi, the lack of paperwork led to confusion at the airport. The language barrier between the team from Ukraine and the customs officials in India created chaos and much tension, with neither side willing to back down. In the end, our shipping agents on the ground managed to sort everything out to everyone's satisfaction, but not without major drama at the cargo terminal. It was nothing short of a Herculean effort, as processes in India were not without significant challenges either. At the end of the day, the Ukrainian ambassador to India, Mr Khodorovsky, was delighted with the outcomes and acknowledged the perseverance that went into the project's implementation. The exhibition was inaugurated by Minister P. Chidambaram, the then minister of commerce in India.

The trade mission and exhibition presented another chance to establish close ties with some of the giants of the former Soviet Union, but once again I was unable to leverage these potentially lucrative investment opportunities. While equity in large Soviet organisations was available at significant discounts, legislative issues, language barriers and past legacies handicapped these opportunities. I was stranded with many ideas but no resources to back them up.

* * *

I was thirty-two years old when I started travelling to Russia and thirty-seven when I exited. Towards the end, it was clear that, despite all my efforts, I had fallen short in coming up with the financial resources, relationships, skills and experience to pull off anything significant. I had approached a lot of friends and investors, but no one was willing to make any worthwhile contribution to a Russian venture. The frustration of not being able to pull off this great opportunity in Russia has been one of my greatest lessons. I learnt that in order to be successful, I would have to build on a much larger scale, through interdependence with people and organisations. More importantly, I would need to build personal credibility, as that is the ultimate commodity in the life of an entrepreneur. The era of being a maverick was slowly coming to an end, by both design and opportunity.

THE MIDDLE EAST

Although my association with the former Soviet Union endured until 1996, the meeting with Rick Michaels and CEA in December 1993 came at an appropriate time. By then I had recognised that a size-able and sustainable business could not be built in Russia without making a long-term commitment to the local market in terms of investments, as well as building human capacity. In the absence of this, I would have had to accept being a marginal trading business, dependent on opportunities as they presented themselves. The idea of specialising in the TMT sector was extremely appealing, but daunting. It would force me to take another step back, but I was prepared to do that in order to further my development.

CNN had revolutionised television viewing with its real-time coverage of the first Gulf War. Before then, analogue terrestrial stations had dominated television in the Middle East, and indeed most parts of the world. With the sudden emergence of free-to-air TV via satellite, television stations began scrambling for capacity on satellites over the Middle East. CNN was catapulted into a different league as everyone tuned in to follow events in Kuwait. Broadcast journalists like Peter Arnett, John Holliman and Bernard Shaw became global household names. The future had arrived. Information was no longer limited to the privileged few; it was a freely available commodity, and indeed a necessity.

Rick had founded CEA in 1973 to provide service to a select group of cable-industry clients who needed financial expertise. The first joint project I undertook with CEA was raising money for their Asian fund in partnership with Barings Bank. Fundraising was new to me and gave me insight into the world of private equity. CEA had an impressive industry track record, but did not have fund-management experience. They partnered with Barings to raise their first fund in Europe, and after that raised two more funds with the British bank. I got involved with marketing the Asian fund to Middle Eastern investors. The fund-management team had just been hired in Singapore, with Peter Chan at the helm. Peter has remained a friend and is now managing a much larger portfolio in his own firm, Crest Capital.

The pitch book for the Barings–CEA fund combined two great histories. On the one hand, there was the impressive track record of CEA's industry experience. On the other hand, there was Barings' pedigree and experience in Asia through Baring Venture Partners.

Barings was Britain's oldest and most conservative institution, serving major clients, including Queen Elizabeth II.

As Carsten and I started meeting investors in the Middle East, the name of Barings drew a lot of interest. However, in February 1995, disaster struck when international media reported that Nick Leeson, a Barings derivatives trader based in Singapore, had been concealing losses resulting from unauthorised trading. In December 1994, the losses had amounted to £200 million, but by March the following year they exceeded £827 million. The bank, founded in 1762, collapsed. Barings was finally sold to the Dutch bank ING, for the nominal sum of one British pound; ING took over all liabilities. We had the unpleasant task of communicating this disaster to our potential investors.

Private equity at the time was not everyone's cup of tea, and other than the large institutions and some private offices in the Middle East, most people were wary of the long-term nature and illiquidity of the asset class. Since commitment levels were set at a minimum of US$1 million, we had narrowed our market to select only qualified, sophisticated investors. Despite this funnelling exercise, we had some amusing interactions, particularly with certain sections of the Indian expatriate community in Dubai.

On one occasion, I organised a presentation at the InterContinental Hotel for a few businesspeople from Dubai's thriving trading community. Carsten started off by giving an excellent overview of the opportunity. After thirty minutes and one Scotch, one of the guests asked Carsten to stop the presentation and sit down. Perplexed, he did as requested. The self-appointed spokesperson then asked what the total cash requirement from the group was. We took a wild guess and said US$50 million. He then looked around the room and said, "Gentlemen, between all of us, we can give you the money; now what do we get in return?" Carsten, completely composed, gave our standard rehearsed answer, "The fund projects an annual return of

25 per cent." The spokesperson quickly interjected: "Mr Philipson, did you hear me say that we were projecting to give you US$50 million? So here is our proposal: you take our money, but guarantee, through post-dated cheques, the principal and the returns." It was one of the funniest experiences during our time fundraising together. Needless to say, that was the last time we attempted to raise private equity funds from the trading community in Dubai.

Notwithstanding the lighter moments, a scandal like Barings was enough to scare away even the most sophisticated investor. I received many rejections, but finally got a break from an Oman-based institution. This was not the end of Peter Chan's woes, however. The Barings debacle was followed by the infamous 1997 financial crisis in Asia, which started in Thailand and spread through all the major Asian markets. The systematic failure of all financial institutions across Asia was unprecedented. It took a toll on all the Asian currencies as governments tried hard to prevent a total decimation of value.

Since private equity funds have an investment period of about three years after being raised, our Asian fund made several investments at relatively high valuations in the eighteen months before the crisis hit. After the crash, the investment value of the portfolio immediately took a dive and struggled to recover. I remained in touch with the fund's performance, and we were far off the mark on the returns. The fund was eventually closed at US$102 million, having reached only 50 per cent of its projected target. I drew an important lesson from this experience regarding the timing of projects and the effect of global economic upheavals on investments.

* * *

Over the years, CEA raised a total of US$1.2 billion in nine private equity funds. After raising the Asian fund, CEA had an adequate track record to raise money in its own name, and the firm entered its golden era. Carsten and I continued raising funds in the Middle East, including a special purpose vehicle that we set up for investing in Seaport Capital Partners in the US.

The Middle East, particularly the GCC, was a market different from any other in the world. CEA's main business was investment banking, basically a brokerage or fee-based business. The principal model was pure vanilla corporate finance, helping companies step up their business through either advisory work or raising capital through debt or equity. Most of the clients were small to medium-sized companies, in varied stages of their life cycle, and so we had to build a diverse range of skills in our small teams to cover the complete range of services. For start-up companies, the advisory work was as basic as drawing up business plans, conducting feasibility studies and then helping entrepreneurs raise capital. In other cases, we assisted more established companies raise expansion capital. The more advanced a company was in its life cycle, the more difficult it was to secure mandates. This was a highly competitive space, as all large deals in the market were contested by the major investment banks, which not only had global industry knowledge and large teams, but also a larger network. The smaller companies seeking advisory work were typically unable to pay retainers. We therefore had to think very carefully about which companies to take on, as an advisory business based purely on a success fee was highly risky, particularly since there was a high people-cost. The opportunity cost of failure was often far too great, especially when it affected the ability to generate income and risked reputational damage. Luckily, my relationships in the region, supported by CEA's sector experience, allowed us to secure some of the most prized mandates.

As we worked on a business plan for the region, CEA realised that the GCC was largely a reverse investment banking market. There was surplus cash but not enough good deals to invest into, with the result that too much cash was following to too few deals. The valuations of good, well-managed companies were superficially high. After considerable research, CEA established a new development model. Rick decided that since we could not bring cash to deals, it would be better to reverse engineer the business model and take deals to cash. The idea was to adapt and re-engineer successful business models of companies in developed markets to better suit the Middle Eastern market. The main challenge was the lack of a pan-Arab market.

This was the birth of Communications Development Corporation (CDC), established as a joint venture between CEA and a few Middle Eastern families. Between 1998 and 2001, we were involved with several projects in the Middle East. Setting up a business in Dubai required a local sponsor and I was fortunate to be introduced to Dr Juma Al Matrooshi. Dr Juma, as we affectionately called him, was an unassuming and modest man who could get just about anything done. We nicknamed him "the magic man". He provided the priceless administrative support needed to build a great franchise in the region.

The projects that Carsten and I executed, first on behalf of CDC and later CMA, included a pan-Arab TV network in Dubai; transitioning Arabsat from C-band to Ku-band; a home-shopping network in collaboration with QVC in Kuwait; a music-based entertainment TV channel from Turkey; a cable-TV network in Oman; a GSM licence in Yemen; two-way internet via satellite in Kuwait; a media-sales company in Qatar; a document-management company in the UAE; a prepaid calling card in Saudi Arabia; call centres in the GCC; radio networks in Egypt; and publishing companies in the Levant.

The TMT sector in the Middle East was changing rapidly in the 1990s. Most countries had monopolies in telecommunications, and the media industry in the GCC was highly regulated. Other markets had opened up, but advertising was very small and the businesses remained marginal. With the success of CNN, a number of satellite TV stations emerged from Lebanon, including LBC and Future TV, and the Saudi-owned MBC set up in Jeddah, but later moved its operations to Dubai Media City. Of the various pay-TV operations that emerged, the pioneer was Saudi-owned Orbit, followed by Sheikh Saleh Kamel's ART and the Kuwait-backed Showtime, a joint venture between KIPCO and Viacom (CBS). The ensuing period was a veritable bloodbath, as the platforms paid enormous amounts of money for content from studios in the US and the UK. The take-up rates for pay TV remained small and the three networks incurred huge losses. To further exacerbate the situation, Dubai launched its own cable TV, followed by all the other countries in the GCC.

All three pay-TV operators eventually moved their operations from Italy to Dubai Media City. People argued over the years about the futility of three platforms for the Middle East, but since the shareholders had deep pockets, no one was willing to relent. It was more about personal ego than business sense. It was only after Showtime's aborted attempt, under Peter Einstein's watch, to list in 2006 that good sense finally prevailed and Showtime merged with Orbit to form OSN, which subsequently bought ART's Asian bouquet.

I watched with astonishment as the television networks haemorrhaged large amounts of money just to stay afloat. To my mind, it was a result of complete mismanagement that none of the networks, other than MBC and LBC, made any money. We offered to advise them, but they were not interested in making their operations leaner or more efficient. If it did not involve spending more money, they were not interested. Clearly, the shareholders did not object to what was happening and had the deep pockets to support the excesses.

Many of our efforts to develop projects failed owing to regulatory obstacles. Two come to mind that would have been excellent opportunities. The first was to set up a cable-TV network in Oman. CEA, the Majid Al Futtaim Group (MAF Telecom) from Dubai and Ominvest from Oman signed a memorandum of understanding to set up the operation in Muscat. We spent a fair amount of time and resources meeting with the Ministry of Posts, Telegraphs and Telephones; the Ministry of Information; the Ministry of Culture; and Oman TV. After eighteen months of follow-ups, we finally had to abandon the project because the various entities could not decide which ministry was eventually going to be responsible for the licensing. Consequently, there was no one to take the project to cabinet for approval. In retrospect, I think we should have partnered with Oman Telecom, as they already had the frequencies and it would have been easier for them to secure the media licence. This experience taught me about synergies and choosing the right partners for projects. It is not just about the ability to invest cash. Being able to navigate other elements that present barriers to entry, like licensing, is equally important.

The second was a cable-TV project that we developed in Beirut. I had first visited Beirut in 1993 and found a city completely destroyed by ethnic violence and a civil war that had lasted fifteen years. Buildings in Hamra Street and in the Achrafieh district were riddled with bullet holes and signs of heavy artillery. For a city once known as the Paris of the Middle East, Beirut was battered and all but beaten.

The Lebanese have always fascinated me for their resilience and fortitude. Lebanon is one of the few countries in the world where you can enjoy snow-capped mountains over breakfast and be at a sunny beach for lunch or tea. The authentic meze in Lebanon offers more than eighty dishes, including tomatoes the size of small melons. I enjoyed many evenings at the Bourj Al Haman restaurant in Beirut looking down into the valley, reflecting on how God could give so much with the one hand yet take away with the other. For all the beauty of the country, there has unfortunately never been any stability.

By 1997, Beirut had undergone a radical, positive transformation. One of the reasons for this was the establishment of the real-estate company Solidere, the brainchild of then prime minister Rafiq Hariri.

In 1994 he set up a joint stock company, offering shares to all property owners, and completely rebuilt the central district in downtown Beirut. At the time, there were conflicting news reports on the questionable methods used by the government to set up Solidere, but, without condoning these methods, the outcome from a foreigner's perspective was spectacular. As an example, once the new airport and road leading to it were inaugurated in 1998, the journey into the city was reduced from over an hour to less than fifteen minutes. I could not believe how a war-torn city could be changed into something so magnificent in such a short space of time.

In 1997 we started discussions with Solidere about the possibility of setting up a cable-TV company in the central district. In 1998 we signed a memorandum of understanding for jointly evaluating the opportunity. The project was opportune, since large satellite dishes were banned on the rooftops for aesthetic reasons. American management consulting firm Booz Allen Hamilton was hired to do the techno-economic feasibility studies. Each element of the report validated what we already expected; it was an exceptionally lucrative project, as the company would be the gatekeeper for triple play, encompassing voice, video and data. Unfortunately, at the end of 1998, Hariri left office and all projects, particularly anything to do with Solidere, were unexpectedly put into cold storage. For us, the cost in terms of actual resources committed and the lost opportunity was significant.

But it wasn't all doom and gloom. One successful project that we were very proud of was Saudi Telecard, a company set up in Saudi Arabia to bid for a prepaid calling-card licence. Telecommunications was largely controlled by the state and, rather than give out a second fixed-line licence or open up the cellular business, Saudi Telecom decided to test the waters with privatisation of low-end services that they would eventually control. Since tele-density was very low in Saudi Arabia, the calling-card initiative was designed to increase the number of customers using the fixed-line network. The idea was to better leverage the fixed-line asset with no investment on the part of Saudi Telecom. The licence allowed private-sector companies to establish an exchange, through which consumers (be they local, resident expatriates or tourists) could make calls using the existing fixed-line network. The commercial terms of the licence allowed the private-sector operators to retain 10 per cent of the revenues collected, while the other 90 per cent went to Saudi Telecom. Saudi Telecard was one of six companies to be given a licence in Saudi Arabia and one of only four to become operational.

It was a great learning curve for all of us. I was busy on a start-up TV project in Dubai, but Carsten and David Green, our in-house telecoms expert hired by CEA from MAF Telecom, took charge of the planning and implementation. Once the licence was issued, I got involved with the debt financing for the project and made several presentations to banks in Riyadh along with our Saudi partners. We finally secured the debt and the project was successfully launched in 2000. Saudi is not an easy market and has many limitations for foreigners, particularly if you do not understand Arabic. It is perhaps the most insular of all the markets in the Middle East, but once you get to know people, it is not so bad. Many foreigners live in Saudi and love being there, but while I enjoyed visiting for business and the occasional Saudi champagne at the InterContinental in Riyadh, I could not ever imagine living there. Since ours was a developmental role in Saudi Telecard, once we had established the company and operations and hired a management team, we moved on to other projects, although Carsten continued serving on the board. We later sold the company to our Saudi partners.

Another country that really fascinated me during my travels was Yemen. We had sourced two projects there for development: the first was the introduction of the Yellow Pages to the country, in conjunction with TeleYemen, and the second was the privatisation of the cellular business. TeleYemen was a joint venture between Yemen Public Telecommunications Corporation, and Cable and Wireless plc. I travelled several times between Aden and Sana'a from 1999 to 2001, reviewing these projects. Yemen was then the poorest country in the Middle East. It was backward and underdeveloped, and the infrastructure and facilities were very basic, yet it was rich in cultural heritage. I remember being pleasantly surprised to find that the Taj in Sana'a provided beer in the minibar, something unique in Yemen during that period.

On one of the trips, David Green and I went to the Haraz Mountains, close to Sana'a. The region is famous for its coffee production and khat, a plant containing an amphetamine-like stimulant chewed by all Yemeni men. We were on top of one of the mountains when we found an antique shop. David was extremely impressed with an antique dagger that was on display. The Yemeni merchant quoted US$2000 for this dagger, which he said was from the Ottoman Empire. David jumped on this chance to own a unique part of history, and the merchant was thrilled to have found his "sucker". I told David not to show any enthusiasm and questioned whether he was serious about the purchase. When he insisted that he was, I told him to leave the store. Before I could say a word, the merchant asked me, "Where are you from?" to which I replied, "India". He frowned and said, "There is no point bullshitting, is there? So please tell me what you will pay and let's get over this misery." I walked out of the store with two antique daggers for the princely sum of US$400.

We participated in a number of interesting ventures during my time at CDC. One project that stands out was the launch of India's CNBC TV18, by Raghav Bahl. The company grew from a small production house into one of the largest media conglomerates in India. I had always been fascinated by CNBC as a brand and was even more intrigued to learn that the business model made it an attractive investment opportunity. CEA invested in TV18 when it was still a production house and witnessed the company establish the first business TV channel in India, under a franchise with CNBC. CEA exited when the company went public, along with AIG and a few other early-stage investors. I was not in favour of this exit, as the returns would have been 300 per cent more if CEA had waited for just another two years.

* * *

As we were building the investment banking business in the Middle East, there was yet another storm brewing on the horizon: the internet. In 1995, there were about fifteen million internet users. Two decades later and that number has grown to over 3.2 billion users worldwide. No other industry has seen such rapid year-on-year growth. Through the mid- to late 1990s, the discussion around convergence radically changed, as the complete model for delivery of voice, video and data began to take on new meaning. Technologies around compression linked to this cyber goliath were creating opportunities that people could not yet comprehend. One immediate and visible effect was that the average age of entrepreneurs dropped to the early twenties. Fast-talking young college dropouts from Silicon Valley were now talking about a redefined future, which would be revolutionised by technology.

As the internet bubble began to expand, we were presented with another great private equity opportunity, this time with Gulf Finance House (GFH). GFH was established in 1999 by a number of financial institutions, some of which were based in Kuwait. Carsten and I had done some advisory work for Mohammed Al Alloush, the CEO of Gulf Investment House, and he suggested I meet Esam Janahi, CEO of GFH. While GFH was being established, Esam wanted, as a first project, to set up a platform of sector funds in the Middle East. Once again, he was a visionary with ambitious ideas way ahead of the development curve in the Middle East. GFH was keen to launch a technology fund and enthusiastic to use CEA's track record to raise capital. There was a sense of déjà vu, as I had seen CEA use Barings to start their own private equity business and now a Bahrain-based company wanted to leverage CEA's experience to raise US$50 million for a Middle East–focused technology fund.

The only caveat was that the fund had to be Islamic. Education and learning have always been part of my journey, so I immediately enrolled for an online course in Islamic finance. Esam asked me to help raise the capital for the fund on the understanding that CDC would be the technical advisor to the fund. This meant that we would do the filtering and funnelling of deals, and provide an opinion or recommendation to the management team on whether or not to invest in a proposed transaction. This was a dream mandate, as it gave us an annuity contract tied to the investment cycle of the fund.

Carsten and I spent a year with the GFH team travelling all over the GCC for the fund's roadshow. GFH had an impressive list of clients across the region and we managed to close the fund in record time. Half the fund capital came from GFH and the Islamic Development Bank through their private-sector arm, the newly formed Islamic Corporation for the Development of the Private Sector. Other investors included top Islamic financial institutions from Qatar, the UAE, Saudi Arabia, Kuwait and Iran. There were only a handful of interested investors, as the minimum investment was US$5 million. Eventually, the Injazat Technology Fund was registered in Bahrain in 2001 and set up in Dubai Media City with Mohamed Mejai of the Islamic Development Bank as its CEO.

As the internet continued to grow, it seemed to me that many people were losing their sanity. We saw some very innovative technology ideas from the Levant, Kuwait, Saudi Arabia and the UAE during this time. The internet had caught on and some of the most incredible business plans were doing the rounds with the hope of being funded. But for every good one there were at least a dozen bad ones. The worst were from people from some of the top Ivy League business schools, who came with start-ups modelled on the US market looking to raise cash from the Middle Eastern market.

There's an important saying in the army: bullshit baffles brains. The business plans we started seeing in this period were complex mazes of utter fantasy, but they somehow managed to fool even the most rational minds. One of the presentations I attended while reviewing an opportunity for Injazat was on an internet portal to sell Islamic securities to investors in the United States. The company needed US$5 million in round one, had made some outrageous projections on potential revenue, and had come up with an obscene valuation. I was flabbergasted. When I questioned the rationale for US investors' appetite for Islamic securities, I was told that I was not getting it. "This is the internet, Mr Wahi. You seem to be missing the point." Point or no point, we shot down many of these deals, remaining steadfast in our thinking and retaining our fortunes through a very tumultuous period.

Although we had some trying boardroom battles with the investment committee over various deals like the one just mentioned, the experience with GFH and Injazat was invaluable for me personally. I came to understand that investment decisions must be made on no rationale other than a clearly defined revenue model, supported by cash flow. Deviation will produce catastrophic results.

The scale of some of the global deals that went down during this period left many gaping with astonishment. When America Online (AOL) and Time Warner merged in 2000 – a deal valued at over US$350 billion and approved by more than 95 per cent of the shareholders of both companies – it was the biggest deal in the history of Wall Street. It saw the shareholders of a well-established bricks-and-mortar company (Time Warner) swap their shares for 45 per cent of the merged entity. The merger ultimately failed when the dot-com bubble burst shortly thereafter, and billions of dollars of shareholder value were lost. In 2002, AOL Time Warner lost US$99 billion in market capitalisation. With the dot-com collapse, the NASDAQ declined by 78 per cent, the largest fall in the index's history. Private companies that had billions invested in them by large technology funds in the US, Europe and Asia were decimated. It was carnage of the worst kind, and unfortunate for everyone in the sector. Even though we had refrained from any dot-com investments, association with an industry that had brought the world to the brink impacted the credibility of our business.

While the sector in the Middle East lagged behind the developed world, wealthy sovereign funds and large investors in places like Saudi Arabia were not spared the madness. Carsten and I had always wanted to manage a fund of our own, domiciled out of Dubai, and we began working on a structure in 2001. The reality of people's errors in judgement when it came to the dot-com bubble did not dawn on us until we began fundraising in Jeddah for our new fund planned for launch in 2002. A few institutions declined to participate on account of the conservative nature of their investment portfolios. We accepted their reasoning and returned home, only to find the names of some of these institutions tied to some extremely risky investments in internet companies like Boo.com. The reality is that bullshit *does* baffle brains; sometimes people can't help themselves and get swayed by "the next big thing".

We made another interesting discovery while fundraising for our new fund, this time in London, in January 2002. Owing to market conditions, many funds were struggling with timely drawdowns from investors or limited partners who had been defaulting. We came up with an innovative fund structure that would draw all the funds upfront, but enhance returns during the investment cycle through fixed money-market securities.

We took the model to several mutual-fund managers, one of which was Bear Stearns. We had the pleasure of visiting their Canary Wharf headquarters, where their technical team gave us a detailed presentation. We spent two hours in an opulent and impressive boardroom, but I did not understand a word of what was being said. I was far too embarrassed to ask questions and acknowledge my ignorance. Luckily Carsten was taking copious notes; his Harvard education seemed to be holding him in good stead.

When the meeting finished I waited for Carsten to summarise our position, which he courteously did. Like a thorough gentleman, he thanked them profusely for their patience and indulgence. As soon as we got into our car, I asked Carsten to explain what had just happened. He looked at me and said, "How should I know, weren't you the one paying such close attention? I wanted to leave after fifteen minutes!" "What about all the notes you were taking?" I asked. "It's been a long trip," he replied. "I was completing my expense reports and trip memos."

We still laugh about this incident. It taught me that it does not matter how big you are, you still need to simplify the details for your client, or you will lose him or her. We often assume that people know what we are talking about. The sad reality is that there is a huge difference between working knowledge and detailed understanding. When dealing with potential clients, assume that they do not know anything about your business. Walk them through everything you do, and explain how it is relevant to their business. If you don't make that connection, you have just wasted everyone's time.

As the markets closed around us in 2002, I realised the time of reckoning had come once again. After taking a battering in the markets, and on the back of shrinking revenues and some bad investment decisions in the UK, CEA decided to consolidate its operations back into the US. Some people close to Rick, and to whom he had delegated responsibility, let him down badly and unfortunately he had to pay the price of their disloyalty. I could only watch with anger as these individuals completely abused the trust that he had placed in them. Watching a man whom I held in such high regard suffer the consequences of betrayal was difficult, but it was an invaluable lesson.

The Middle Eastern partners approached me with an offer to continue building the business without CEA or its team. When I declined out of loyalty to Rick and Carsten, the partners were amazed and understandably upset. Loyalty can be a huge burden. It is more than a word; it is your actions, your religion and your honour. I did ask my father and Saloni if they thought I was crazy to pass up the opportunity, but they both agreed that following the just path, no matter how much harder, was the better option. I did what I believed was right, irrespective of the consequences, and thus continued on the path towards my destiny.

ASIA

In April 2002 I was once again at a crossroads. This time around, I was forty-two and a lot better prepared, and had established credibility both with investors and in an industry. Sidharth was fourteen and at boarding school in India, while Shweta was eleven and in school in Dubai. The decision this time would be significant, as it would perhaps be the last major change of my career. I went back to the drawing board and looked at the landscape and the opportunities around me.

I now wanted to combine my sector knowledge with my experience in emerging markets and try to set up businesses from the bottom up. I had seen, both in Russia and through our investments in portfolio companies of funds, that real value creation was in start-ups in emerging markets, and that the riskier the terrain, the higher the risk–reward ratio. It was clear to me that this was my destiny.

In February 2001, my father-in-law, Promod, had been diagnosed with stage-four prostate cancer. It came as a shock to everyone, as he was absolutely healthy. Saloni returned home in March to be with her parents. I had asked her to forget about any responsibilities towards our family and spend whatever time she needed with her father.

Then, exactly a year later, my father was diagnosed with throat cancer. The doctor asked me to fly to Delhi, as they did not want to give him the news without my being there. Saloni and I met the doctor along with my mother and two sisters, Sunanda and Shalini, after which we went into my father's room. When he saw all of us, he must have realised that something was wrong. I watched my father's expression as the doctor, with exceptional sensitivity, broke the news. He was absolutely stoical as he listened to the prognosis. He looked up at the doctor and said, "The good news is that we know the problem; now let's hear the solution." The doctor suggested chemotherapy. He asked my father to think about it and perhaps get a second opinion before going ahead with the treatment. Again my father surprised me by saying, "I don't need another opinion; I came to you in the first instance because I have faith in you and am happy to put myself in your care." He has always been a decisive man and procrastination was never an option, even when he faced the greatest challenge of his life.

The doctor, though accomplished, was sceptical, as he knew that he was dealing with one of the most well-known corporate leaders of all time. He nevertheless accepted the response and they began my father's treatment.

This was perhaps the most trying period in my life. As the only son, my first reaction was to shift my base back to India, so that I could be close to my father. Saloni was in a similar position with her own father. Unfortunately, in his case the cancer had not been diagnosed in time and had started to spread. Both of us were torn over what we should do and, after many sleepless nights of deliberation, began seriously considering a move back to India.

Between the bouts of chemotherapy, I spoke about my intentions with my father. He was unable to speak, as he had almost entirely lost his voice, but with gestures and the help of a slate board, he asked me not to make the mistake of relocating to India. He told me that there was nothing I could do for him that my mother could not and that I needed to go back to battle and continue on my own path. This was a tough time for my parents, but they did not show any weakness, as they knew it would break my will to continue with my work. Our parents' moments of selflessness are perhaps what parenthood is all about. We take our parents for granted, as they continue to make silent and painstaking sacrifices each day so that we can accomplish our dreams. It was another turning point in my life, as things would have been very different had I moved back to India.

Saloni's father finally succumbed to his illness on 8 September 2003, twenty days short of his sixty-fifth birthday. Towards the end of his life I was given a closer insight into my wife's family and how they came together to deal with the crisis. The devotion and commitment shown by my mother-in-law, Anjula, and her three children, Saloni, Shalini and Gaurav, was heart-wrenching. My wife was extremely close to her father and his death took a big toll on her. He was a man of the highest character and integrity. Although he had been extremely hard on me while I was courting his daughter, his passing had a big impact on me; and even more so when my mother-in-law honoured me by asking me to perform the last rites with Gaurav, an act that was absolutely unprecedented in the Hindu culture. These acts only come from superior human beings who have transcended all barriers to follow what they believe to be right. My mother-in-law exemplifies these virtues and is a lady for whom I have the utmost respect.

My own father defied all the odds and kept surprising the doctors with his willpower and tenacity. He was finally declared cured of cancer in 2007, after having been in remission for five years. His battle was made somewhat easier owing to the commitment of my mother and Saloni, and the unfailing love and devotion of my two sisters. Shalini, whom we affectionately call Shaloo, lives in Delhi and was there by my parents' side all through this very trying period, often assuming the role that a son would normally play in our culture.

In May 2002, I established CMA in the British Virgin Islands and set up an affiliate in Dubai. Once again, Saloni joined the business and provided invaluable support in getting it off the ground. Although I had taken the decision to continue our operations from Dubai, from 2002 onwards I went home almost every month for two to three days to be with my father. He often told me not to come and said that we could connect equally well via telephone, but for me it was not the same. Having gone to boarding school from a young age, I had missed out on a lot when I was growing up and these visits enabled us to grow closer. It was the start of a new phase in my relationship with my parents, as they began discussing things in a more spiritual context, and examining their lives and the mistakes they had made. It dawned on me that, irrespective of what we do and where we go, we remain emotionally interdependent with our parents and need to keep nurturing this gift from God.

This phase was challenging emotionally as I struggled to balance my personal concerns with my fledgling business. It was not easy and Saloni helped by taking on many responsibilities, both at home and at the office, so that I could focus on building the foundations of yet another major transition. I wanted to start developing projects from the bottom up and spent innumerable hours writing feasibility studies and sharing ideas with my friends and potential investment partners.

The first start-up I tackled was with my long-time friend Rajiv Podar. I first met Rajiv when I was in the army and we remained in touch after I moved to Dubai. He comes from a proud lineage of business families, is a fourth-generation industrialist, and a down-to-earth and outstanding leader with high personal integrity and values. Rajiv and I did some business together in Russia and shared some exciting stories during our travels. He continues to maintain a strong presence in both Russia and China, and has invested significantly in building business opportunities between those countries and India.

We had been talking about a document-management business for a while, and eventually decided to set something up in Mumbai. P Document Management Solutions was established in 2003 with a warehouse in Vashi. The business model was a real-estate arbitrage in Mumbai where companies could free up expensive real estate and store their paperwork at an external location, at a fraction of the cost. The main driver for revenue growth, however, was the digitisation of content.

The business got off to a good start under Rajiv's leadership and that of his management team in Mumbai. As expected, the first year was tough because it was a sunrise industry and because Indian businesses are surprisingly conservative when it comes to corporate documentation. As business began to ramp up, we started putting our expansion plans into motion. During this period, the investment climate in India was extremely buoyant. With Rajiv's international networks, it wasn't surprising that before long the company received a takeover bid from a multinational logistics company that was looking to enter this space in the Indian market. The board reviewed the offer and we decided to exit in 2007.

It may perhaps have been too early for us to exit, but I do believe that our decision was the right one and everyone came away smiling with a "10x gain" from the transaction. I found the experience of working with Rajiv extremely enriching and it brought us even closer as friends. While there are many schools of thought about doing business with friends, my experience has been that if expectations, rights and responsibilities are clearly managed, success can be accomplished. However, the overriding value is trust, and as long as that is unwavering, you are likely to succeed with any business relationship you establish.

As we were building the document-management business, I met another entrepreneur, Lars Jeppesen. It was as if I was destined to do business with Danes, the first being Carsten. Lars was at that time running a successful IT business, Valuevad, distributing document-management solutions like Kofax, which was owned by the Dicom Group, a Swiss-domiciled global document-capture and enterprise content-management solutions company. Lars had successfully scaled up the business and was looking at expansion capital on one side and a buyout of some of his shareholders who were keen to exit the business on the other. I helped Lars through the process of preparing the company for capital-raising, but it was a tough market as the tech sector was reaching its nadir. While we were meeting potential partners, Dicom made Lars an offer to buy him out with an attractive valuation on the proviso that he stayed on for three years as CEO.

While the Valuevad sale was underway, Lars got an opportunity to establish a software-distribution business in Sri Lanka to distribute Microsoft. The opportunity was far too great to turn down. I discussed this with another close friend, Ali Bagash, who, apart from being a successful entrepreneur, is a man with a golden heart. Ali was also an investor in the special purpose vehicle through which we had invested into Seaport Capital Partners in the US. He was principally in real estate and oil trading, but, through his family holdings, had a large and diversified investment portfolio of listed and unlisted companies. He did not think twice when I told him about the opportunity. He came in as the principal investor, as he had the large credit lines needed to provide guarantees to Microsoft, as well as access to trade finance on bulk orders required by the company.

When we were going through the feasibility, the main concern was political stability, as Sri Lanka was in the midst of a civil war that had started in 1983 (it would continue until 2009, when the Tamil Tigers were finally defeated). The other issue in Sri Lanka was rampant piracy. This was actually the bigger concern, as market education and regulatory recourse were still in their infancy. Microsoft at that stage covered Sri Lanka through their Indian distribution network and were themselves cautious about the business case.

What finally clinched the deal for us, from an internal investment decision perspective, was the size of the market and the fact that we had a person on the ground whom Lars could trust. Wasantha Weerakoon, who joined as general manager, had worked closely with Lars in the Middle East and was largely responsible for building the business. I met with the Board of Investment (BOI) in Colombo and we registered Tech One Global as a BOI-registered entity with three staff members in 2003. Over the last decade, the company has grown into one of the largest SMEs in the IT sector in Sri Lanka. Based on our success in Sri Lanka, we went ahead and established similar operations in Bangladesh, Nepal, Brunei, Maldives, Singapore and the Philippines. In 2016, Tech One Global was awarded Microsoft Partner of the Year in the Philippines, Bangladesh, Brunei and Nepal.

As the business grew, we brought in Wasantha as a partner and aligned his interests with those of the business. In the meantime, Lars completed his buyout obligations at Valuevad and joined Tech One Global as CEO and managing director, providing the leadership we needed. Lars relocated to the Philippines, a personal choice as his wife was from there, and this gave us the management support we needed in South-East Asia, where we were generating increasing interest and revenue.

Given the evolution of software distribution to cloud computing, we evolved our business model to become more solutions based and began product development. The company also partnered with Certiport for IT education in Sri Lanka. Certiport offers, among other courses, Internet and Computing Core Certification (IC3), Microsoft Office Specialist (MOS) and Microsoft Office Specialist 2003 (MOS 2003). These programs integrated well with our core business, as they are structured around Microsoft products.

Since the distribution business is based on high volume and low margins, we needed to boost activities that would increase our margins. To achieve this, we acquired a document-management business in Sri Lanka, an affiliate company owned by Wasantha and his family. The transaction was achieved through a share swap that gave Tech One Global ownership of Sanje Lanka, and Wasantha received additional equity in the holding company. Building on this strategy, Lars spearheaded a new initiative to create our own products for document management. Enadoc was born eighteen months after conceptualisation and is now gaining momentum as a leading innovative, cloud-based, enterprise document imaging and management system. Under Lars's excellent leadership, the joint company now has over 600 employees across seven countries, with plans to grow into another three in the near future. Tech One Global was a classic example of a home run, where the value creation was exponential for the shareholders, both in terms of wealth creation and dividends.

Over the years, as the business scaled up, we received a fair amount of investor interest. Some of the offers were tempting, but the four partners decided not to dilute or exit. We had developed a magic formula, built on trust, and we did not want to interfere with our ability to stay entrepreneurial and nimble. That did not mean we never argued; our board meetings were always interesting and tough, but the beers afterwards made up for everything.

* * *

As mentioned previously, I had met Zafar Siddiqi in 2002, at which time he was producing content for various television networks in Asia and was lobbying for the CNBC franchise for the Middle East. Zafar had, at that time, engaged a UAE-based firm to help him raise capital, but was facing significant resistance particularly because there were very few TV businesses making money. At the end of the day, despite promises, the UAE firm was unable to help him. And so Zafar retained CMA to assist him with fundraising for CNBC Arabia. I took a very pragmatic approach and introduced him to a few families with whom I had done business and who all had an understanding of the media business. Some of these families were from Qatar. As expected, CNBC Arabia was finally funded by Qatari investors and was launched in 2003 in Dubai Media City. After its launch, I continued as an advisor to Zafar and his senior management, assisting with strategic aspects of the business.

Soon after the launch of CNBC Arabia, the Pakistani government announced plans to issue additional TV licences and requested intent from interested companies. Zafar again retained CMA, this time to help complete the documentation for the licensing as well as issue an information memorandum to raise capital. CNBC Pakistan was capitalised with investments from the UAE, Kuwait and Pakistan, and finally established in 2004. I do believe that these projects were an early indicator that our destinies were aligned, as we started working together on building interdependence, a sound partnership and a true friendship.

AFRICA

With these two networks established, I began looking around for other territories in which to launch CNBC. It was then that Cliff Tendler, director for business development at CNBC Arabia, suggested sub-Saharan Africa. Cliff's wife Pam was South African and he had spent some time there. He provided vital insights into the media industry in South Africa and played an important role in developing the business case for coming to Africa. He stayed with the project for the first year, but moved on when he got a better career opportunity.

While Zafar and I were reflecting on the merits of this opportunity, Eddie Mbalo, CEO of South Africa's National Film and Video Foundation, visited Dubai. Over dinner, he extended an invitation to me to visit Johannesburg. Eddie was our first contact in South Africa and played a pivotal role in introducing us to several decision-makers there.

I set foot in Johannesburg for the first time in October 2004 and was completely bowled over by the state of infrastructure development in South Africa. Eddie had used his good offices to set up an excellent schedule of meetings with various institutions, including the Industrial Development Corporation (IDC), the Independent Communications Authority of South Africa (ICASA), the Gauteng Economic Development Agency (GEDA) and the Gauteng Film Commission (GFC). Cliff had set up some additional appointments with MultiChoice, a few advertising agencies and some of his friends, including people from Summit TV (now BusinessDay TV).

Sub-Saharan Africa is a complex terrain of about forty-eight countries with a population close to a billion people. Governments within the region have established several economic groups like the Economic Community of West African States, the Southern African Development Community, the Common Market for Eastern and Southern Africa, the East African Community, the Economic Community of Central African States and the New Partnership for Africa's Development, formed to promote regional integration and the development of trade. While most countries are anglophone, several are francophone and Portuguese-speaking. Sub-Saharan Africa has an extremely chequered past, since most countries in the region were colonised variously by the Portuguese, Dutch, French and British.

There is a strong misconception among people unfamiliar with sub-Saharan Africa that it is one homogeneous entity. The countries in sub-Saharan Africa are in actual fact fragmented and diverse in terms of development. South Africa is perhaps the closest to a developed country, while most others are in various stages of development. In terms of demographics, Nigeria has close to 185 million people, Ethiopia 90 million, the Democratic Republic of the Congo

77 million, Tanzania 55 million, South Africa 50 million and Kenya 45 million, while over 25 countries have populations below 10 million. Most of the countries in the region have been marred by a long history of poor leadership and the indiscriminate plundering of resources resulting in abject poverty.

As I travelled across the continent, and in keeping with my experiences of emerging markets in Asia, I realised that in most cases the biggest malady was the greed of those in power. Even in the largest economies in sub-Saharan Africa unemployment was rising and currencies were tumbling. While some of this was the result of global events, a large part was self-inflicted. There were, however, pockets of development and growth during this period, particularly in countries like Rwanda and Mauritius.

I was also exposed during my initial visits to the different shades of democracy. This did not surprise me at all, as I had witnessed the evolution of democracy in India. Political systems evolve, and as long as it doesn't infringe on basic human rights, one style of democracy can be just as good as another. This was tactfully articulated by Russian president Vladimir Putin in an interview with CNN in June 2016 when he said of the American Electoral College system: "Now, do you really think presidential elections [in the United States] are democratic? Look, twice in US history a president was elected by a majority of electors, but standing behind those electors was a smaller number of voters [super-delegates]. Is that democracy?" Why I use this example is because African democracies are evolving and will mature to what works best for each individual country.

Despite all the uncertainties and volatility caused by poor leadership, what was apparent was the great economic opportunity that existed in sub-Saharan Africa. This was my first impression as I travelled through the major economies like South Africa, Kenya, Nigeria and Ghana. What was also apparent was that over the years there had been much irresponsible reporting, leaving the rest of the world with a skewed picture of the continent. Problems were magnified, while economic development and growth were understated. Furthermore, there was no pan-African television channel to report on the successes in this important part of the world. Here was an opportunity to tell Africa's story and change perceptions of the continent. This was perhaps the starting point for our interest in sub-Saharan Africa.

However, when we carried out the pre-feasibility study to get a top-line assessment of the opportunity, the project did not stack up at all. The only driver in favour was that there was so much economic activity in Africa that, editorially, there was more than enough to report on. But, among other problems, there was limited distribution and a non-existent pan-African advertising market. MultiChoice was the only credible platform for delivery of content via a high-end pay-TV service that catered solely to the top demographic. The only other pay-TV service was Vivid, operated by Sentech, and there was no possibility of getting a terrestrial frequency. Other than South Africa, which had a mature advertising market, there was no information on advertising across sub-Saharan Africa.

After a few trips, we concluded that the project was far too risky and perhaps the best course of action would be to pass up the opportunity. It was small wonder why no other TV network had set up, or been successful, until then. Nevertheless, in March 2005 we received a communication from GEDA that they wanted to meet with us to discuss the project further. A delegation arrived in Dubai and communicated a strong intent on behalf of the Gauteng Provincial Government (GPG) for us to establish a presence in South Africa. One of the compelling factors for the government was their plan to set up a media centre in Johannesburg for the 2010 FIFA World Cup, which the country was to host. The idea was for CNBC to be based in the media centre after the World Cup, so that a media cluster could be developed. We voiced our concerns about the project limitations to the delegation and they assured us that the GPG would review the points and revert on how to mitigate some of the constraints.

It took us almost eighteen months from that meeting to finalise our plans and analyse the market from all aspects. It was encouraging to see the overwhelming response from every country to which I travelled, particularly Nigeria. Engineer Mustafa Bello from the Nigerian Investment Promotion Commission met me in Abuja and assisted with the company set-up. I had the opportunity to meet with various government leaders from the departments of trade, industry, commerce, information and communications, and they were all extremely supportive of the initiative.

Despite its enthusiasm, Nigeria was an extremely difficult market to understand. The challenges started from the time we landed. The chaos of the immigration process at Lagos airport was unparalleled. It took forever. The air conditioning and escalators did not work. There were touts everywhere plucking the lucky few out of the immigration lines and ushering them towards the immigration desks and through a painstaking VIP service that attracted loud jeering from everyone still in the queues. I had to suffer the long lines during my initial visits, but once we established an office in Nigeria, we got our own protocol officer to fast-track us through immigration.

The chaos, however, did not end at the immigration desk. Baggage claim was an even bigger nightmare. It could take anywhere between sixty and ninety minutes to get your bags. Once out of the airport, you had to walk some distance to wait for your car and then you just prayed for light traffic on the drive from the airport to Victoria Island. The airport and traffic were mere inconveniences, however, compared to the main issue, which was the lack of infrastructure and power. For a population of over 180 million there are only 4 000 megawatts of available capacity, compared with 35 000 megawatts for 50 million people in South Africa. Over 50 per cent of the Nigerian population does not have access to electricity. It is estimated that over US$125 billion of economic opportunity is lost each year owing to inadequate infrastructure alone.

Despite these impediments, the Nigerian economy is slowly but surely growing in the right direction. Each successive government has been more progressive, and with the growing need for transparency, expenditure is finally finding its way, albeit slowly, into infrastructure projects. When we first arrived, there was absolutely no doubt in anyone's mind that at a macro level Nigeria would eventually surpass South Africa as the largest economy in Africa. We were proved correct in 2014 when, after the rebasing of the economy, Nigeria overtook South Africa's gross domestic product by a wide margin. (In 2016, owing to currency and lower oil prices, Nigeria dropped back to second place, after South Africa.) Nevertheless, at a micro level, the challenges pertaining to our business were many and complex.

The issue across all of Africa was that legislation in the media and communications space had been blindly following global industry trends. Distribution of television was either on an analogue terrestrial service with limited frequencies, or on MultiChoice, by default the only other available distribution platform. While most countries had white papers on digital migration, because it was not a priority for governments, implementation and financing were far from finalised. Some of the smaller countries had issued licences to private TV stations, but these were rare and capacity concerns for getting distribution for niche television stations like ours were disconcerting. Despite being the largest market, South Africa had shown surprisingly little haste in implementing its digital migration.

South Africa eventually did start the licence process for regulating the direct-to-home space previously dominated by MultiChoice, but the offering limited foreign ownership to 20 per cent. No major international media company was interested in entering the bidding process in a marginal capacity that offered no protection to foreign investors. Having thus virtually shut out anyone with major experience in the business, the Department of Communications and ICASA awarded five new licences in September 2007 based on the criteria that had been set: one each to MultiChoice, On Digital Media, Telkom Media, Walking on Water (WOWtv) and e.tv. As we were looking at launching CNBC Africa at the time, I had also reviewed this opportunity and tried to put together a consortium to partner the local players. However, after several rounds of discussions, we decided to stay out of something that appeared to be a bloodbath in the offing.

Our fears were proved correct when e.tv did a content-supply deal with MultiChoice and did not implement their licence, Telkom Media collapsed, and WOWtv never got off the ground. This left On Digital Media, which launched with a lot of fanfare. However, with no compelling content or management experience, the project folded and was finally taken over in 2014 by the Chinese-owned StarTimes. The entire exercise had come full circle: after spending hundreds of millions of dollars, MultiChoice remained the undisputed king.

* * *

For a channel provider, the circumstances in Africa are relatively easy from a regulatory perspective. Direct-to-home operators are responsible for the content they carry and therefore have to make sure that their content complies with the culture and laws of the country in which they are operating. Being almost a monopoly, for several decades MultiChoice has been the gatekeeper of content into Africa, and has self-regulated all the content providers, exercising undisputed control over the industry.

While we did not face any problems with approvals, we did have to go through several rounds of clarifications in different countries, particularly where the laws around satellite free-to-air channels were not clear. For instance, the Nigerian government facilitated our launch in 2007, but decided retroactively to audit our licence requirements in 2009. It took them a year to complete the audit and give us a green light for our operations. Most governments viewed CNBC as a neutral genre, more as an opportunity to change perceptions than a threat. For instance, in 2008 we were the only channel providing a balanced view of the violence that followed the Kenyan election results, and were the only channel permitted to continue broadcasting live from Nairobi.

The CNBC content model revolves around a lot of stock market–related information and data. The exchanges in various countries are, therefore, by default strategic partners of the business as the two are interdependent. During the pre-project phase, I met with several stock exchanges in Africa. Most exchanges were small, with limited listings and consequently small trading numbers. This was a major limitation to investing in some of these countries in the first phase of the project as the capital markets were underdeveloped and the easy choice was to focus on South Africa, Nigeria and Kenya.

The JSE is arguably one of the largest and best-run stock exchanges in the world, its high standards achieved over time, with first Russell Loubser and then Nicky Newton-King at the helm. It was my first preference to establish our studios at the JSE, but after several rounds of discussions, we could not find the space to do so, either at the exchange or in the two buildings around it. We finally took up residence a stone's throw away, at Sandown Mews on Stella Road. I did not give up hope of being at the exchange, however, and we finally set up our studios there in May 2014, becoming the first TV network to broadcast live from the JSE.

The Nigerian Stock Exchange (NSE) was in a state of evolution. While the market was primitive, it was evident that there was latent opportunity waiting to be harnessed. When I visited the NSE in 2005, the exchange was still trading over-the-counter. IT infrastructure did not exist and information was provided on floppy disks, yet the interest in the market was significant. It was clear that the major gap was in the ability to access information and trade. Things gradually began to change, particularly after Oscar Onyema took over as the CEO, and within a short space of time the NSE had undergone a drastic transformation. I had the great honour of ringing the closing bell of the stock exchange in Lagos on 26 June 2012. (A month later, on 24 July, I was invited to ring the closing bell at the Lusaka Stock Exchange in Zambia, and on 14 May 2014 I was given the privilege at the JSE.)

Incidentally, I had one of my funniest experiences at the NSE in 2005. Soon after the World Economic Forum on Africa in Cape Town, I travelled to Lagos. When I arrived at reception, the security guard called through to the CEO and said, "Boss, there is a white man here to see you." He may have thought that I was out of earshot, but I laughed my guts out that day, as it was the first time in my life that anyone had called me white. The word "relative" never had a more appropriate example.

While I was making progress on the scope and scale of the project, the major holdup was that we did not have distribution. MultiChoice was not convinced about the need for a pan-African business news channel. At that time, there was a South African business news channel for local news and international business news channels like CNBC US and Bloomberg for international news. They did not think there was enough demand in sub-Saharan Africa to warrant a dedicated business news channel. This seemed to be the general mindset towards any pan-African business opportunity in 2006. To my mind, it was short-sighted.

Since they had significant experience in watching other niche channels on their platform, MultiChoice believed that a brand like CNBC would complement the local business channel Summit TV, and that collaborating with them would be opportune. I had several meetings with the CEO of Johnnic Communications, which owned Summit, and tabled a proposition for them to partner us. Unknown to me at the time, there were boardroom politics going on at Johnnic and it finally emerged, after the CEO left, that none of my proposals had ever really been discussed. I do not believe that this was a priority for them at that stage, given that they were dealing with several other issues, including the unbundling of their own business units.

We continued to believe that CNBC Africa could become the platform for changing perceptions of a misunderstood continent. No doubt, it would be an uphill battle to integrate business news across the entire continent, but this is what legacy projects are all about. MultiChoice's indecisiveness forced us to look at a secondary distribution strategy that revolved around a free-to-air satellite transponder, on PAS-7, with Sentech. This was a shot in the dark, but after many discussions with CNBC International, we jointly decided that the opportunity was compelling, and that we would have to relook at our business plan and decide whether we could move forward without carriage on MultiChoice.

Zafar and I met with the late Nelson Mandela just before the World Economic Forum on Africa in June 2006. This was a historic day for us both. Mr Mandela was delighted to hear that Zafar and I were from Pakistan and India respectively, and that we were trying to unite through an initiative in Africa. His words of encouragement were invaluable; he felt that this project was priceless from an African perspective. He told us that groundbreaking projects in Africa would need perseverance and a long-term plan, but that we should continue on our path despite the challenges.

This meeting was a defining one in many ways. During the 2006 World Economic Forum, Zafar and I spent considerable time discussing the pros and cons of what we were planning to do. Over a drink on the last day, Zafar looked at me and said, "Whatever happens now, let's make this happen. We are not going to look back." We threw caution to the wind from then on, and to all those around us that evening we announced that we were going ahead with the launch of CNBC Africa. I had been working on this project for almost twenty months and the decision we made that night lifted a huge burden of indecisiveness.

The next morning I went back to rewriting our business plan and we looked once more at the numbers based on a longer gestation period and a model that would rely on satellite free-to-air broadcast. I presented the plan to the IDC and we went into the next stage of due diligence. The revised plan had me focusing on all the other aspects of the business and not just distribution. While we made the contingency plan, I still hoped that we would be able to convince MultiChoice to give us carriage.

During this period, I also had the good fortune of interacting with the minister in the Presidency, Essop Pahad. He welcomed me to his home in Bird's Haven, South Africa, when I requested to meet with him to explain our project and some of the challenges we were facing, particularly our carriage agreement with MultiChoice. He was very encouraging but made his position clear from the start. He said, "As government, we will encourage you to invest in the country and the continent. We believe that this is an extraordinary initiative, however, as a word of advice, we can only assist with what is in our control." I stayed in touch with him for many years, including after his retirement from government. He was one of the selfless people who offered advice and encouragement every time I asked for it. He gave us the will to press on regardless of the obstacles. When we inaugurated our studio in Sandton, we could think of no better person than Essop to cut the ribbon.

The real support for our project came from the GPG, under the outstanding leadership of Premier Mbhazima Samuel Shilowa, provincial finance minister Paul Mashatile and Geoff Qhena of the IDC. Both the GPG and the IDC were convinced that this was a strategic initiative that should definitely be pursued. The IDC carried out a detailed due diligence on the project and finally agreed to come in as an equity partner. In October 2006, we held a joint press conference with the GPG, the IDC and the founders (Zafar and myself), and Premier Shilowa welcomed us to South Africa.

One of the boxes that I needed to check at this point was the choice of a black economic empowerment (BEE) partner; this particular nuance was similar to laws in the UAE and Malaysia. BEE was the post-apartheid solution for bringing about economic inclusion and wealth distribution to the black, Indian and coloured populations in South Africa. While there was no obligation to embrace BEE, it was clear that if one did not achieve the milestones as per the BEE scorecard, both in terms of ownership and employment opportunities, it would be difficult to do business with the government. The harsh realities of the pre-1994 era are well documented and this initiative, in itself, was an imperative for us.

I had, over the previous two years, been trying to identify a suitable BEE partner for the venture. In this context, and on a lighter note, I became familiar with terms like the "usual suspects", coined because there were several reputable names that had become synonymous with sponsoring BEE credentials. A project like ours had generated substantial investor curiosity, both in South Africa and in Nigeria, but media, in relatively uncharted waters, raised a level of apprehension, which in many ways brought sanity to our process. What we were looking for in a partner was an understanding of the media business and someone who was not entering it for the wrong reasons. The normal expectation from traditional investors would be low risk and quick returns. This is never the case in media and definitely not when one is setting up a trailblazing venture in a complex and underdeveloped market.

As we were completing our financial deliberations, I was approached by Sam Bhembe for an investment into the company. I had first met Sam when he was executive vice president at the IDC and it was his division that reviewed the IDC's investment into CNBC Africa. He had delegated Chris Mullin to carry out the due diligence. Chris was so thorough in his understanding of the complexities we faced that by the time the IDC made its commitment, I had started requesting Chris to respond to queries on behalf of the company. Chris unfortunately left and moved on to Capricorn Asset Management, which to my mind was a big loss for the IDC. During the same period, Sam moved to Nedbank as a senior executive, but, since he had knowledge of the project, he was keen to make a personal commitment.

Sam had been involved with the media vertical at the IDC and understood the space in which we were operating. While his was not the typical big-business family name, he was eager to build something with us. This was exactly the kind of partner that Zafar and I were looking for. He made a personal contribution to the project that was relatively small at the launch, but we helped him raise his stake in the company through a second round of funding in 2008, which gave him enough skin in the game to remain actively involved. His advice to management and his contribution to the company at a board level were invaluable. His contribution validated our decision, particularly when he left Nedbank in 2014 and started playing a more active role in the operations of the business.

We took our time identifying the premises to house the broadcast facilities. As mentioned, my first choice was to set up within the JSE precinct. I visited all possible facilities but we couldn't find a space that would be sufficient for our planned infrastructure. At this stage I even contemplated taking space at Telemedia's facilities in Rivonia and asked Peter Bretherick whether they would be able to come up with a proposal. Telemedia were reconstructing a segment of their offices and Peter came up with a comprehensive plan, but the development offered was mainly underground and had no natural light or ventilation. This was a major negative and we decided to decline the offer. After many site visits, we found our current location at Sandown Mews in Sandton. The building was close to Reuters and the JSE, and was in the centre of the business district. What was also compelling was that it was designed as a smart building and had sunken flooring and high ceilings. This was a perfect space, as it was basically a rectangular shell that we could pretty much design to suit our needs.

We designed our offices using Middle Eastern architects but local resources. Kalim Siddiqui had designed the Dubai offices of CNBC Arabia and did an excellent job working with local contractors and delivering on schedule. I recall the early days when the project consultants came up with ridiculous quotations for high-end oak designs and other non-essential frills that would have increased the project cost significantly. This was not surprising, as they were being paid a fee based on a percentage of the total cost. We finally got them to understand that this was an ordinary office like any other and needed to be a purpose-made, operational and sturdy television station.

Our original date for launch of the channel was 1 April 2007. We took possession of the premises at the end of October 2006. What I had not factored in when we started was the very South African tradition of "builders' holidays". While we were selecting the contractors for civil works, no one said anything about downing tools from 15 December to 10 January, the period when the construction industry in South Africa goes on leave. I patiently waited through this period and we finally started our civil works on 10 January 2007.

I am a great believer in Murphy's Law and was not surprised when our engineers informed me that "air conditioning" as per South African terminology was merely "evaporative cooling". This meant that our server room, studios and other technical facilities would not have proper air conditioning. In light of this, we had to order a chilling plant for the building and wait for two months for the plant to be shipped and delivered. Installing the chilling plant on the fourth floor of the building was one of the greatest challenges. Despite these challenges, the civil, electrical and mechanical works were finally completed at the end of April 2007.

The other major area of concern was the system design and architecture. We had recently established CNBC Arabia and CNBC Pakistan, and had requested Hassan Saeed Hassan, head of broadcast operations in Dubai, to assist with the technical design of the station. The only requirements that we gave Hassan were that we would not use any technical resources from overseas, and that the systems integrator had to be South African. Hassan prepared a very comprehensive request for proposal, but most vendors quoted without understanding the complexity of the project and chose to err on the side of caution by over-inflating all costs. We finally made it obligatory for short-listed vendors to visit Dubai to view the facilities there, before resubmitting their proposals.

Not a single company in South Africa had designed a modern newsroom or a server-based television station before. Hassan spent innumerable hours analysing the quotations and finally sent me his recommendations. I worked with the management of Inala Broadcast during this period and they met all our requirements and were the most proactive of all the vendors. After a series of meetings and negotiations, we finally awarded them the contract. Inala deputed Antony Bijsters as the project lead from their side, while their general manager Colin Wainer oversaw the complete implementation. I was keen to retain Antony for our business, but he offered his brother Mike instead. Mike is still with us.

In October 2006, we had leased temporary space at the Regus offices at The Campus in Rivonia, the first home of CNBC Africa. We started with four people and gradually grew to about forty by March 2007. With the delay in construction, we had to defer the joining dates of some of the staff but had our complete team by 1 May 2007. By now part of the office space in Sandton was ready and most of the technical staff were able to move there at the beginning of May. It was a frustrating time, as people were quite unsettled by the delays, which also impacted the time for trials and training.

However, when we eventually moved into the offices in Sandown Mews the staff were thrilled to see the look and set-up. The team were in their seats by the middle of May, in time for the new launch date of 1 June.

After thirty months of painstaking planning and hard work, we finally launched the channel on 1 June 2007 from our headquarters in Johannesburg. South African president Thabo Mbeki honoured us by coming to the studio for the launch and we had one of the best launch parties that I have ever attended. The five men largely responsible for getting the project up and running were Kalim Siddiqui, Hassan Saeed Hassan, Trevor Ormerod (COO), Anton de Wit (head of broadcast operations) and Gary Alfonso (head of programming). I remember standing in the Final Control Centre with some of them before the launch, amid the chaos in the studio, and saying, "I don't care if you have to put your fingers in the plug points, but that signal better go out tonight." The signal did go out, with the precision of a well-integrated television station. It was a proud day for all of us.

The launch of CNBC Africa was a glorious beginning, but there were many challenges to come. No sooner had we launched than we were hit by the worst recession of all time.

The global financial crisis began in 2007 when the US housing-market bubble burst, leading to the sub-prime mortgage crisis. Some of the largest banks tumbled, and the crisis relentlessly followed countries that had high debt exposure. The real trouble started with the collapse of Lehman Brothers, one of the most respected financial and brokerage institutions in the world, in September 2008. Once again, I witnessed the demise of a firm with a history dating back to 1850. It paved the way for the largest global crisis since the Great Depression of the 1930s. It seemed that it had taken roughly seventy-five years for memories to fade, and for all the decisions made to ensure good governance over the years to be systematically repealed.

Each time there has been a financial crisis the overriding causes have been greed and lack of proper governance. This time, greed was so great that home ownership was encouraged and loans were given to people who could not afford the mortgages. There was a systematic failure of governance, conflicts of interest, and lack of regulation by financial institutions, insurance companies and rating agencies. They simply allowed the rot to spread across the entire system, to the extent that pension funds and governments had large exposures in the so-called secure and highly rated collateralised debt obligation (CDO) products that became the buzzword in the investment world. If you were not in the market either buying or selling CDOs or their derivative products, you were not in the game. It was great as long as everyone was making money and the cycle or chain did not break. Carsten and I often called this the "greater fool theory". As long as there was a greater fool sitting above, ready to buy the assets from you, everything was fine. If you were the one at the top of the pyramid, you were destined for a "long drop" – literally. The worst part was that some of the biggest names that perpetuated these crimes got away with a mere rap on the knuckles and affordable fines. Hypocrisy and irony were evident in the fact that the people responsible for the financial mess were subsequently bailed out by government funds.

The crisis affected most parts of the world with varying degrees of intensity depending on the debt burden or the debt-to-GDP ratio. Since the US was exposed, the US dollar took a dive and markets around the world went into an uncontrollable downward spiral. As expected, everyone went back to the reserve currency – gold – the price of which went through the roof.

The impact for small businesses was that all banks came under a lot of pressure to evaluate their debtors' books, and loans became both expensive and difficult to secure. Small businesses began to shut down as they did not have the working capital to ride out the storm. Unemployment began to spiral globally, which added further pressure to the rapidly declining consumer market. The unfortunate reality was that while banks took write-downs on their investment portfolios, they continued to make money on their lending arbitrage. While the interest rates for deposits had fallen close to zero, the lending rates continued to be very high, giving the banks much higher spreads than in 2007.

The impact on our business in Africa was severe. After the global markets crashed, exports from Africa slowed down and the price of commodities, except gold, plummeted. The first expenses that companies cut when they face a crisis are marketing and advertising. Since our media business is completely reliant on advertising, we faced the onslaught from the word go. The company clearly needed to manage its costs judiciously, as well as seek additional shareholder support, for which we went back to the drawing board to relook at our strategy. It was an incredibly trying time for me as I tried to keep the ship on an even keel.

At launch, CNBC Africa had its headquarters in Johannesburg, a bureau in Cape Town, an East African bureau in Nairobi, Kenya, and two bureaus in Nigeria, in Lagos and Abuja. We had planned to add additional bureaus each year so that we could get comprehensive editorial coverage. Additionally, we had news updates on the hour and the content strategy was to build the local content from six to eight hours over the next two years.

In light of the recession, I took a decision in 2008 to stop bureau expansions, as it was an expensive undertaking and it was important to get the company to break even before expanding further. We also consolidated our grid, and instead of starting at 6 a.m., we moved the first show to 8:30 a.m., so as to maximise the workforce as much as possible into a single shift. While we were making these adjustments, another bolt hit us unexpectedly. A sponsorship contract signed by the GFC was unceremoniously and unilaterally terminated. This wrongful and untimely termination put substantial pressure on us, including bringing us bad publicity. Our competitors hypocritically had no intention of letting go a chance to raise insignificant issues, and questioned government spending on media, of which all of them were major beneficiaries. Our lawyers advised us to take the GFC to court and seek reimbursement, as we had all the paperwork to prove that we had done no wrong. However, our board was rightfully of the opinion that we needed to move on and succeed in spite of all the impediments. This hurt us in the short term but was a prudent long-term strategy that paid us dividends in the future.

With this relentless onslaught, I had no recourse but to go through the unsavoury task of retrenchment and consolidate our operations further. Additionally, I had to go back to the shareholders, including myself, for more money. This is often a tough task for a start-up. History has shown that the number one reason for failure is inadequate capitalisation. Luckily, all our shareholders supported the initiative and we doubled the initial capital required for the company and continued contributing additional cash as and when needed.

Recapitalising the company was critical to ensuring that we were adequately funded, but the real painful exercise was the letting go of people. Retrenchment is unpleasant for everyone, and the difficult task fell on Roberta Naidoo's shoulders as she was heading finance and administration. She, along with Michelle Chetty, our HR manager, went about this emotionally draining task with representatives of South Africa's Commission for Conciliation, Mediation and Arbitration (CCMA), and completed it with transparency and efficiency. Roberta proved her leadership ability during this crisis and worked tirelessly around the clock under the most difficult circumstances to keep the ship stable, managing the expectations of both staff and stakeholders. In January 2013, for her competence and leadership, we appointed her as managing director of the ABN Group.

As the markets began to improve, we reopened our expansion plans and by 2016 had established bureaus in twelve countries, with a view to eventually getting into twenty. This expansion was part of my strategy to provide broader editorial coverage and diversify our revenue base. The East African Community had become a major economic bloc and to take advantage of that I established our East African headquarters in Rwanda. The choice was largely owing to the progressive nature of the Rwandan economy under the leadership of President Paul Kagame. With guidance from Francis Gatere (CEO) and Clare Akamanzi (COO) of the Rwanda Development Board we were able to establish ourselves within twenty-four hours – a feat that speaks volumes about the ease of doing business in Rwanda. We launched our headquarters on 4 February 2016. Rwandan finance minister Claver Gatete inaugurated our studio and President Kagame honoured us by being on our first panel at launch. By the middle of 2016, other than our strong presence in South Africa, Rwanda, Kenya and Nigeria, we had expanded to Zambia, Namibia, Mozambique, Uganda, Mauritius, Gabon and Ghana. In its nine-year history, the channel had become truly pan-African.

* * *

In 2009, I had approached the Forbes family to launch *Forbes Africa*. We unfortunately had to put the project on the back-burner due to the recession, particularly as publishing companies all over the world were shutting down and traditional print media was under immense pressure. However, I went back to the Forbes management in 2010 and restarted the discussions. When I approached my shareholders in ABN, they were sceptical. The IDC had had some bitter experiences in the publishing business and immediately turned it down, while others asked me if I really thought it was the right thing to do. Having checks and balances at board level is always good. It makes you more prudent, but it can be difficult when you are trying to build a business that is losing money and at the same time asking your partners to contribute more cash towards new opportunities. My conviction, however, was based on a comprehensive understanding of the market.

During my travels around the continent, I had gauged the demand by talking to peers about launching an aspirational magazine like *Forbes*. The general sense was that people would want to be associated with the brand. My gut feeling about this brand was overwhelming and I was happy to invest the complete capital requirement on my own. However, both Zafar and Sam agreed to co-invest. In early 2010, we established ABN Publishing with a view to launching *Forbes Africa*. Setting up ABN Publishing also gave me a chance to bring some of our senior team members into the equity pool. This was a critical moment for the group, as it is vital to align the long-term interests of your senior management with the interests of your company.

My son, Sidharth, had just returned from university, and when I asked him where he wanted to be based, he immediately and without hesitation chose Africa. I handed over the *Forbes Africa* project to him to cut his teeth, under the direct supervision of Roberta Naidoo. After months of negotiations with Forbes Inc., we finally signed the agreement in March 2011, with a planned launch date of 1 October 2011. The main question was the choice of managing editor. I met with many people and we seriously considered a few. For one reason or another, none of them worked out. I then asked Bronwyn Nielsen if she was ready to take the challenge. Bronwyn, in her usual manner, carefully considered her options but ultimately declined.

One morning, I was in the boardroom with Gary Alfonso, Roberta and Sidharth going over possible names when I asked what everyone thought of Chris Bishop. While all of us recognised that it was a huge risk, as Chris had never edited a stand-alone magazine, I had worked closely with him on the Liliesleaf documentary, which had earned him a lot of respect as a gentleman and a journalist. Gary had a close understanding of Chris's strengths as a journalist and volunteered to take the offer to him. Chris was ecstatic and said he would gladly take it gratis, if need be. I thus appointed Chris as the managing editor and, as expected, he brought a fresh look and character to *Forbes Africa*. It was exactly what I had wanted. With Chris at the editorial helm, and with Sidharth overseeing the project from the business side, I had nothing to worry about. The product was a resounding success and almost broke even in its first year.

In early 2013, I was in Cape Town when I decided to launch *Forbes Woman Africa*. My gut feeling was that there were innumerable inspirational stories about women in Africa. Since we were covering forty-nine countries, if we were to wait to put these stories in *Forbes Africa*, we would have to wait a long time. It was, to my mind, a compelling product. I also decided that I wanted Karima Brown as editor-in-chief. Karima had been with CNBC Africa hosting a weekly show, *Political Exchange*, and to my mind she had the gravitas to lead the new title.

Once again, management and the board were apprehensive. Of all the ideas I have proposed, this one received the most resistance. After careful research, review and discussion, however, I was able to convince everyone to take it forward. *Forbes Woman Africa* launched along with *Forbes Life Africa* with a lot of fanfare in October 2013. Unfortunately for me, a month after the launch, Karima was offered the role of group executive editor of Independent Newspapers; it was a once-in-a-lifetime opportunity. I could see that she was torn between her commitment to me and her desire to grow professionally. I told her to take the offer without hesitation. The responsibility for all three magazines suddenly fell on Chris Bishop's broad shoulders, until we met and recruited Methil Renuka. After taking over the baton for *Forbes Woman Africa*, Renuka became the true architect of a fantastic magazine.

The greatest challenge we faced when launching the *Forbes* magazines was once again distribution. Three or four big media companies own or control all the major retail bookstores in South

Africa. The practices followed are anti-competitive, and not without conflicts of interest, and made our start difficult. However, once the magazines gained traction, the retailers had to carry them for the sake of their own credibility. We have faced similar issues in other parts of Africa, and in some places retailers will mark up the selling price at will. Until a proper distribution network is established on the continent, these issues will remain. Nevertheless, *Forbes Africa* is now a well-established brand and in 2015 became the number one magazine in Africa among affluent readers. I was at the River Club in Johannesburg for a round of golf in November 2014 when one of the support staff in the restaurant asked me if I had stopped sending magazines to the club. He did not want us to stop as he read it from cover to cover and found the stories inspiring. Nothing gave me more pleasure than to hear those words, as it was evidence that our readership was growing across all demographics.

Innovation has become the buzzword in modern-day business parlance. Innovation, however, is not merely an idea. Innovation is a reality; ignore it at your peril. If consumers are at the centre of our universe, innovation is recognising and proactively making sure that both processes and products are more efficiently delivered to them. Everything you deliver by way of products and services will impact the consumption patterns of your consumers, and the greatest impact is made by technology. The rate of change in technology is becoming more and more disruptive. Technology affects the way all business is done, and industries need to rapidly evolve to align themselves with the future consumption patterns of their consumers. Every year communications and broadcast equipment becomes more efficient, more compact and cheaper. Adapting to change is a necessity, as one's competitors are unlikely to be waiting around. At a meeting with our senior executives on future trends, my son ended his presentation by saying "bankruptcy is a Kodak moment". Truer words have never been spoken. If you do not ask whether future consumers are going to choose your products, you will at some stage become obsolete. It does not matter whether you think your product is at the cutting edge, it *will* have an expiry date because there are millions of businesses trying to improve processes and products, and evolution cycles are getting shorter.

In the context of the media business, a major transition is taking place towards digital technology. Future generations of consumers are going to consume media in a very different manner, and while it is difficult to predict whether the computer screen will become de facto television, it can no longer be disputed that most media and information will be consumed on hand-held devices. It is therefore imperative for media companies to start evolving their models to meet the challenges of the future.

The core issue for those of us in Africa remains the rollout of broadband infrastructure and the corresponding cost of bandwidth. Currently, Africa lags on both counts. Even a developed market like South Africa does not have adequate bandwidth at low cost, making consumption of media on hand-held devices expensive. The issue becomes more challenging as you move further into the continent. At the moment, it's even difficult to have an uninterrupted conversation with our office in Lagos as calls drop regularly.

The other side of the coin relates to the revenue model for digitisation. Consumers in Africa are reluctant to pay for using the internet. But trends are changing as evidenced by the growth in online shopping as an alternative to conventional shopping. It will, however, take considerable time for the front-end and back-end logistics of the business to be properly established.

To meet this challenge, I assigned Andrew Herd to start putting in place the building blocks of our digital strategy, but it was only after Sidharth joined the business in 2011 that I decided to push the project further, as his understanding of the digital space far exceeded that of anyone I had met. We established ABN Digital in 2012 as the digital arm of the ABN Group and, after getting the back-end through some extremely complex technical issues, CNBCAfrica.com launched in April 2013. The service is currently available free of charge so that we can build loyal viewers. What exceeded our expectations was the complete shift from traditional advertising to online advertising. By 2014, the project was at break-even with double-digit growth in both revenue and viewership. Andrew Herd had been appointed general manager of ABN Digital in November 2013 and, once again, I was rewarded in having one of the most committed and forthright individuals on my senior team.

We were ahead of the curve in our move to digital publishing. We saw early on that the consumer market was transitioning to reading magazines and books on hand-held devices. E-readers like the iPad, NOOK and Kindle were becoming the preferred choice. We made a conscious decision to make our magazines available in an electronic format and, while subscriber numbers remain low, this strategy allows us agility to change should we need to shrink our printing costs as physical books and magazines gradually die out.

* * *

Between 2011 and 2013, I started three other companies under the ABN Group umbrella. ABN Productions was launched in 2011 to organise editorial events for CNBC Africa, *Forbes Africa* and other third parties. As we expanded our bureaus, this became an increasingly important arm of our business. The model allowed us to get editorial content for CNBC Africa virtually for free, while accruing some revenue to justify our costs in each country. Around the same time, I founded the All Africa Business Leaders Awards (AABLAs), which recognise corporate leadership and business excellence on the African continent. What started as a small event is now a huge continent-wide endeavour with three regional components covering East, West and southern Africa, and a grand finale held in South Africa.

As an entrepreneur, you seldom seek recognition. The work you do and the impact it has is evidence of your success. However, from time to time there are unexpected gestures from people that validate and reinforce your vision. At both the regional contest of the AABLAs in East Africa in September 2014 and the finale in South Africa in November, the winner of the Lifetime Achievement Award, Dr Reginald Mengi, asked the audience to give me a standing ovation for setting up such an incredible platform on the continent. He applauded the fact that the AABLAs recognise people who are making a difference in Africa and tell their stories, which would otherwise not be heard. It was indeed an emotional moment that I savoured for many days thereafter.

As an aside, and also in 2011, Sidharth started the Forbes Person of the Year. This has become one of the most coveted awards on the African continent and prominent recipients have included Sanusi Lamido Sanusi, James Mwangi, Aliko Dangote, Akinwumi Adesina and Mohammed Dewji.

The ABN Training Institute was launched in March 2012. I had been keen to start journalism and broadcast training programmes since CNBC Africa's inception, mainly because of the shortage of skills in financial and broadcast journalism in Africa. When we started CNBC Africa, Bronwyn Nielsen saw an opportunity for us to offer media training to help political, government and corporate leaders learn how to interact with the media. This was the starting point for the training institute, which Bronwyn ran in conjunction with her role as CNBC Africa's prime-time anchor. In 2013, she agreed to join CNBC Africa full time in a senior executive position and took responsibility for building ABN Training.

I launched ABN Pictures in 2013 to produce documentaries on subjects relevant to the African continent, including tourism, corporate leadership, company profiles, events and issues facing Africa. The idea had started with two independent projects that I had commissioned: the documentary on Liliesleaf farm, produced and presented by Chris Bishop and scripted by Jill de Villiers; and a documentary on the life of my parents.

The latter was my way of showing my appreciation for all that my parents had done for my sisters and me. The documentary was overseen by Saloni and produced by an Indian production house. The producers viewed years of footage and interviewed many people in the different cities in which my parents had lived. We screened the documentary at the SCOPE complex in New Delhi, before an audience of 500 of my parents nearest and dearest relatives and friends. It was an emotional day, the success of which made me think about the number of people out there who might also want to document their lives.

Jill de Villiers had been head of programming at CNBC Africa since 2008. When I approached her with the idea for ABN Pictures in 2013, she was more than happy to take on the challenge of producing documentaries and long-format programming, as this was one of her core strengths and her passion. In the first year, we completed documentaries on the Greek government-debt crisis, the Tata Group, the global debt crisis, Raymond Ackerman, and many more. The vision of this company is to become Africa's leading producer of documentaries, and Jill and her team are well on their way to achieving this.

In 2016, nine years since the launch of CNBC Africa, the ABN Group was recognised as the leading business media conglomerate on the African continent. This was no mean feat, accomplished through the hard work and dedication of our people. Many of those who have left the group played as much a part as those who joined later. Each one added some value during the incredible journey. At CNBC Africa's ninth anniversary I was overjoyed to see so many familiar faces that had been with the company from the beginning.

While there was churn, it was heartening to see so many stalwarts, all of whom had contributed to our success and whose lives we had been able to transform.

EDUCATION IN EMERGING MARKETS

In emerging markets, shortage of skills is a major impediment to setting up sustainable businesses. Consequently, capacity building is core to any growing business and we looked at several ways to do this, through professional training and by bringing in international trainers and specialists to upskill our teams. To this end, Zafar and I set our sights on starting a school of journalism in Dubai, which would support the huge demand for talent from media companies in the Middle East and Africa.

In 2006, I approached several tier-one universities in Australia and the UK for potential partnerships in the Middle East. Since we did not have a track record in the education sector, very few universities even bothered to respond. It was not until I invited the director for international development at the graduate business school INSEAD for dinner at my house that I realised that the top universities would never enter into partnership with private businesses, particularly small to medium-sized business groups.

This discovery, however demoralising, was both a great lesson and a reality check. The rationale was simple and compelling. Unlike other products, education in general, and tertiary education in particular, is core to individual human development. Our college or university experience is as important to us as the ultimate certificate, since it permanently impacts on our future career and life. It is therefore very important that the standard of education and the value of the institution are not diminished. Because of this, Ivy League institutions will seldom partner individuals or businesses to open offshore campuses, as it would take away from the experience of being at the home campus. Some of these institutions had, however, started to offer limited programmes and executive education in different parts of the world. Over a period, some of them had established centres in Singapore and the Middle East, but with exorbitant price tags. These projects were clearly set up for non-commercial reasons by the host countries, as there was no way they could recover the huge commitment fees and royalties to the Ivy League institutions.

Therefore, while my strategy was to take global brands to emerging markets, the model in education had to change completely. Learning from my experience with the tier-one institutions, I wrote to all the second-tier universities in the UK and Australia and received varying levels of interest. Most of the universities we contacted were government-owned and therefore had a limited approach towards transnational education. This was largely because state-owned universities did not have the mandate and subsequently the budgets to allocate to international expansion. We therefore needed to think outside the box to develop a long-term model that would benefit both the university and ourselves.

The university that really caught my interest was Murdoch University in Perth, Australia. Though not highly ranked, they had an outstanding media and journalism school and the senior management was very keen on expanding their offshore presence. They had already set up offshore collaborations in Malaysia and Singapore; in the former with a private-sector college and in the latter with two institutions, one governmental and the other private. Murdoch's media and research centre had been involved in complex research projects for multinationals around the world and its head, Professor Duane Varan, was an absolute delight to talk to. Murdoch had been in conversation with many South African media institutions and had even participated in some research projects with MultiChoice. All these achievements were important, as they demonstrated a practical orientation towards education that is critical in today's world.

What was refreshingly different at Murdoch University was the senior management. Our first point of contact was Professor Gary Martin, who was then the deputy vice-chancellor for international development. Gary had travelled extensively to develop international collaborations and understood the nuances of starting an offshore partnership. In Singapore and Malaysia, I saw some fundamental mistakes in the way the collaborations had been set up. Most of the partners in those countries represented more than one international university and therefore had a supermarket model. As long as the prospective student enrolled at the college, it did not matter to them in which university programme the student was registered. The college was therefore not building any particular brand and was not committed to any specific university.

We approached Murdoch with a core-campus model, which was basically an exclusive-franchise model. We would build the brand exclusively and run the campus in Dubai as a dedicated branch of the parent campus. Murdoch was delighted with the suggestion and we went ahead with developing the feasibility for the project. What was particularly interesting for them was that under this model they had no risk, as the complete investment and implementation risk was to be carried by Zafar and me.

At this point, Dubai was changing its regulations for setting up universities. The Knowledge Village had been established in 2003 for the development of human resources in Dubai. This strategic initiative was bolted onto two of Sheikh Mohammed bin Rashid Al Maktoum's visionary projects: Dubai Internet City and Dubai Media City. Several educational institutions had shown interest in establishing themselves in the Knowledge Village, which was a limited area within the Dubai Media City precinct.

When we started our discussions, the regulatory body still resided within the Knowledge Village, although it was made clear to us that, as part of the master development plan for Dubai, a separate area had been earmarked near the Dubai Silicon Oasis, which would be home to all the international universities being established. The only issue was that the regulatory side had not been fully developed in advance, and, true to Dubai's reputation, things were happening at lightning pace.

The new legislation concerned two types of organisational structures. The first was based on the premise that the international university was investing on its own, in which case it was responsible for all academic, infrastructure and investment responsibilities. However, most international universities did not have a mandate to invest overseas and therefore needed an investment partner.

The second regulatory structure therefore split responsibilities between the international university and an academic infrastructure provider (AIP), a title recently changed to educational services provider. The university would be responsible for academic management, while the AIP would be responsible for infrastructure, investment, hiring of staff, marketing, business development and all other non-academic activities on campus. Since Murdoch University was not required to invest under our agreement, Zafar and I established Global Institute Middle East as the AIP and operating partner of the Murdoch University campus in Dubai.

We were hoping to launch the project in 2007, but because of all the regulatory delays we had to defer to 2008. In many ways this was a blessing, as we were able to broaden the curriculum and scope of the campus in Dubai. From initially focusing on journalism, we expanded to include commerce, business, IT, an MBA and a master's in human resources.

In March 2007, I asked my sister Sunanda's son, Raghav Lal, who was based in Chicago, to consider returning to Dubai to cut his teeth on the project. Raghav thus became the first employee of Murdoch University Dubai. We set up our temporary offices at the Knowledge Village in October 2007 and hired a core team to start the process of recruitment and marketing the brand. In April 2008, Dr John Grainger joined as the academic head of the business school and gradually the team started growing.

During this period, Dubai International Academic City (DIAC) was established in 2007, the world's only free zone dedicated exclusively to higher education. DIAC developed a clever low-cost model that was great for investors. Since it takes time and a large investment to build a university campus, DIAC built twelve buildings with sufficient capacity to incubate start-up universities, so that they could rent space in the first phase of their operations and then gradually move to their own premises, once they had the critical mass necessary for a stand-alone campus. Like many other start-up universities, we rented a floor at DIAC and began outfitting in April 2008.

At this time, my daughter stepped up and did all the artworks for the university. After taking a quick 101 course on aboriginal art, Shweta painted over twenty pieces for the campus. We were all thoroughly impressed with her effort and gave her a small token amount as a thank you. I was deeply moved when she took the money and gave it to our driver, Saleem, so that he could pay for his daughter's MBA at Murdoch Dubai. Her act of kindness touched our hearts, and the hearts of many others, as it was completely unprompted and unexpected. It gave Saloni and me satisfaction of a different kind, as it was confirmation that our children had developed the right values.

Just as we were launching the university in September 2008, the Dubai real-estate bubble burst and markets plummeted. While we had seen the severe impact of recession during the Gulf wars and the dot-com crisis, the 2008 crash in Dubai was the worst, as even the government was badly affected. Much of the development and growth since 2003 had been on the back of real-estate projects. Owing to mass speculation, prices had superficially increased to a point where they became unsustainable, resulting in a market collapse. People defaulted on loans and the banks were put under severe pressure. A large number of expatriates lost their jobs and went home; some fled overnight leaving bad debts in the market and expensive cars in the airport car park.

When Murdoch University Dubai opened its doors in September 2008, we had thirty-nine students. For an infrastructure that cost us millions, our revenue for the first half of the year was minimal. It was time to reflect on our prospects and we questioned just about everything relating to the project. One of the problems we faced was leadership on the Dubai campus. We had hired an individual who, although academically impeccably qualified, did not really understand the needs of a start-up business. I had to carry out the painful task, with Gary Martin, of letting go someone a lot older and more experienced than myself, but if we hadn't made that decision, we would have been destined for failure.

I decided to offer John Grainger the position of academic dean and pro-vice-chancellor, but was told at the time that he was in hospital undergoing minor surgery. I asked my assistant to check if I could call on him and subsequently visited him in his hospital recovery suite. He was still under the effects of anaesthesia when I made him the offer and I don't think he completely understood the question, because he just nodded and went back to sleep. I presented John with a contract to sign the next morning, when he was fully *compos mentis*. He was very excited by the opportunity, but confided in me later that when I had initially suggested to him, in the hospital, that he should "clear his desk", he had thought I was going to fire him for being off sick. With John at the helm, there was a marked change for the better on campus, but the market conditions remained tough.

The only things that kept me going were the good team we had hired and my unfaltering belief that the project was viable. We just had to stick it out. In 2009, we were given the bad news that our institutional partner from Kuwait was in trouble and wanted to exit the project. This was a very difficult time for us, as not only did we have operational issues, but we also had to buy out one of the share-holders. On 28 December 2009, Zafar and I took on the major risk and bought out our Kuwaiti partner at a time when the campus was burning approximately US$350 000 per month.

Since our royalty payments to Murdoch University were in Australian dollars, in 2007 our bankers had advised us to convert a part of the equity to Australian dollars. Acting on their advice, we converted a considerable amount. However, in 2009, to complete the buyout and meet some of our working capital requirements, we had to convert Australian dollars back to US dollars when the Australian currency was at its weakest point, losing over a million dollars in forex. It was not out of character to suddenly find that all the relevant account managers from our bank had conveniently left with absolutely no apology or remorse.

At this point, I had two major projects (CNBC Africa and Murdoch University Dubai) sucking in cash faster than I had planned, with revenues not ramping up. It was a real test of my resolve, as everything had gone pear-shaped, with no end in sight. Unbeknown to most, if there was a time when I lost the most sleep, it was during this period between September 2009 and March 2011. At a time like this, you realise how lonely it is for an entrepreneur trying to make his or her dreams come true. In my mind, failure is not an option, and so I had to rely on self-belief and put a strategy in place to get the businesses through the challenges.

The strategy I continued to drive hard was three-pronged: manage costs, build the brand and continue diversifying revenue streams. To this end, we started the Foundation Programme, which is a pathway programme from school to university. It was an immediate success as many students who had not made the grade in high school now had a second chance to join the university by passing the foun-dation course. Dan Adkins ran the programme, which was in many ways our saviour. It not only provided additional revenue, but also became a healthy conduit for building student numbers. In addition, John started a Master of Education programme and built it into a resounding success, and the gap between revenue and expenditure started narrowing. Raghav transitioned responsibilities from project executive to management information system (MIS), and finally to head of business development and marketing.

The team under John Grainger worked well together and slowly but surely I could see our goals were being realised. One of the critical success factors was John's approach to students. He built a culture where students and parents were valued as customers and a high-satisfaction index was critical to benchmark performance. He led from the front and was respectfully nicknamed Professor Dumbledore by the students; the resemblance less the beard and hat, I might add, was striking.

After relentless hard work and perseverance, we finally broke even in August 2013, five years after we began operations. In many ways it was a case study for how a start-up could achieve success in record time during the worst global economic downturn. Most universities established at the same time as us faced hardships that they could not overcome; some shut down and others scaled back.

In addition to our own team, what did stand in our favour was the outstanding leadership from Murdoch University's senior management in Australia led by Gary Martin. Gary clearly understood that everything was stacked against us for the first three years and attempted to assist as and when possible. He believed that the only way Murdoch would be successful was if their partner was successful. This was a value that I had not found in many people, but he lived by that value right until the day he stepped down from his role as acting vice-chancellor in January 2012. Although it should not be the case, as partnerships are between organisations and not people, much of the cooperative and collaborative spirit within the partnership disappeared after Gary left. Future leaders of the university regrettably did not understand or value how much blood, sweat and tears had gone into setting up this strategic project.

* * *

As I travelled through Africa, one of the glaring gaps I noted is the lack of focus and priority given to skills development. These gaps are visible across the board, as there is a shortage of quality educational institutions on the continent. While South Africa does have quality universities, they all have capacity constraints. Many families that can afford to send their children overseas, to universities in Europe, North America and Australia, do so. However, the rest have to suffer the consequences of an unfortunate status quo.

Nigeria, given its huge population, is an attractive market. Furthermore, Nigeria is one of the highest spenders when it comes to international education. Each state has its own programme for international training and many universities in Europe and North America benefit from a high number of Nigerian student enrolments. The country with the greatest affiliation is the UK. The infrastructure and associated costs in Nigeria are currently not in sync with the needs of a start-up education business, particularly if it is foreign-owned. The regulatory process is cumbersome and the length of time over which accreditation can be achieved is not clearly defined.

Given the constraints in Nigeria and the potential for attracting Nigerian students to an international campus, I took the decision to set up our first African campus in Ghana. I asked John and Raghav to join a team headed by Chris Pilgrim, the senior vice president of special projects, to carry out a feasibility study in Ghana. The results were encouraging. Zafar, as always, supported the project and also agreed with my recommendation to give equity to the senior management team. We established TNE as the special purpose vehicle to manage and control the assets of the education business in Ghana.

To be successful in West Africa, we needed a UK university partner. Once again, I sent out many mails to universities and this time the response was a lot better. For one, we had an operating university in Dubai, and secondly, most British universities have a clear African strategy. In January 2012, I travelled to the UK with Saloni to meet with various potential university partners. Most of the meetings were exploratory, and the responses were generally very positive. Shortly after returning to Dubai, I received intimation that the vice-chancellor of Lancaster University was keen to visit our Dubai campus on his way back from China. This was indeed great news. Sometimes when you meet people, you immediately get a sense of comfort. The minute I met Professor Mark Smith I had a strong gut feeling that I would like to get to know this man better and I was keen to explore the possibility of entering into a partnership with him. Mark clearly understood the investment model we had proposed and appreciated the value of an offshore campus. While the University of Lancaster had several offshore projects in India, Pakistan and China, it had not established a core campus outside the UK and Mark was keen to progress the discussions.

Mark invited me to make a presentation to his senior faculty heads and administrators in Lancaster in March 2012. I took John Grainger, Chris Pilgrim and Raghav Lal with me and we spent two days in meetings, with both larger groups and individual departments. At dinner on the second day, Mark told me that our proposal had been placed before their senate, where it had received a unanimous vote to proceed with the alliance. It took us a few months to conclude our negotiations with Lancaster University. Professor Robert "Bob" McKinlay, the deputy vice-chancellor, rightfully and light-heartedly said, "The agreement from our perspective was two pages of sense and thirty pages of fluff."

The time had now come to staff our project in Ghana. I asked John Grainger whether he would be interested in taking on another challenge – this time in Africa. In his usual upbeat style, he accepted willingly and gradually started handing over responsibilities for Murdoch Dubai to Dan Adkins. In time, John moved to Ghana and took charge as the first resident provost of Lancaster University Ghana and president of TNE. Raghav was appointed group vice president and project director for Lancaster Ghana. John and Raghav had worked together in building and growing Murdoch University Dubai and I was sure that they would be able to develop the new campus in Ghana with the benefit of lessons learnt during the first project set-up.

Once the agreement was concluded, our teams started the process of accreditation through the National Accreditation Board, ably assisted by Bob McKinlay and Lancaster's pro-vice-chancellor international, Steve Bradley. After the presidential elections in December 2012, a new cabinet had taken charge in Ghana. This was opportune, as all parties were motivated to encourage investment flow into the country. However, even with the best of intentions, there were many bureaucratic delays in obtaining site approvals and complying with building regulations, but with Raghav and other members of the team on the ground in Accra, we were able to expedite the process. The team did an outstanding job with the set-up in Ghana and the project was completed on time and on budget, which was very creditable. The Lancaster University Ghana campus was officially launched on 28 October 2013, in Accra, by teams from Lancaster and TNE. Both Mark Smith and I were there to wish our faculty, staff and students the very best. This was a milestone event, as we became the first British university to have an offshore campus in sub-Saharan Africa.

Over the first year, we faced some interesting challenges in Ghana. For one, the government had made several bullish statements about its potential oil revenues and began an extremely aggressive strategy around announcing new development projects. However, most of the initial foreign direct investment that came into the country evaporated with little accountability. By the time the government realised that their optimism was a bit overstated, it was too late and the country went into a downward economic spiral. The currency collapsed from 1.9 to the dollar when we invested in 2013 to 3.7 in just one year, almost entirely eroding our investment.

The overall business model for Lancaster University Ghana was similar to the one for Murdoch University Dubai. The division of responsibilities remained unchanged with the investment and financial risk undertaken by Zafar and myself as the founders. While the business model was essentially an integrated franchise, Lancaster University played a significant role in getting the approvals and accreditations for the programmes. They were always available on the ground when needed and we enjoyed numerous visits from various members of their senior academic faculty. Lancaster was rightfully concerned about the quality of programme delivery in Ghana and in phase one decided that they would like their academics from the UK to teach their postgraduate degree programmes.

As expected, one of the key challenges we faced was finding good staff. We launched our TNE Foundation Programme, verified by Lancaster University, in our first year of operations. I asked Johan Claasen, who had been our head of media programmes in Dubai, to head the Foundation Programme. Johan was another member of my team who had shown implicit faith in my leadership and vision. In 2012, I had asked him to move to South Africa to head the ABN Training Institute. He agreed, but after a few months I could see that he was not happy and that I had perhaps given him a responsibility outside his comfort zone and not focused on his strengths as an excellent teacher and educational administrator. Johan never complained and tried relentlessly to secure training contracts from state broadcasters in several African countries, but the process was just far too bureaucratic. Johan became ill with a potentially life-threatening illness and I realised that I had made a mistake. And so I asked him if he would prefer to go to Ghana to do what he did best. He took the offer to lead our Foundation Programme without batting an eyelid. In 2015 the British Accreditation Council (BAC) accredited the programme as the first BAC-accredited foundation programme in sub-Saharan Africa.

Within two years, our staff contingent in Ghana grew to seventy-five. The skills we found most deficient were in IT and finance. A large part of the initial support for both these departments came from Dubai. This was not sustainable, however, as building local capacity is an imperative. In all our businesses, one value I always insisted on was the development of local skills. Initially, we needed to bring in a few expatriates, largely for governance and consistency. At our budgeting meeting in October 2014, I asked the team to recruit the best candidates from leading Ghanaian companies, as we were just not able to attract talent at the mid-company level.

In the first two years, we also saw an increase in prices across the board. Inflation has its consequences and the costs of basic commodities went up dramatically, particularly fuel. As a result of irregular but frequent power outages (known locally as "dumsor"), almost 60 per cent of our power went to running generators. Fortunately, we incurred most of our costs in Ghanaian cedis and therefore had minimal exposure to foreign-exchange losses. Our redeeming feature was that we achieved our student enrolment numbers and consequently our revenue targets. By October 2014, we had a student body of 200 and by January 2016 that had risen to 400. As predicted, almost half the numbers came from Nigeria, validating our research and business plan.

Once again, the success of the venture was largely due to the commitment of the senior management team, whose members complemented one another with diverse and synergistic skills: John Grainger leading the organisation and managing academic responsibilities; Johan Claasen managing the Foundation Programme; Chris Pilgrim with business planning; Raghav Lal with project implementation and business development; Sudeep Sachin in finance; Biju Veetil and Janeesh Karammal in IT; and Sanjay Rodrigues with internal audit and MIS. The team, however, would not have been able to deliver without the complete participation and support of the senior management of Lancaster University in the UK, particularly Mark Smith and Steve Bradley, both pillars of strength and committed to our joint vision of success.

No sooner had we launched Lancaster University Ghana than I began to look at setting up a centre of excellence for energy in East Africa. I met with various universities, but after several visits to Scotland in 2014 and 2015 I realised that the University of Aberdeen was the right partner. Professor Seth Kunin, the deputy vice-chancellor international, started building the foundations of a partnership with us, but he moved on to Australia at the start of 2016, leaving the project under the dynamic stewardship of Professor Sir Ian Diamond. While there is a lot of work yet to be done, we hope to launch the University of Aberdeen campus in Rwanda in 2017/18.

My journey across emerging markets has been interesting to say the least. Setting up trailblazing ventures in different countries, in difficult economic cycles and amidst political volatility is never easy. The only positive constant has been my various teams, which have all performed like well-coordinated packs of lions on a mission to succeed – and succeed they have.

4

LESSONS

I once came across this interesting quote: "Good judgement comes from experience, and experience comes from bad judgement." This perhaps summarises our lives in many ways. In our childhood, we learn what is taught to us by our parents and our schools. This is our formative education. Next, we learn from our experiences, good and bad, from our successes, our heartaches and our disappointments. Positive experiences have a high impact on our lives, as we learn to recognise our strengths and start to leverage them. But negative experiences can be equally impactful, as we begin to recognise that most crises could have been avoided if we had planned beforehand and perhaps acted differently. We therefore cannot blame circumstances alone, or unilaterally blame others, for the inadequate measures we take. When events and decisions out of our control impact our lives adversely, we are as much to blame, as we could have prevented or limited the damage to ourselves through proactive interventions.

That said, making mistakes from time to time is an important part of learning. Adventurous, entrepreneurial self-starters and trailblazers who act on their own initiative often make errors in judgement. There is nothing wrong in that. Those who have never made any mistakes have probably not done anything groundbreaking. I have always believed that you should experiment and make mistakes early in life, so that you absorb the shocks when you are young and are wiser for the future. The only caveat I have is that you should not repeat mistakes. Those who repeat mistakes are either negligent or did not understand what they did wrong in the first place. Both are unforgivable.

History is a great teacher. The very purpose of teaching history in school, usually a compulsory subject until Grade 10, is to educate students about the past so that they get a good sense of where they come from, how the past affects their present, and how they can shape their destiny. A great part of our destiny is formed unconsciously in the classroom, as each of us consumes and retains what interests us the most. This knowledge creates a latent orientation that subconsciously remains dormant until an event or opportunity brings it to the fore and we suddenly find that it has become integral to our existence.

Our instincts as human beings are also shaped through our experiences. Our actions and reactions to events or situations are an outcome of our experiences. In biology, we learn of reaction to external stimuli, the way an organism is able to react to a threat and do what is necessary to survive. Applying this analogy to our lives, our instincts provoke behaviour aimed at protecting our organisations and ourselves. Over time, our reactions to circumstances create a pattern of predictability that in many ways becomes the stamp of our existence.

As part of my training in the army, there was a great focus on military history, specifically military campaigns. We studied legendary examples from World War II, like General George S. Patton's heroic conquests in North Africa and General Douglas MacArthur's island-hopping strategy to regain the Philippines and consequently dominate the Asia-Pacific theatre. These were unconventional actions in response to exceptional circumstances. While unrelated to the Indian context, these examples gave us insight into the decisions made by military leaders and their consequences. We looked at strategic mistakes, too, like Hitler's Operation Barbarossa, arguably his greatest blunder. Barbarossa is my all-time favourite, as it is a clear example of fighting on too many fronts and not learning from history (in this case, the experiences of Napoleon and others with Russian winters). We also studied examples from wars relating to India, to enable us to learn from our own context. What all of these case studies had in common was that they taught us about trends and adaptability. As technology and weapons systems advanced, generals were forced to adapt and integrate strategy and tactics with technological advances to ensure that they remained relevant in modern-day warfare.

Business is no different and the experiences of corporates and business leaders throughout history offer important lessons. While most cannot be applied directly to modern-day business, because there are far too many variables to take into account and because much has changed, the underlying principles are the same. When formulating policy or carrying out risk assessment, we need to be able to adapt to a changing paradigm and apply history in a manner that makes it relevant to our current needs. Otherwise our structures will be archaic and irrelevant. Some factors, of course, remain constant. One is the importance of leadership and followership, both of which are integral to any business or activity.

Having lived a varied and full life, I have learnt many lessons that I would like to pass on. Most leaders and entrepreneurs face similar challenges, but perhaps under different circumstances. It is, therefore, not about modelling your life on someone else's experiences, but rather about learning from and adapting the experiences of others to your personal circumstances. Ultimately, this is what allows us to do what is in the best interests of our organisation and ourselves.

LEARN TO DREAM

Major human achievements are only possible if we have the ability to dream, and then follow our dreams. Whether going to the moon, climbing Mount Everest or building a computer, the first people to succeed had a vision of what they wanted to achieve, and then set out in relentless pursuit of their vision. If you want to find a pearl, you cannot lie on the beach sipping a piña colada, hoping that the right oyster will come to you. You have to jump into the ocean and seize what you want.

One of my greatest assets has been my ability to visualise, dream and think beyond the present and the ordinary. Two incidents while I was at school alerted me to my ability to visualise. The first was when, while doodling in class, I drew the complete configuration of the human heart, including all the valves, without ever having seen a picture of a heart. The second was when I drew the shape of the Concorde aircraft, again without ever having seen one and before it even came into service. These visualisations did not result in my becoming a heart surgeon or a pilot, but they left me with a strong belief in my ability to conceptualise.

At every stage of my life, I had dreams about what I wanted to do. Some were realistic; others were pipe dreams. Over time, I learnt to distinguish between the two. The dreams that I felt were realistic, I worked hard to achieve. What underlies my belief in myself as I enter the last lap of my career is that I have accomplished, with flying colours, everything I have set my mind to. So what did it take to do this?

The most important factor was courage of conviction, which essentially means believing in what you want and putting everything you have at your disposal into finally achieving it. You can test this by setting yourself small goals, then planning what you need and

The Wahi family gather to celebrate my parents' 50th wedding anniversary in 2007

The Doon School, Hyderabad House A, Class of 1975. I am seated, second from the right

Army training at the National Defence Academy, 1979

Colonel Jagannathan (centre) and the 113 Engineers, 12th Infantry Division, 1981. I am on the far left

The icebreaker, MV *Thuleland*, prepares to set sail from Goa to Antarctica in 1987

Receiving the Vishisht Seva Medal during the Army Day parade, 26 January 1986

Visiting a penguin rookery in Antarctica during the 7th Indian Scientific Expedition in 1987/88

Our son, Sidharth, was born on 13 April 1988. Two weeks later I resigned from the army

Saloni and I are blessed by her parents, Promod and Anjula Mehta, at our wedding in 1985

With Saloni at our first function with Frontline, Sunanda and Rajeev's business, in 1989

The couple who started my second innings after the army, my sister Sunanda and her husband Rajeev, in 2008

With Sid and Rick Michaels at CEA's 40th anniversary in New York, 2013

(Left) Minister P. Chidambaram inaugurates the largest trade exhibition hosted by the Government of Ukraine in New Delhi, India, March 1996

CDC's UAE partner Dr Juma Al Matrooshi (left) and his wife Razieh (second from the right) with our family in 2008

The CDC investment banking team, 1998. From left: Amani El Jandali, David Green, me, Carsten Philipson and Colleen Murphy (missing are Maha Abadileh and Abdullah Shahin)

Pioneers in Islamic private equity. At the launch of Injazat Technology Fund in 2001 with Esam Janahi (second from the right) and Carsten Philipson (far right)

With my brother-in-law Gaurav's wife Sakshi, Saloni, Gaurav and my sister-in-law Shalini in 2012

With Saloni and my sister Shalini in 2007

With my long-time friend Rajiv Podar in Johannesburg in 2009

With Tech One Global co-founders, Lars Jeppesen and Wasantha Weerakoon, in Colombo, Sri Lanka, 2015

Our other Tech One Global co-founder, Ali Bagash, with Saloni and Gazala Bagash in 2012

With senior executives of Global Institute Middle East, the operating partner of Murdoch University Dubai, in 2010

The Global Institute Middle East team at Dubai International Academic City in 2014

Zafar Siddiqi and his wife, Seema, with Saloni
and me at the Murdoch University Dubai launch
in 2008

With Saloni, Murdoch University Vice-Chancellor John Yovich and my parents,
Colonel and Mrs Wahi, at the Murdoch University Dubai launch, 2008

With John Yovich, Sheikh Nahyan bin Mubarak Al Nahyan (then Minister of Higher Education), Zafar Siddiqi
and Dr Ayoub Kazim at the launch of Murdoch University Dubai, 2008

With Murdoch University Deputy Vice-Chancellor Gary Martin, Director General of Dubai's Knowledge and Human Development Authority Dr Abdulla Al Karam, Chancellor Terry Budge and Zafar Siddiqi, 2009

Saloni and I share a proud moment with my nephew Raghav Lal in 2009

Shaking hands with Nelson Mandela in May 2006. This meeting inspired the launch of CNBC Africa

The start-up team for CNBC Africa and members of CNBC Arabia in October 2006

With former South African President Thabo Mbeki on a landmark day, the launch of CNBC Africa on 1 June 2007

Sam Bhembe, former Gauteng Premier Mbhazima Shilowa and me at the launch of CNBC Africa, June 2007

At the Cape Town launch of CNBC Africa. From left: former Western Cape MEC of Environment, Planning and Economic Development Tasneem Essop, former Western Cape Premier Ebrahim Rasool, Mrs Rasool, me and Saloni, June 2007

From left: Roberta Naidoo, Zafar Siddiqi, Gauteng Premier David Makhura, me, Sam Bhembe and Sid, 2015

With Geoffrey Qhena, CEO of the Industrial Development Corporation, a great partner of CNBC Africa, 2012

Sid, Saloni and me with President Jacob Zuma at CNBC Africa headquarters in Sandton, 2012

Ringing the closing bell at the Nigerian Stock Exchange in June 2012. CEO Oscar Onyema is on my right

In May 2014, I was honoured to blow the horn for the closing bell of the Johannesburg Stock Exchange

Speaking at the 2012 AABLA finale in Midrand, South Africa

With President Paul Kagame at the launch of our East Africa headquarters in Rwanda in 2016

Senior executives of the ABN Group, 2014

With Patrice Motsepe, Zafar Siddiqi and Chris Bishop at the Forbes Africa launch in 2011

Sid speaking at the launch of *Forbes Africa*,
October 2011

It was a pleasure to welcome Steve Forbes to the
ABN Group headquarters in Johannesburg in 2011

With Shweta, Sid and Saloni at the *Forbes Woman
Africa* launch in October 2013

Sid, my mother-in-law Anjula Mehta, Saloni and me
at the *Forbes Woman Africa* launch, October 2013

Shweta awarding a sponsorship for the Mauritius
Designers Council, 2013

Gauteng MEC of Economic Development Qedani Dorothy Mahlangu and Tata Africa CEO Raman Dhawan present the AABLA 2011 Lifetime Achievement award to Pick n Pay founder Raymond Ackerman

With former KwaZulu-Natal MEC of Economic Development and Tourism Michael Mabuyakhulu and national Finance Minister Pravin Gordhan at the AABLA finale in Durban, 2013

Gauteng Premier David Makhura with the 2015 AABLA winners

With Saloni and my parents, Colonel and Mrs Wahi, at the AABLAs in 2014

Saloni at the Thuthuzela orphanage in 2013

Sid and I present Aliko Dangote the 2014 Forbes Person of the Year award with 2013 winner Akinwumi Adesina (left) in Nairobi

The ABN team on Uhuru Peak, Mount Kilimanjaro, 16 March 2013

With Chris Pilgrim and Murdoch Dubai student Hazim Darwish on the way up Mount Kilimanjaro in March 2013

Raghav Lal welcomes everyone to the launch of Lancaster University Ghana, October 2013

Inaugurating the Lancaster University Ghana campus with Kwame Dattey, executive secretary of the National Accreditation Board, and Vice-Chancellor Mark Smith, October 2013

With Saloni and Shweta after she joined Murdoch University Dubai in 2015

The TNE team prepares for the expedition to Everest Base Camp in 2015

Sid with his fiancée, Sannah Rajpurohit, 2015

My niece Aparna Lal did an internship with me, but went on to become a banker. Here Saloni and I bless her and her husband, Varun Malhotra, at their wedding in 2014

Celebrating Shweta and Vishesh Tandon's wedding reception in Johannesburg, February 2016

finally committing yourself to them. You will realise that no target you set for yourself is unachievable, as long as you are willing to make it a priority. Some people believe that golf is a difficult game to play, but once you've gone to a driving range and worked on your swing, it is just a matter of time before you get onto the course. I have seen people achieve single-figure handicaps within a year. If you want to play golf well, you need to find the time and resources outside of all your other commitments to make it happen.

My father registered me at the Doon School, one of India's finest all-boys' boarding schools, in 1959, just a month after I was born. At that time, he had no idea how he was going to afford it, or the sacrifices he would need to make. It was just his dream. He worked hard to make sure that when the time came and I passed the entrance exam, he was able to keep the commitment that he had made to himself. If he had not registered me and I had not attended Doon, I would have known no better. But my father dreamt of giving me what he believed was the best education in the country, despite the fact that he had not had the benefit of such aspirational schooling himself. When I was told I had the option of going to Doon, I worked hard and made sure I excelled in my entrance exam. This is a small example of the need to set a challenging agenda at each stage of your life, in order to shape your destiny.

Aside from personal dreams, you also need to plan and set goals for the future. Where do you see yourself in twenty-five years' time: are you a scholar, a musician, an actor, a sportsperson, an entrepreneur, a preacher, or something else? Your aspirations should dictate what you do with your life and how you spend your time. Sometimes dreams are born from opportunities that present themselves. For example, you may travel somewhere and decide to build a school there, or move there to teach, and so on.

When I travelled to Africa, the need to change perceptions of the African continent was an opportunity for me. There was no precedent for a successful pan-African business news channel and no compelling case to compete with a small local TV station in South Africa. From the start, Zafar and I shared a vision to establish a business TV channel that would span the whole continent. After launch, I expanded our vision to a multifaceted business media conglomerate spanning TV, print, online, events and training. It was then only a dream that I articulated in a presentation in October 2007. Some seven years later, as part of a review of our business, Sidharth checked off each of the boxes in the original 2007 rollout plan. It had taken several years of hard work and the subordination of everything else, but the vision had been realised. A well-thought-out strategy, choosing the right people and aggregating the necessary resources were instrumental in bringing my vision to fruition.

It was no different with our education vertical. The original dream was to build a university in Dubai, but after the initial hardship and subsequent success, I expanded the thinking to establish a whole network of universities. We were going through a severe recession and losing money in the first venture when I presented a strategic plan to create ten universities across Africa. Given the circumstances, even the optimists on the team began to doubt my sanity. It would have been an act of insanity if we hadn't subsequently planned and built capacity to execute my vision.

For each of these dreams, we developed properly formulated, well-thought-out plans, as well as detailed feasibility studies, to clearly define the path that would turn the dream into reality. We then made sure that the right people, who had earned my absolute and complete trust, were in place to execute the plans. This was core to the success of my dreams. At times, I retained people on my team, waiting for the right moment to launch them into something different. When given the opportunity, most of them flourished. The senior executives charged with overseeing budgets were initially difficult to convince, but over time they have come to see method in my apparent madness.

These were all personal dreams. They did not shake the world or make any waves, but, through their realisation, they brought me much personal satisfaction. You live only once, so you must live well. Do not short-change yourself. It does not matter what your dream is: think big, aim big and strike big. Work hard and commit yourself to your dreams. The only limitations in life are a lack of imagination and an inability to work hard and to achieve what you set out to do.

BUILDING TRUST

My life has been largely about building trust with the people who have helped build my future. I have always maintained that trust is an implicit feeling of confidence in another person's intentions towards you or your cause. This feeling comes after years of observing consistent behaviour patterns.

Almost without exception, children trust their parents. This implicit confidence comes from each parent's inherent desire to protect their children through every phase of their life. Your umbilical cord with your parents, particularly your mother, is only cut when they die. Until that day, parents will do anything to safeguard their child. This is why the first word that comes from a child's mouth when he or she is in pain or in trouble is "Ma". There is an almost uncontested, intrinsic belief that if you are in trouble your mother will be there for you. This belief is sustained over the years as you receive her consistent support, irrespective of your actions and behaviour.

It is a lot easier to have a feeling of trust for someone related to you by blood. Under these circumstances, it would be rare for him or her to let you down. For relationships formed through business, friendship or any other interdependence, the question of trust becomes more important. To build anything significant, you need a team of people. To get the team to follow your dream, there has to be implicit trust from both sides. Do I trust that this person will act in the best interests of the business and me personally? Am I meeting all the commitments that I have made to the individual in question? This two-way review of positive outcomes is what builds trust.

What then are the qualities you should look for and what is your role? How we interact with people is largely dependent on the cumulative experiences of a lifetime. I have spent my entire life either being part of teams building start-up businesses or building teams to manage my own start-up businesses. No matter the situation, when it comes to people, I follow a few fundamental values. The first is informed by my father's belief that people are essentially good and that you must trust them until they prove otherwise. The second is that people must be capable of handling the responsibility given to them. Thirdly, to be a good leader you must be a good follower. The model is not very difficult to understand.

In the first instance, I have trained myself to always see the best in people, to work with their strengths and to continue to encourage them, despite any mistakes they may make. When dealing with mistakes, I first look at the intentions behind the action. If the intention was good, to the greater benefit of the organisation, and not malicious, I will not act against the individual. Whenever you are faced with a decisive moment, close your eyes and look at intention. If the intention is not personal gain, the person may simply have faltered in judgement, and that can be remedied.

As to the second value, an organisation built on meritocracy will always be robust. If the person given responsibility has the relevant education, training and experience, then they will not make mistakes based on a lack of capability.

Regarding the third value, I always pay attention to how people behave when they receive instructions. If they debate the instructions when there is time to debate and if they understand them well, it is unlikely that they will misinterpret the instructions. These people will do the same when they lead. A good follower is not someone who blindly obeys instructions. A good follower is someone who understands the mission, debates and questions everything that is unclear, challenges what he or she disagrees with, and implements only when fully aligned with the final decision.

Trust deficits arise when there are inconsistencies in a relationship; for example, when people say one thing and do another, or overcommit and are then unable to deliver. To my mind, trust is fundamental to good leadership. If you do not trust someone, then do not allow that person to remain a part of your organisation. As a corollary, if someone is part of your organisation, then the implication is that you trust that person. The sooner people realise that, the more efficient your organisation will be. Similarly, since it cuts both ways, if people do not trust the organisation's vision or leadership they must have the courage to leave. A relationship of mistrust will never work.

Trust is built over a lifetime. I was sitting with my long-time friend Rajiv Podar one day, finalising the terms of a business arrangement, when he looked at me and said that nothing needed to be documented because "you are like the Reserve Bank of India". This, to my mind, is one of the greatest compliments one can get from a friend, and it was a feeling that I reciprocated, as Rajiv's ethics were no different. We had, over the years, built a relationship where our word was all that was needed. Our dependability rested on the fact that we both made sure that we always honoured commitments, irrespective of any individual consequences.

In my experience, people do not have to say that they trust you or vice versa. Trust is established through actions and transparency related to the circumstances that bind you. It is when people's behaviour in your presence matches their behaviour when your back is turned. When people share things with you without hesitation, you know that there is a relationship of trust. I have generally been rewarded by placing trust in people. There have been a few instances where people have abused my trust by saying the right things and then acting inconsistently with their words. In all such cases, I have walked away from the relationship and never looked back. What I have learnt over time is that people who let you down once will do it again and therefore it is in your best interest to sever those relationships, particularly when the question of integrity is involved.

LOYALTY

I have spoken about the importance of people in my life and the need to build interdependence. People will always be central to your success and failure: integral to your success and there to cushion your fall in failure. Both aspects are critical. You need your team to take credit and enjoy the fruits of success, but you also need their shoulders when you are weak or stumble; they will be your crutch through difficult periods. Never forget this.

There is a fallacy that money drives people's loyalty to the organisation and to its vision. Money is a commodity and at some stage the people around you, particularly those in seniority, will be comfortable from a material standpoint. If you have chosen well, they will also be intelligent, capable, innovative, dynamic and ambitious; and some may even be more capable than you. Their loyalty will stem from their belief in your dream and their trust in your ability to pull it off with the requisite resources.

Loyalty is not a one-way street. Loyalty is an intrinsic honour code between people who are united by a common mission or cause. No one will ever be loyal to you if for a moment they think that their loyalty will not be reciprocated. I have seen several managers who have failed to stand by their teams when targets have not been achieved. This betrayal of professional integrity is the worst trait in a poor leader. You should stand up for your people irrespective of the consequences; after all, you chose them. If you are unhappy with any member of your team, or do not believe that she or he is capable, then manage expectations clearly by asking that person to move on. However, if they are on your team, then stand up for them; they will pay you back a thousand times over.

The truest test of loyalty comes during "crunch time". In 2008, when the global recession hit, there was complete mayhem. Our media business in Africa faced its biggest test as we were caught between adverse market conditions and a major contract with government that was terminated with no warning and for no reason. For a start-up enterprise, this was my greatest nightmare. When we went back to the shareholders for additional funding, one of the suggestions was to bring in international consultants to review the business and relook at the senior management team before getting contributions. I dug in my heels and explained to my shareholders and board that the issue was not management, but circumstances, as I knew how hard everyone was working to keep the ship afloat. After several meetings, the shareholders and board eventually came round to my point of view and we stood by our senior team, a decision that I remain proud of to this day. The confidence that I placed in the ability of the team was clearly justified when we finally broke even in 2015.

In return, I have been rewarded with some of the most loyal team members. This show of loyalty has been consistent across all my businesses. Management meetings at times were rough, especially when they questioned my decisions, but once they came to see my logic, they were supportive. When they felt I was making a mistake, I had to take a step back and allow them to overrule me. I particularly enjoyed the meetings in which they opposed me, as these provided me with the necessary reality checks. Loyalty does not preclude disagreeing with each other. Rather, it is about being respectful of each other's point of view and allowing the correct view to prevail. Once my colleagues step out of the boardroom, I can rely on them to implement our collective decisions fearlessly, irrespective of their origin.

When we took the decision to launch *Forbes Africa*, the shareholders questioned the business case. Print media was struggling all over the world, especially after the crisis in 2008. Our institutional partners did not agree with the plan to get into print and would not approve it. I sat with the team for hours, rationalising why it was a good idea for Africa. After much debate and box-checking on all the relevant issues, they gave me the thumbs up. We implemented the project and the magazine was a success from the very first issue.

Loyalty, like trust, is not earned in a day. It is a value that is formed through the tempering of time. Relationships must go through severe tests before these values can be taken for granted. However, lack of loyalty towards an organisation can usually be seen early in a relationship. There are several telling signs, the most important of which is the lack of alignment of objectives. People who believe that their personal goals are far more important than the goals of the organisation are not going to be loyal to the organisation in the long term. They will follow their own path, irrespective of what it does to the business. This attitude should not be confused with people wanting to pursue their own dreams. That is every person's God-given right and should be encouraged. However, being transparent about your intentions, doing everything in the best interests of the business and acting honourably for as long as you are part of an organisation, and beyond, is what loyalty is all about.

HIRING THE RIGHT PEOPLE

A great lesson I learnt in the army was about the importance of preparing soldiers for what they had joined the service to do: defend their country irrespective of the consequences for themselves. Preparing them for battle, an event that may or may not happen in their lifetime, involved a combination of understanding their aspirations and why they were willing to make the ultimate sacrifice; explaining to them what it would take for them to be successful; looking after their needs; and, above all, training them relentlessly. Armies that win wars do so because their officers and soldiers are better trained than the enemy, and have the right motivation. Winning wars is about good people and good leadership.

The Indian Army has a complex recruitment process for both officers and enlisted soldiers. I attended my thirty-five-year NDA course reunion (56 NDA) in December 2014. A significantly impressive number of 56 NDA course graduates had gone on to become generals, admirals and air marshals. Two in particular, Air Marshal R.K.S. Bhadauria and General Ashok Ambre, were now commandant and deputy commandant respectively. It was the first time in the history of the NDA that these two senior positions were filled by men from the same course. It is a rare occurrence in any establishment, particularly one as politically sensitive as a defence academy. An important statistic presented by the commandant at our reunion related to the quality of officer cadets inducted into the Indian Army. On average, 400 000 young men apply to join the NDA each year; 10 000 of these receive invitations to attend interviews with the various Services Selection Boards situated around the country; and, of these, only 300 are selected to join the NDA to serve in the armed forces. The NDA is the eighth most difficult institution in the world to get into. Those who join are the best of the best.

Business is no different. To be successful in business, you need a team that is committed to the goals of the organisation and willing to make the necessary sacrifices to achieve these goals. Building an effective team requires systematic and continuous engagement. The journey begins with ensuring that the right people are hired. The hiring process can be extremely complex, especially when building a multinational start-up. Not only do recruits need to be capable, but they need to understand the dynamics of interacting in a multicultural and multidimensional workforce. Looking back at the businesses that I have built, or have been a part of building, one of the essential hallmarks has been the high quality of the people with whom I have worked. If you have hired well, and at times paid above market, you will see a good return in a short space of time.

As I have mentioned elsewhere, in my business I have done away with the word "job" and replaced it with "responsibility". You may have a job, but you have to fulfil a responsibility. I have had to work hard to instil this idea in the minds of my employees – key people do not sleep until they have completed the task and fulfilled their responsibility. For this idea to be effective, you have to make people believe in it. In most parts of the business, I have been able to get the desired results, mainly from the senior team but also from some members of middle management. I have attempted to build this concept of responsibility into our business culture, and time will tell how it evolves.

When Carsten and I set up the CDC in Dubai, we hired some of the best talent from around the world. Being in the business of asset management, investment banking and corporate finance, our projects required us to work around the clock. We had staff in both Tampa in Florida, and Dubai, and we would transfer work overnight to one another, making the business more efficient. We behaved like a family when we were together, yet retained our individual lives. Owing to cultural and ethnic differences, our members of staff did not necessarily understand one another, but they were extremely respectful of each other's capabilities. I do not recall a single person leaving for monetary reasons or work dissatisfaction, or being asked to leave, once they had joined the company. The only time people left was when they were leaving Dubai.

Hiring is not about employment; it is about employability. Governments provide employment for various reasons. Businesses hire based on employability. In its most basic form, this involves mapping the responsibility of a position onto the skills, motivation and attitude of a particular person. The accuracy of the mapping largely depends on the process, criteria and the time allocated to get the right outcomes. Whenever we did well with our hiring, the real winner was the process that was followed, particularly when we took our time in properly assessing the candidates.

My entire life has centred on building start-up companies. The challenges for start-ups are unique, particularly if the businesses are set up in emerging markets that you are entering for the first time. For CNBC Africa, the cross-section of people that we hired was extremely diverse. I was reminded repeatedly by the HR team that one of the important considerations was BEE, and that we had to meet employment targets around ethnicity. As a general principle, I have always advocated indigenisation, as no matter how long it takes to train people, it is more prudent in the long run to hire locals, since I believe that expatriates will always eventually return home, leaving skills gaps in the organisation. However, in general, for the private sector to be forced to hire on any criteria other than merit is fundamentally flawed. South Africa was particularly challenging, as a large portion of the black population did not have any training or qualifications as a result of a legacy of discrimination. The BEE requirement created its own challenges, as skills in the financial journalism sector were extremely scarce, irrespective of ethnicity, as very few local journalists had ever stood before a video wall and even fewer technicians had any knowledge of a server-based tapeless TV station. The skills to establish and drive a pan-African TV business simply did not exist on the continent. Adding a filter of ethnicity thus made the task of hiring virtually impossible. Nonetheless, we had to comply and make it happen.

Interestingly, the across-the-board skills gap actually made it easier in the long run. We recognised the dire need to train people and took it upon ourselves to do so. The enormity of the task was onerous, as we were attempting something no one had done before. We nevertheless managed to get a great team together when we launched CNBC Africa. We supplemented skills shortages by bringing in temporary qualified experts and trainers to train local staff and, in some cases, by taking locally hired staff overseas for training. With a view to the future, we started an internship programme, which enabled us to meet BEE requirements, as we were able to build long-term employment opportunities through a sustained process. By 2015, eight years after starting our operations in South Africa, we had met all our employment conditions.

The quality of the people around you is a reflection of the values you inspire. I coined the acronym LIACC as the basic principle for recruiting staff. It stands for loyalty, integrity, attitude, competence and commitment – the core values that I look for when recruiting and retaining people.

It does not matter in which part of the world or industry you operate, finding good people is always the greatest need and challenge for companies. In most cases where people either were asked to go or left of their own accord, it was on account of bad attitude. Start-ups need employees who have a can-do attitude and levels of commitment beyond the ordinary. Identifying such enterprising people takes time and patience, but once you find them, it is about making sure that you do not lose them. One of the hallmarks of my success has been my ability to retain those senior staff who not only provide exceptional leadership, but also offer continuity in the implementation of my vision.

RETAINING PEOPLE

The human resources department is, to my mind, the most critical department in any organisation, as it nurtures the most important asset in the business: people. Since people are the main assets of a company, it is necessary to devote adequate time and resources to manage the expectations of the workforce. Getting to know your people and understanding their motivations is fundamental to success. Many organisations only pay lip-service to this, but over the years I have tried to make sure that we implement very strong policies and procedures around the development of our people.

I believe that my interest in HR has not gone unnoticed by the people who work with me. I spend a significant amount of my personal time with members of my team, getting to know the "crown jewels" in the organisation, so to speak, around whom the future will be constructed. It is critical for leaders to spend time understanding the aspirations of their people and mentoring them on their future growth path. If people do not understand the vision and growth plans of the company, they will most certainly not be able to understand their own future in relation to the company, and will eventually leave. This is even more important during a crisis, because when there is turbulence people get anxious about their own survival and often act in an irrational manner. It is therefore necessary to continually talk to your people, both formally and informally, in order to align their interests with the goals of your company.

Performance appraisals are critical, as this is usually the only formal process by which you can manage your team's expectations. It should not be a one-way process in which the reviewer does all the talking. It is equally important to get accurate feedback from staff members on whether their own career objectives are being met and whether the organisation can provide tools to make them more productive. People will leave an organisation if they detect an indifference towards their growth or aspirations. Young people especially will leave if no one respects their ideas about how to improve the team.

I get my teams to conduct proper performance appraisals by personally checking every personnel file in the company twice a year. This forces my HR teams to make sure that the files are updated and that issues arising from performance appraisals are properly followed up by HR along with the designated line managers. Over time we have changed several policies or procedures based on staff feedback. Interestingly, I have come to realise that while compensation is important to people, often what is equally salient is that their views are factored into the decisions made by the company.

There will be times when you need to act decisively following your staff reviews. In the past, we have sometimes been sympathetic towards people who unscrupulously abused the trust placed in them. We failed to act because of the various personal and emotional excuses they gave us, muddying the waters and preventing us from taking the correct action. I have always believed that you should give people a chance to change or improve. However, when it comes to basic ethics and values, I have to agree with Ayn Rand: our character is embedded in our identity or DNA and is formed very early in life. If people lie, deceive or steal, they will do it irrespective of the number of opportunities you give them. In fact, they will bear a grudge against you for having discovered their flaws. Whenever I have spared someone over an ethical violation, it has come back to haunt me as the person has always let me down again. You should take corrective action against value infringement and terminate people when it occurs, irrespective of the seniority of the person or the short-term difficulties this may cause. In the long term, the organisation is best served by decisive action.

Compensation is a key conversation point in many appraisals and should be discussed as part of the review. Except for a few exceptionally committed journalists and academics, money is one of the main drivers of a person's desire to work hard. Progressively, every generation aspires to economically do better than the last. You want to provide a higher standard of living for your family than you had, and therefore what you earn is important. This is perhaps the most aligned motivation from a company's perspective, since people who are ambitious will work hard knowing that the success of the business will also result in the achievement of their own dreams. In the start-up phase, however, it is not always easy to give compensation increases, particularly when the business is losing money. Despite that, I have always tried to give salary increases in line with market benchmarks, particularly to those who have consistently performed well, or those with unique skills that are critical to the organisation.

I have encouraged heads of departments to recommend compensation increases for people who they believe are crown jewels and should be retained. These decisions are prudent for shareholders in the end. We have at times lost junior or mid-level staff members to our competition, but such attrition will always happen in any market or industry, irrespective of pay scales.

In 2011, I started a company stock-option plan in South Africa and brought all our senior members into it. In 2013, when we set up Lancaster University in Ghana, I once again aligned the interests of the top team by giving them significant equity in the business. This is one of the most effective long-term strategies designed to retain good management. It helps motivate the senior team to get the company to profitability fast, so that they can share in the long-term growth of the business. For more junior team members, the key incentives are different and are linked largely to travel and further education. I will discuss this in greater detail under mentorship.

In my experience, no matter where in the world, and with only a few exceptions, people do not leave organisations solely for monetary reasons. Sometimes they do not feel challenged enough. Losing good people for this reason is a shame, but it is an inevitable part of career growth. Small and medium-sized businesses typically have a narrow pyramid structure with only a few vacancies at senior level. These vacancies are created only when people move on. It is, therefore, part of the evolution of small companies to lose people to larger organisations that offer a greater breadth of opportunities. I have always encouraged people to try new things, to enjoy living each day and to make their lives more rewarding for themselves and their families.

For my part, I never give up on good people even after they've left the organisation, provided they do not do anything unethical after leaving my side. Alexander Leibner left ABN as head of marketing, but after trying different things, including a stint in Germany, he rejoined us a year later as head of ABN Productions. Similarly, our head of finance at Murdoch University Dubai, Sanjay Rodrigues, left us and came back a year later as group controller. I have no ego in such matters and stay in touch with people who have earned my respect, with the hope that I will get an opportunity to work with them again. In most cases, they have reciprocated in a similar manner. People will experiment with their lives and have every right to do so. You just need to make sure that they know the door is always open for them, irrespective of where they go.

MENTORSHIP AND PERSONAL DEVELOPMENT

Closely linked to performance appraisals is the need to follow up on discussions with staff members. Irrespective of their positions, people, particularly those over the age of thirty, are keen to know what is in store for them as part of the long-term growth of the company. It is therefore important for senior members to know their own career paths before they can make plans for the junior members of the team.

I have always made a point of speaking to my senior team members about their long-term plans. I implemented an open-door policy, which made it possible for all members of the team to come to me for mentorship sessions, during which I would advise them on their career and personal development. The intention of these sessions was not to discuss their responsibilities or their relationship with their line managers, but to help them identify goals and then assist with a plan to achieve their goals. I often started by asking people where they would like to be by the age of fifty and then worked backwards from there. Most people do not plan that far ahead, and in some cases they have no plans at all.

I advised people to put together a plan in writing and to periodically monitor their plan throughout the year, to see which milestones they had achieved and which they had missed. For those who took it seriously, I saw some major changes, including reforms to lifestyle, such as giving up habits like smoking and instead working on their fitness, and wealth creation, such as investing in property. In some cases, I encouraged people to move within the group, so that they could better achieve their goals. These mentorship sessions helped people understand where we were going as an organisation and gave them insight into the various opportunities that could potentially open up within the group.

The mentorship sessions also afforded me the opportunity to spend time with people who I ordinarily wouldn't get the chance to spend time with in the normal course of business. Some of these insightful conversations were extremely beneficial, as the feedback allowed me to make changes to things that were acting as bottlenecks in our system.

As we were not always able to reward staff with bonuses, particularly in the media vertical, we leveraged training courses and MBA programmes. Through periodic skills audits we were able to identify gaps in skills and provide skills training using both in-house talent and external trainers. Since we own universities and a training institute, we made media training available for the administrative staff to improve their presentation skills, and provided business courses for staff who did not have a business or finance background. I also got team members to participate in conferences and exhibitions to bring them up to speed on the industry and build relationships. I gave most members of the executive team a target to represent the company and speak at one industry conference each year. This helped our staff achieve prominence in the industry, building their own profile and at the same time bringing the company recognition.

In 2012, I took a decision to start sending members of our senior team to Harvard Business School for short courses. In 2013, Roberta Naidoo completed a course on the future of the media industry, and in 2014 Bronwyn Nielsen took one in finance. Besides the obvious benefits, my intention was to facilitate a global platform for my senior team, so that they could interact with the best in the industry and build an international peer group. This recognition is invaluable and a great motivator. Many companies manage to initiate staff-development programmes once they are profitable. To offer these programmes while you are still a start-up making losses requires belief in building a strong corporate culture that places the development of your team at the core of the business.

Our industries, particularly media, are changing rapidly. Technology is a key driver of change and some changes are happening so fast that it is becoming difficult to keep up. I grew up in a generation that saw the dawn of the home computer. My first computer was a Commodore 64 that had sixty-four kilobytes of RAM. We now have laptops that have greater processing capacity than the super computers from my time in college. The only ones who really understood the implications of these changes were the young members of our team who grew up using technology. With this in mind, I started the process of integrating middle management with the senior executive teams. What was most disconcerting was the obvious paradigm shift in habits and language, even between the people in their twenties and those in their mid- to late thirties. In many ways, I was becoming the dinosaur.

To be a great company, I realised early on that integrating our young managers was integral to long-term sustainability. I started the YLP to make sure that we could provide a platform to connect flamboyance, energy, passion and innovative ideas with a comprehensive understanding of the vision and strategy of the company. We went through a very rigorous process to identify candidates for the YLP. While the selection filter had many criteria, the only real attribute that I was looking for was the right attitude. It took a year to complete the programme and the results revealed the comprehensive understanding on the part of the younger generation as to where the business was heading. They simply nailed it, in terms of both content and technology. As expected, the glaring gap was in their understanding of human resources and finance. This validated my theory about the need for a blended management structure.

At the end of 2014, I asked for a shadow board to be established, chaired by my son, who despite his youth had a comprehensive understanding of both the industry and finance and was the perfect person to bridge the gaps. To give the board teeth, I gave complete authority to members of the YLP to question every decision taken by the senior management, as well as encouragement to hold their own board meetings to supplement the company board meeting. Select members of the senior executive team would attend the shadow board meetings purely as observers.

Another initiative that I started in our media business was the concept of reverse mentorship. It is important to mentor your teams, but it is equally important to create a forum where competent members of middle management are given an opportunity to give you their perspective on where the business is going and where it should be going. To this end, I appointed six mentors. I meet with them quarterly to listen to their advice. Some of the suggestions that I have received so far have been priceless. These interactions have not only brought me closer to the middle management, but have also afforded me the opportunity to deal with small but important matters in a timely manner. This is an experiment, the success of which will only be determined over time. However, we live in a new, modern world and we need to act differently and try new things if we wish to become a great company.

INNOVATION

Innovation has become a buzzword. The reality is that technology is disrupting the way in which we serve our customers across all businesses. The bottom line is that innovative and creative companies are better able to provide their customers with more efficient products and services, in a cost-effective manner. No company can insulate itself from the risk of becoming irrelevant. Telecommunications companies are acting as banks, telephones have replaced cameras and the largest car-rental business in the world is a software company. The list of revolutionary business models is endless. Companies that do not look at the impact of technology on their products and services will become outdated, and will eventually perish.

It is difficult to conceptualise the future. In an interaction with some of my professors at Murdoch University Dubai, they shared the fact that the speed of change is so rapid that the undergraduate curriculum studied in the first year of a degree course will likely be obsolete by the time the student graduates. How scary is that?

During my meetings with our franchise partners, as part of their due diligence they would ask a number of questions about our market, strengths and so forth. Given that we were talking about well-established global brands, I would ask them just one question: "Where do you see your business in twenty years?" Any hesitation in the response from their senior management was evidence that they had not given the challenge enough thought. Whether IT, education or media, the consumption patterns of our consumers are changing rapidly and we need to make sure not only that our product remains at the cutting edge, but also that its access to the market is in sync with the latest trends of delivery.

As a first step in our businesses, I have prioritised this as a key deliverable by integrating our youth with senior management in all major discussions. This will ensure that we incorporate future trends into our strategic plans. In our media vertical, we have taken adequate measures to ensure that both CNBC Africa and *Forbes Africa* are available online. Education is evolving rapidly and all non–Ivy League universities will have to adapt their business models to factor in transnational education and move to online, distance or blended learning. In our IT vertical, we are moving the complete licence-distribution business to "the cloud". In time, the traditional distribution model will become irrelevant. Technology companies have to become systems integrators, an area in which we have already invested. Additionally, we have developed our own software, Enadoc, for document management, which will provide us with the necessary diversification as the conventional distribution business declines.

An understanding of changes in technology and consumption patterns is critical, as we need to make sure that our investments factor into the future and not just the past.

DO YOUR HOMEWORK

When you go into battle, the chances of success are always higher for the army that is better motivated, equipped, trained and prepared. We had a motto in the NDA and the Indian Military Academy: "The more you sweat in peace, the less you bleed in war." Preparation for battle lies in training and having a detailed understanding of all the battlefield variables, particularly the terrain in which you will be fighting. This requires years of building resources, engaging in reconnaissance and understanding every possible contingency that could arise.

For a business in an emerging market, it is exceedingly important to carry out a detailed due diligence of everything relating to the project as part of the project feasibility. I have spent a fair amount of time doing these analyses before setting up any new business. Other than the obvious market research and assessment of talent, a few specific areas that require detailed evaluation include:

- licences, if needed;
- tax regulations, including but not limited to withholding taxes, transfer pricing, tax treaties and tax benefits, if any;
- ownership laws relating to foreign ownership and affirmative action (such as BEE in South Africa and the Bumiputera policy in Malaysia);

- labour laws and regulations for hiring expatriates, or quotas for local workers;
- central bank regulations for restrictions on outward remittances, typically in countries like South Africa, Nigeria and Bangladesh; and
- choice of business partners.

Entrepreneurs often cut corners on some of the above, with a view to save money and/or time. When things go south, they realise retrospectively and to their detriment that they made mistakes on critical points. Having to go back and fix things will always be more difficult and expensive than if you had got the right advice in the first place.

I learnt a bitter lesson in Odessa when I put considerable resources into a retail project without properly doing my homework. While the banking system was weak in Ukraine and the law did not allow foreign ownership of land, there were plenty of opportunities. I invested in a local project without spending enough time getting to know the history or verifying the credentials of the partner. I was swayed by their contacts and their ability to move fast. The business was up and running in record time and soon became profitable. Despite appearing successful, however, the business was declaring losses. The only credit I got on all my trips was a recurring recitation, "Mr Wahi, you bring luck to us. Every time you are here, the place is full of customers. The minute you go, the customers stop coming." The net result was that I had no recourse on any aspect of the business. All receivables were in cash and all agreements were in Russian. I lost my investment and eventually had to walk away. In hindsight, if I had spent a small fraction of the investment doing my homework, I would never have made the investment in the first place. Remember the old saying: "If it seems too good to be true, it probably is."

It is critical to build in some internal filters when selecting a project for implementation. The costs of resources in start-up projects are significant, especially the opportunity cost of time. It could take you a year or two to complete the evaluation, feasibility and approvals, and even after all that you may not be able to set up the project. In that time you could have gone somewhere else and been in business with a different project. There are several examples of ventures that we analysed and then abandoned for various reasons. Earlier, I detailed the cable-TV projects in Oman and Lebanon that we eventually discarded owing to regulations and changes in government. Then there are instances where we ourselves walked away from ventures. In the education sector, there are two examples of projects we abandoned after completing the due diligence.

The first was in India. The education sector in India is huge and the opportunities are significant. There appeared to be a major drive to deregulate the sector and open it up to private universities. Several companies had established operations in India through different forms of collaboration with international universities. The regulator in India told us that there was no problem, and that once approvals were obtained the business could be established and run for profit. The charter and law, however, clearly stated that educational institutions had to be run as not-for-profit operations. So while the law said one thing, its interpretation by officials from the regulator was totally different.

I retained a law firm in India to come back with an opinion on the law and the structure under which a university could be established. What stood out from the report was that education was indeed a not-for-profit sector, but that people were making a fortune from it anyway. What became evident was that several large corporates had entered the education business as part of their corporate social responsibility in order to get a tax benefit for investing in the sector. They were given large amounts of land at lower-than-market rates on which to build the educational institutions, which in turn gave them a long-term benefit in the form of escalating land prices. Finally, they set up management companies that provided services to the education business and through which all business profits were withdrawn. A great structure, except that it was illegal and the operators would have to continue paying bribes if they wanted to stay in business. Another major shortcoming was that the bill for foreign universities had been approved in parliament but did not allow for royalties or repatriation of profits. The final icing on the cake was when we were asked to contribute US$10 million to secure goodwill for the allotment of land that was a prerequisite for the licence; unfortunately, we could not figure out a way to account for this goodwill in our financial statements. These policies work if you have a significant presence in India and can manage the specific nuances efficiently. For a stand-alone small enterprise, these requirements are onerous. We decided to walk away.

In Malaysia we encountered a different problem. The Bumiputera policy requires 51 per cent local ownership. We retained lawyers to advise on a structure and they came back with a proxy structure that would pass muster, but was legally dubious. The problem was that if any issue came up later, we would have to not only concede our ownership to someone else but also suffer reputational damage along with our partner university.

My view is that regulations in these countries will eventually change and once they do we can always go back and reassess the opportunity. In both cases, we had to spend time, effort and money on the due diligence, but in the end the decision to walk away was sound, as the consequences of setting up and facing a problem later were potentially far higher than what we lost in the due diligence.

It is also important to select good advisors for the due diligence and to ensure that the team they allocate has some understanding of the business about which they are advising. Frequently, advisors allocate teams that become specialists at your cost. If the team does not have proven experience, don't hire them. The best choice is to engage reputable international companies to support you. Not only will the project have credibility, but also the quality of advice will generally be better and there will be a fair degree of reputational accountability for anything that is provided. In Sri Lanka we engaged KPMG for our set-up and later Ernst & Young for the acquisition. In Dubai we used PricewaterhouseCoopers (PwC) for our set-up and Al Tamimi & Co. for our legal work. In Africa we used PwC for our tax and structure and hired Webber Wentzel for our legal due diligence. In all cases, we received excellent support.

CHOOSING INVESTORS

The choice of shareholders is integral to the long-term success of your business. It is not just about getting money, but also about the long-term sustainability of the relationship. You need to determine, in advance, who you need as a shareholder and why. Similarly, it is important to understand why someone is investing in your business; how long they intend to invest for; their ability to contribute future rounds of funding that may be needed; and how their investment fits into their long-term strategy. When it comes to choosing share-holders, emotional decisions seldom work out and expectations are often mismanaged over time. The worst situation to face is if you have a shareholder who is not strategically or emotionally invested in the long-term development of the business.

Most entrepreneurs need money when they start their business. Some start at home, have their spouse join them and work through low-cost models until their product is ready to be launched, or until sales allow them the luxury of securing offices and hiring profes-sionals. In my case, Saloni was part of everything I did and she looked after the complete back-end of my business from day one, which took a lot of pressure off of me. The result is that you have someone whose interests are aligned with yours, working close to the business, and together you manage to keep your overheads as low as possible.

We both made sacrifices when we needed to, and shared the spoils when the time came. I recommend spouses to work together, particularly if they have complementary skills, as the chances of success increase exponentially.

The next consideration is the equity that you may have to trade in lieu of a product or service for which the provider wants stock and not cash. Alternatively, you may not have cash to pay for a product or service that you require and thus may be forced to trade stock. Investment bankers and franchisors sometimes prefer to take a combination of cash and stock in start-ups, so they have a potential upside if the business is successful. CEA was a prime example of a company that successfully built up its own balance sheet over time. Finally, there may be services critical to success and professionals who don't mind taking a risk. These are usually the people who believe in the product and in your leadership, and who align behind you to build something with you. They may be happy to take equity in the business, rather than be paid a salary. All these models deal with "sweat equity" or a "carry", and lower the cost of the project.

Keeping the project cost low does not necessarily mean that the business is destined to be small. It just means that if the business is modular or scalable, then set it up with baby steps so that you can prove the concept first. There are two options for raising cash for a project. You can either raise all the money upfront, giving away a large part of the ownership, or bear the hardship of growing the business slowly; in other words, get it to a point where the revenues are well established and then reap the benefits of a higher valuation. For SMEs, the second option is always better, especially if you are an entrepreneur who has the tenacity to take on hardships.

Often, when you decide you want to start an enterprise, the first people who come to your aid are your parents, family and friends. They know you well and believe that you have what it takes to pull off the idea. In my case, I had decided never to approach my parents for any capital for my business ventures. I just banked whatever they gave me on a personal level into secure deposits that then acted as my "drop dead" money, or cushion. It was far more than what I expected from my parents, and I felt blessed knowing that even if all my ventures failed, I still had a home and something that would get me back on my feet. This was obviously a big bonus, as it gave me the security that many other entrepreneurs do not have. However, this did not make my journey as an entrepreneur any easier.

Much also depends on what stage of life you are in when you raise money for projects, and your record of accomplishment. When I went to Russia in 1991, very few people were ready to back me. However, as I gained expertise in the TMT sectors and established projects in emerging markets, several investors were ready to back any venture I started.

When I met with investors in Sri Lanka at the time of setting up Tech One Global, they did not have the confidence to invest in their own backyard and turned down the opportunity. They did not believe that the civil war would end, and also did not believe that software piracy would ever be eradicated, particularly from within large corporates, SMEs and government businesses. In light of this, we decided to set up as a low-cost, modular business and build organically. The business began to generate so much cash that we expanded our complete operation organically, including our acquisition into a document-management business. The business had relatively low overheads and the only time we needed any funding was when we wanted to support a specific project. Over time, banks began to give us facilities that were then priced into the project cost.

In the case of CNBC Africa, I knew that the project had a long gestation period and we needed institutions that were ready to invest on their balance sheet and that were not private equity funds. Media companies are long-term projects, and if any shareholder has a short investment time horizon, it can disrupt the project completely. South

Africa's IDC turned out to be a perfect partner as they had a long-term development focus in the media sector and did not have a finite time horizon to exit.

Another important decision you need to make at the start of a project concerns the stages of funding needed and the calculation of the break-even point of the venture. Some entrepreneurs prefer to raise funds through different rounds of financing, particularly for large projects that have modular growth. This is actually an excellent way to hedge value, as you continue to raise subsequent rounds of financing at higher values, thereby benefiting either from the higher values or through dilution protection, or both. The down side of this model is that if, for any reason, you get into a rough economic cycle, the ability of the project to raise money may be close to zero. Several start-ups with good ideas have gone under because they were either undercapitalised or failed to raise additional rounds of financing. My preference, therefore, has been to err on the side of caution and raise the financing upfront, but this is largely because my projects to date have each been under US$30 million in equity.

In the case of CNBC Africa, even after this prudent strategy things did not work out, because we were hit by several unforeseen events and had to double the projected capital requirement. We were fortunate that the IDC made all their calls, as did Zafar and I, and we were able to support the capital needs of the company. Perhaps one of the reasons the IDC continued to support the company was because the founders were also putting their own money into it. They saw that they were not the only ones feeling the pain of a project facing a cost overrun.

It was perhaps for these reasons that we single-mindedly pursued the IDC as a shareholder. It is not that we never have disagreements; we have had some differences of opinion during our capital increases, but they have always been supportive and encouraging while looking at the bigger picture. The IDC by virtue of its mandate is a long-term partner and has significant experience with start-up businesses, an important feature for entrepreneurs. Despite the frustration at times, I do not mind the bureaucracy that comes with the IDC. It is important to understand that institutions are governed by policies and guidelines and cannot take decisions the same way private investors do. This is a small price to pay for the otherwise outstanding value of our partner.

In the case of Murdoch University Dubai, as already mentioned we brought in a Kuwaiti institutional partner as a shareholder, but soon after the financial crisis started they expressed a desire to exit the business. I advised them to stay on. Their problems, however, were far too complex and so Zafar and I had to buy them out, at a considerable personal risk as there was no debt in the market. I had to liquidate some of our personal assets to make the purchase, but did so willingly, because I believed in what we were doing and did not want to abandon the project.

Another important ingredient is the role of debt in the business and your ability not just to raise debt for the company, but more importantly to service it. Debt is a major liability in the short term, as in emerging markets one has to service high interest rates, thereby increasing the cost of the business. For our education venture in Ghana in 2015, for instance, the banks asked for 26 per cent interest on local currency borrowings. This was simply unsustainable, so we had to fund the expansion through equity.

In the long term, however, debt allows you to own a larger part of the business, as you do not trade money for shares but rely on a fixed return instead. However, it can be a double-edged sword. On the one hand, if the business becomes extremely profitable and successful, you will have the resources to retire the debt and still own the business. On the other hand, if the business goes down, the banks will have some recourse through personal sureties and liens on assets that could adversely impact on you personally. In this case, equity would have been the better source of capital, as you would not have had liabilities beyond the investment in the company. It is therefore important to get a balance between debt and equity, and at all times make sure that you have the ability to service your debt.

Over the years, I have come to believe that, given a choice, you should seek out as an investment partner a financial institution that has a developmental focus in the region in which you are setting up the business. Institutions have a long investment time horizon, and as long as you keep them informed of progress and remain committed to the venture, they will usually hold an umbrella over your head. It has also been my experience that financial institutions provide you with political insurance in emerging markets, so that more often than not the playing field remains level and you do not become a victim of erratic changes. Finally, institutions are not managers within your business and are rarely interested in taking management control of a business unless forced to do so under dire circumstances.

COMMUNICATIONS

Communications is a complex subject and I am only going to touch on some examples of actions we have taken. The hallmark of a good leader is his or her ability to communicate both verbally and in writing. In any business, communicating with your stakeholders is extremely important, so that news, both good and bad, is delivered in a manner that is consistent with the company's position. The worst way for news to circulate to stakeholders is through the rumour mill. This does significant damage. As a general policy, I have historically provided a business update to staff every quarter. Over time, I have delegated operational messages to the managing directors and kept my own focus on strategic messages. This has helped to keep our people constantly informed of developments in the business.

Having been through challenging cycles – including two Gulf wars, the Asian financial crisis, the internet bubble and the global financial crisis of 2008 – the one compelling lesson for me has been the importance of communicating with stakeholders. We did make mistakes in some instances, but over the years we have learnt a lot about this crucial subject.

The most important parties to external communications are your clients and it is the responsibility of the company to make sure that clients are always aware of things that could affect your relationship with them. When we were fundraising for the Barings–CEA fund in 1994, and news about the collapse of Barings reached us, the first thing I did was to send out communications to our clients. I informed them all that although our partner was facing problems, the fund would not be affected and more details would follow. We updated them when ING took over, which gave comfort to potential investors that an equally strong partner with a long history in asset management was coming on board. Finally, we informed them once the fund documents had been revised and we were back in the market to raise money. Even though most prospective investors did not invest in the fund owing to prevailing market conditions, they were definitely pleased with the communications that they received.

During the 2008 financial crisis, I met with my board members and shareholders every month to update them on all aspects of the business. I needed their complete support to pull the ship through a tumultuous period and they needed to be sure that they were not throwing good money after bad. These sessions were extremely interactive, and with their indulgence and understanding I was able to get complete support from the shareholders at every stage. The main message at all times was that we had a plan and the right team to implement it.

One of the critical communications strategies relates to the messages that go out to your staff, particularly during a crisis. Having to retrench CNBC Africa staff in South Africa in 2009 was especially difficult. There was no easy way to let people know that some of them were going to be laid off. According to South African law, we had to provide the CCMA with a strategy, rationale and plan for the retrenchments. The entire process then had to be conducted under the supervision of a representative from the CCMA. As part of the implementation plan, if you intended to lay off a driver, for instance, you had to advise all drivers that their trade was under review for retrenchment and that one of them would be losing their job. Out of our staff complement of 140, we were planning seventeen retrenchments but had to serve notice to over seventy-five people. We communicated frequently with those affected and kept our doors open, but this was an incredibly difficult time for staff morale and, irrespective of what we said to people, the corridors were full of unhappy faces. What we did achieve, however, was a fair process that was as transparent as it could be.

Another difficult time for us in South Africa was when the GFC terminated its contract with us. As already mentioned, this made headlines, as all competitor media companies were happy to trash us. Communications experts in the US advised me that at times like this, less is more. We stuck with their advice and focused on the key message for the network: that editorial independence had never been compromised and that no one was ever able to influence the content of our channel. This was key to our reputation as a broadcaster and we maintained a strong position. It was not our responsibility to explain the government's reasoning for terminating the contract. That was up to them, and the Gauteng minister for economic development responded with the government's position on the termination. Even while the government was acting against our interests, I stayed in touch with the minister and made sure that he had all the necessary information to respond to the media, as he was new in his role and most of the people involved with our contract had moved on. Once again, this worked in our favour as journalists, and, despite their best efforts, our competitors were unable to create any controversy from the situation.

An interesting lesson that came from my reverse-mentorship sessions with my team was the need to communicate internally when people abruptly left the organisation. It turned out that some people, particularly those who were asked to leave or who left acrimoniously, would bad-mouth the company. Our mistake was that we did not inform staff of the reasons why a particular member was asked to leave or resigned. While "washing dirty linen" in public is never a good idea, in an organisation one needs to be transparent, particularly in a small business where employees are an extended family and have a right to know. We evolved a strategy whereby, each time someone left abruptly, we would hold an information session and disclose the nature of the disagreement. This did wonders for staff morale, as they now had the complete background to each case and could take a relatively dispassionate view on the rationale for the dismissals.

STRATEGY REVIEW

Business is a battlefield. To be at the top of the food chain you have to have a clear strategy. It means ensuring you have the best, most innovative people; a distinctive product prepared with a clear understanding of the market and consumers; the most effective technology; effective communications; and a robust resource plan. This strategy, together with able leadership, will produce the desired results. The strategy, however, needs to be reviewed in a timely manner, so that plans are consistent with market intelligence and changing industry paradigms. I have been a great advocator of focused annual strategy meetings to review performance against goals, with specific attention on ensuring that we remain focused and are not getting distracted.

The approach to the strategy meetings is bottom-up for assessment and alignment of operations with vision, and top-down in terms of making sure that the vision remains relevant. Each member of the executive team presents their department's performance, so that a collective picture emerges about what is being done well and needs to be complemented, what is going wrong or could go wrong and needs attention, and finally what needs to be realigned or recalibrated.

Outcomes from the strategy meetings are channelled in many directions. The first is towards the management and staff, so that they have the strategy and plan that has been agreed upon by the senior executive team. The second is to the board for governance purposes, to ensure that they have an opportunity to comment on any change in strategy that could affect the company. The board may in turn refer matters to shareholders, particularly if decisions that could affect the capitalisation or resources of the company have to be taken.

In 2012, after our strategy meeting for CNBC Africa, we went back to recapitalise the business to take advantage of the rapidly growing economies across Africa, as well as to shore up our defences from increased competition. We bolstered our balance sheet to build capacity in ten African countries, upgraded our technical infrastructure and took steps to fight growing competition. These actions were taxing in the short term, particularly since shareholders had to contribute additional funds, but we were able to strengthen the business from a long-term perspective.

In 2014, we reviewed the changing landscape in the distribution of television content across the continent and prepared our plans for the rollout of additional content through digital terrestrial television. Strong revenue growth indicators supported these plans across the new markets. Since the business had grown largely in South Africa for seven years, we went back to zero-based budgeting to look at what we wanted to achieve and reallocated resources accordingly. We reconstructed the budgets, looking at what we needed, rather than merely projecting a linear increase from previous years' expenses. This exercise allowed us to cut costs, make the operations leaner and reallocate resources geographically.

In the case of Tech One Global, if we had stayed content with our growth in Sri Lanka, we would have done well in the first five years, but our business would have shut down by now. We expanded each year into a new market, built human capacity and acquired a new business to bolster our position to better face the challenges of an evolving software-distribution industry. These actions were a drain on short-term cash, but we were able to build scale in a manner that allowed us to mitigate risk through diversification geographically and through increased product offerings.

Strategic planning is integral to success. Never forget the old adage, "Failing to plan is planning to fail." Get your top team together as often as needed and make sure that you pay attention to what they say. If you have hired the best and if you believe they complement you, then make sure you listen to them and incorporate their views into any plans that need implementing. If they are not part of the preparation, their hearts will not be in the implementation and execution.

CASH IS KING

The greatest lesson for anyone involved in business in any capacity, whether as an entrepreneur or a professional manager, is respecting the value of cash. The sustainability of a business eventually boils down to one fundamental indicator: cash flow. It is the lifeblood of a business. You can have the best of everything in terms of product, management and market, but if you don't generate cash, the story is over. Many organisations have been brought to their knees because they could not manage their budgets.

One of the biggest mistakes made by entrepreneurs when they set up businesses is that they do not plan their cash requirements adequately. The general tendency is to attract investors with aggressive revenue targets. However, once the unrealistic targets are not met, the business immediately comes under pressure, because it is invariably inadequately capitalised.

My attitude towards cash flow has always been proactive. I normally look at monthly cash-flow projections for a twenty-four-month cycle rather than a quarterly or annual cycle. As we complete one month, a new twenty-four-month projection is prepared. This extremely prudent exercise has paid off – not only has it kept all the businesses solvent, but it also has been a good way of updating shareholders on the cash needs of the business.

Cash is needed not only to support the day-to-day costs of the business, but also to fund future investment needs. Failing to plan for future investment needs, whether for expansion, capital replacement or strategic growth, has serious consequences.

It's no different for profitable companies. Entrepreneurs must guard against confusing a profit-and-loss statement with cash flow. It is a major flaw when non-finance executives have gaps in their understanding of the need for working capital to bridge cash-flow deficits. Just because profits are reflected in the accounts does not automatically mean that the company is doing well or is healthy financially. At times, there are such high receivables on the books that the business becomes unviable simply because it is unable to collect its payments from customers and therefore cannot meet its own commitments.

It is extremely important to take into account all the variables that can go wrong and make sure that you have an idea of the probable cash position and a plan for how to bridge the deficit. The payment terms with most clients in the media industry range from thirty to ninety days. With government delays in countries like Nigeria, you're looking at between 180 and 360 days. This can have a serious impact on a business. This is where banks should logically step in and help. However, most banks do not understand the media industry and therefore shy away from supporting start-up companies in the sector. This is largely because banks need collateral against facilities and media companies do not have collateral other than intellectual property.

Over time, however, banks will see the trends and, once a record of accomplishment is established, will begin testing the water slowly but surely. In our media business, we were lucky to have Standard Bank hold our account. They had a great team and worked with us to build on our needs, not just in South Africa but also throughout the continent.

This was not the case from the beginning, and we had to rely a lot on shareholder financing to keep the business afloat. The recession in 2008 caused major problems for the start-up media business, as most companies curtailed advertising expenditure in an attempt to cut costs. We had to go back to the drawing board and review our budgets. As a first step, we took out non-core activities and trimmed our financial plan, based on revised costs. We then went back to all the shareholders and recapitalised the business.

Each business has its own nuances, but cash-flow management remains critical, whether there is a deficit or a surplus. In the case of our IT business, Tech One Global, after the first few years we began to generate a significant amount of cash, because the business performed exceptionally well. We used a large part of the generated cash for expansion and diversification (of product and geographically) to build long-term sustainability and shareholder value. In some instances, shareholders prefer to take dividends, but we decided to keep reinvesting, particularly in the early years while we were building scale. We also acquired additional businesses, as the long-term impact from prudent and synergistic investment activities builds better shareholder value. Once again, these decisions and plans were part of a deliberate strategy and were made well in advance.

Our proactivity has been one of the reasons why we have never once had a delay in our staff payroll. This has been one of my standing directives to all the companies in the group. Inept management of cash can affect credibility and reputation, and is the number one indicator of unsound business practices.

MIS AND RISK MANAGEMENT

An important aspect of setting up businesses in emerging markets is establishing a strong MIS and risk management department.

Most businesses fail to track performance of both budgets and operational milestones against the business plan. It has been empirically proven that, once established, most start-up businesses face significant deviation between projections and the actual cost of operations. This is mainly because there are unforeseen variables, the occurrence and consequences of which cannot always be properly determined. For instance, we could never have predicted in 2006 that the world would face a major financial crisis in 2008. Even after the fact, the impact of the recession that followed was more severe than anticipated on both our media and our education businesses.

In such situations, it is important for both the entrepreneur and the shareholders to receive periodic updates on the business, so that they can all be available as and when needed and support the business from all sides. Having an independent MIS and risk management person or department in your company may appear to be a luxury, but only they can provide a periodic reality check. The advantage is that problems are highlighted as they arise and the management team can be given guidance if needs be, before the problem turns into a crisis.

The MIS function is therefore a critical component of the business and proper resources must be allocated, so that shareholders and management are periodically updated on any issues that may have arisen or are likely to arise. Shareholders also have adequate warning if they need to make additional capital calls for the business. The worst way to operate is to spring surprises on your stakeholders. For the management team, the monthly MIS report provides a reality check on their performance and gives department heads adequate time to evaluate challenges and take corrective action. Finally, it allows management to compliment staff who have performed well and who may need to be encouraged to contribute further.

Linked to a robust reporting system is the need for a strong risk management system. Risk management is an assessment of the systematic and non-systematic risk that a company is exposed to during its life cycle. The risk profile of a company changes with the company's growth. For instance, the initial risk for an entrepreneur is whether he or she can raise capital for his or her project. Once raised, the capital is no longer a risk (unless the intention is to raise capital in stages). The risk then lies in implementation. Once the project is established, that is no longer a risk. Other factors then take over, including staffing, revenue, technical, obsolescence and competition. It is therefore important for the management and shareholders to understand the risks faced by the company at different stages so that they can implement plans to mitigate those risks.

We have analysed risks in all our businesses and conduct quarterly risk-assessment updates. We make sure that we have an understanding, well in advance, of any eventuality that could bring the business to its knees and try to take preventative action where possible. We also use these updates to assign responsibility to the correct level of management, depending on the severity of the risk.

No business can mitigate all risks and provide redundancy for all possible failures. However, critical risks have to be considered and dealt with at the right time. At CNBC Africa, we needed a disaster recovery plan to ensure that the broadcast never stopped. We therefore developed a complete contingency master plan, for which the head of broadcast operations is responsible, which will ensure that our signal is restored within sixty minutes of a halt, no matter its cause.

Risk also relates to churn, compensation, implementation of specific projects, regulatory approvals, insurance and business practices or policies affecting reputation. These factors are critical for a company and need to be managed effectively. Managing risks sometimes requires an outlay of cash or a plan of action should the risk occur. In any event, the main aim is to protect the business and minimise adverse effects.

As a matter of habit, and particularly because we have geographically dispersed and diversified operations, I ensure that the MIS and risk management team members have a direct reporting line to me. This also keeps a check on senior management, particularly relating to accurate and timely disclosures.

PATIENCE

I am often asked about the single most important personal attribute required for success in emerging markets. My response has unequivocally been the need for patience. The days of carpet-bagging are long gone. People looking for quick returns, rather than investing for long-term value creation, are unlikely to succeed in emerging markets.

With very few exceptions, emerging markets do not have the same level of regulations and processes as the developed world. These processes could be as simple as setting up a new company or getting a tax number to begin trading. While most countries have an excellent trade-promotion office handing out glossy brochures depicting the merits of investing in their country, the challenges surface when you actually start the process.

For instance, in 1991 it was a nightmare to even open a bank account in Russia or Ukraine, never mind set up a proper foreign-owned corporate structure for a joint venture. It was up to me to find a way around these difficulties. In Oman and Beirut, we had to wait for years to hear about the licence conditions for cable TV. In Malaysia and India, we had to seek clarification on the regulations for setting up an education business. In South Africa, we had to wait two years to secure our carriage agreement. It took us two years to launch the university in Dubai. These were just the delays encountered in the setting-up phase of the operations.

Bigger frustrations arise in setting up meetings with key decision-makers, awaiting decisions from governments and navigating the environment when there is a lack of transparency. These are all significant impediments to progress and are sometimes exasperating. Many potential investors give up on the discussions and move on to markets that are better suited to their own style of operating. It takes time to win the trust of people and to understand their culture and style of working. In Yemen, it proved impossible to see a government official at his office, but when we invited him to have lunch and khat in the afternoon, he was happy to join us. In Russia, some of the most productive meetings took place in saunas. In South Africa, I had to wait outside government officials' offices for hours before they would see me as they could never keep an appointment. Some would not even apologise for being late. However, once the meeting began, it was usually extremely productive. But then the absence of any proper follow-up would again impede progress. Collecting payments from governments is like drawing blood from a stone and yet they are often huge clients, so you can't invoke penalties or show any form of disrespect.

People who work in emerging markets have to therefore understand the needs and adapt to the local way of doing business. It is important to hire local staff or have a local agent who can help you navigate the cultural sensitivities and work on follow-ups. Emerging markets are no longer suited to people who are interested in short-term investments and just want to make a quick buck. You have to be prepared to invest for the long term and earn the trust of the local community, whether government, clients or, most importantly, staff. If you want to reap the benefits, you need patience.

GIVING BACK

I come from a country that is full of contradictions. India has one of the most dynamic and educated workforces, adequate agricultural output to feed its entire population and still export, and enough minerals to sustain its industrial sector. However, it has terrible infrastructure to support development and has one of the highest poverty rates in the world. Statistics reveal that roughly 33 per cent of the Indian population lives on less than US$1.25 per day and that about 180 million people live below the poverty line. Africa is similar in its contradictions and statistics. With all the economic development and prosperity on these continents, you would expect the levels of poverty to decline. This is not the case.

The divide between the haves and have-nots is unfortunately getting wider, and it is becoming increasingly difficult to close the gap. From water and sanitation, health care and food, to shelter and education services for the poor, positive change does not seem to be on the horizon. Year after year, election manifestos make promises that never materialise. Money earmarked for the poor continues to be misused and channelled to the wrong quarters.

During my life, I witnessed my parents engaging in a lot of charity work. From starting schools for the poor and vocation centres for training young women, to helping destitute children with clothing and education, my parents tried their best to make a difference. As I was growing up, my parents encouraged me to do things with compassion. When we progressed from one class to the next, most children would sell their old textbooks to the next class. My parents would give our books to children who could not afford them. My mother in particular had a soft spot for downtrodden women, destitute children and the aged. One of her unfinished dreams was to set up an old people's home. I saw the same qualities in my younger sister, Shalini, who delighted in helping all the poor children that lived around our home. She has a heart of gold.

Saloni has an equally soft spot for the needy. When I was in the army, rations were delivered to all the officers' homes each week: there were set allocations for eggs, milk, bread, vegetables, meat, and so on, far in excess of what the two of us could consume. There were quarters for domestic staff behind our home at the CME in Pune.

In her spare time, my wife cooked and distributed food to all the people living in the staff quarters. A line of children would come over every Friday afternoon for their specially prepared treats.

Over the years, we continued contributing to charities wherever we were based. We learnt about the needs of others by word of mouth and assisted those known to us or charities run by people we trusted. We also contributed to several projects in India, including the electrification of villages, and set up scholarship programmes at a vocational centre for girls in Dehradun to help young girls pay for their vocational education. In addition, we established an annual scholarship programme to help the children of Class IV employees (skilled or semi-skilled manual workers) at the NDA get educational bursaries. Shweta engaged in philanthropy at a very young age. She volunteered to help children at a handicapped school and raised money for children affected by cancer, as well as for the 2010 Haiti earthquake victims.

In 2011, I decided to set up proper structures under the ABN Group in Africa and formally established the ABN Education Trust. The objectives of the trust are: firstly, to provide annual bursaries to a few children from disadvantaged homes to study graduate programmes in financial journalism at prominent universities in South Africa; and secondly, to support orphan children in Johannesburg, with a view to eventually support orphanages across the continent, wherever the company operates. Over the last five years many of our team members, in particular Roberta Naicker, Nola Mashaba and Sian Schlebusch, have joined my wife in raising funds for the trust and in leading several initiatives, including assisting the Thuthuzela orphanage in Alexandra township.

We chose to focus on financial journalism because it is core to our business. By developing students in financial journalism, we are cultivating a segment of journalism that is underdeveloped. And we are able not only to put kids through college, but also to give them internships and jobs.

Saloni and I made a personal decision to support the Thuthuzela orphanage. Thuthuzela takes in children who are deserted at birth, usually by single mothers. Some of them are HIV-positive and most are severely malnourished. These kids need help, without which they will die. Thuthuzela has become our calling and as a family we allocate the majority of our contributions to them through the trust. I will never forget the look on the children's faces when we presented them with a bus for their commute, or when we contributed towards a new permanent home that gave them a decent roof over their heads.

The importance of giving back does not need explanation. People are generally busy with their responsibilities and routine, and therefore do not prioritise support for charitable causes, even if they want to. By setting up formal structures, however small, companies can at least afford their staff the opportunity to participate in whatever way they choose. It is our responsibility to help the needy and create a culture of kindness towards people less fortunate than ourselves.

5

ENTREPRENEURSHIP

Perhaps my greatest joy has been working for myself for most of my life. This gave me the freedom to pursue my own dreams. Freedom for an entrepreneur, however, does not mean that you can do what you like, work when you like or behave as you like. Freedom to be an entrepreneur actually entails endless responsibility. Entrepreneurship is about creating an enterprise for eternity. This means nurturing your business in a manner that safeguards it for all time. This journey is long and difficult, and requires passion, energetic persistence, determination and sacrifice.

I have always had an extremely fertile mind. I spent many hours thinking about the things that I wanted to do. We did not have television or the internet growing up, and so most of my interests developed through avid reading. My father invested heavily in books and encouraged me to read widely, sometimes across subjects that were a little too advanced for my age. For instance, while I was still in junior school, he gave me a book on management by Peter Drucker. I read the book from cover to cover, and even though I did not fully understand the contents, I developed an interest in economics at a macro level. For my Senior Cambridge studies, besides economics, I took science (as a major), as well as physics and mathematics; two subjects that I loved and that I think formed the basis of all the logic I ever learnt.

I realised even as a child that material things do not impress me. I would save all my pocket money and buy small gifts for my mother. Insignificant as they may have been, giving gave me great joy. I also enjoyed giving away things to people less fortunate than me, something that I learnt from my parents at an early age. These habits became part of my nature and a way of life. I would step up to contribute to charitable causes whenever people in distress approached me. These small acts of kindness became an integral part of my character.

But the characteristic that became increasingly dominant as I grew older was my determination. I had an overwhelming desire to succeed in whatever I attempted. When I joined the Doon School, in many ways I had to play catch-up with my peers. As my father was in the army, we lived a very nomadic life that was wholesome but not without its limitations. I was extremely conscious of the divide and worked hard to close it. I learnt fast that if you want to achieve something, are passionate about it, and ready to work diligently and with perseverance, you will succeed. By the time I left school in 1975, I had distinguished myself as an all-rounder.

There were, however, some areas in which I didn't excel. I was useless in the arts. Despite all my best efforts, I could not act, sing, paint, debate or play a musical instrument. The music teacher at school told me that I was below average in the arts, but that he had seen me on the sportsfield and felt I should focus my activities on my strengths. As a consequence of my weakness in the arts, and imagining, rightly or wrongly, that this was inherent, I stayed away from these pursuits throughout my life. Perhaps to make up for my own inadequacy, I encouraged my children to participate in the arts from a young age and am thrilled that they both developed an interest.

Other values that formed the basis of my character were my sense of propriety and my commitment to doing what was right, irrespective of the consequences. I became fanatical about doing the right thing, sometimes to my own detriment. Right through boarding school, I did my best never to do anything incorrect; even small indiscretions were taboo. As an example, students were only permitted to walk across the school's main field if they were wearing their games clothes. If a student was wearing any other gear, they were expected to walk around the field, not across it. Despite the extra distance, I conformed to this rule until the day I left school, and condemned those who didn't. I was brutal with anyone who broke the rules. In my understanding, there were no grey areas and I did not believe that rank allowed for exceptions. Consequently, I found myself alienated from many of my peers, but became a role model for my juniors. The experience helped me realise that I was not scared of being alone in pursuit of what I believed to be right. It was up to me to lead by example. In my school-leaving scrapbook, my school captain, Sanjiv Mehra, aptly wrote that I was one of the few prefects who stood out for upholding discipline in school, but encouraged me to accept others for who they were.

* * *

My schoolmates were not surprised when I joined the NDA and later the Indian Army. Nothing changed while I was in the army. I volunteered for everything and absorbed things like a sponge. I saw it as an opportunity to learn, and in your formative years, nothing is too big or too small. I did night patrols and courier duties, and on one occasion even travelled on a manual railway trolley to inspect a 200-kilometre segment of railway line between Jodhpur and Jais-almer. My task was to identify suitable locations for tank crossings for the armoured regiments. I performed each mission with a dedication that at times far exceeded the requirements of the task. My motto was excellence at any cost.

During my tenure with the Armoured Engineers, soon after Operation Brass Tacks in 1986, I was asked to assess whether our SKOT armoured personnel carriers (APCs) were fit for battle. To the amazement of many of my colleagues, I went and checked each spark plug, seal, lining and detail of every vehicle. They drew the line and refused my request for the vehicles to be submerged in water to check their amphibious capabilities. Nevertheless, I found that we did not have a single vehicle that was functioning to its required performance specifications and my official report declared the APCs unfit for war. When my commanding officer, General (then Colonel) Gandotra, sent for me, I thought he was going to be furious, but he complimented me on my work and made sure that things were dealt with in an expeditious manner.

On another occasion I was asked to complete the canteen audit. It was customary for officers to simply walk through the canteen and sign off whatever documents were presented. My audit process, however, was thorough and my report was comprehensive. But because it took up too much time, I was subsequently relieved of audit duties. It was fine by me not to be on the audit team, but I was not going to sign off on anything that I had not verified. For me it was a matter of principle; my dictionary had no place for ambiguity. Through all these activities, my core values became more and more evident, and my colleagues came to accept my unfailing rigidity where principles were concerned.

My first posting in the army was in the Rajasthan desert, on an operational task. The mission was classified and my regiment was inducted into a zone on a need-to-know basis. Brigadier (then Captain) N.P.S. Chauhan had a sign painted and hung on our perimeter fence. It read: "Trespassers will be shot." This was an extremely difficult period for all of us; for the first two years there was absolutely no leave and in the third year leave was given only under special circumstances. I was twenty-one years old and the solitude and confinement I experienced during that time inculcated an important quality in my psyche: patience. Life can be a challenge when you are forced to stay in a small, 112-pound tent, in fifty-degree heat, for extended periods of time. The only social interaction was dinners with my superior officers that were invariably a one-way dialogue where they spoke and I listened to their stories. I caught up on my reading and fortunately had a cassette recorder that my father had bought me on one of his trips to Japan. This desert experience tempered my mind and I was able to sharpen my ability to focus to the point of obsession; it's a great personal attribute that has helped in my work and in my dealings with the people I care about.

As explained previously, I left the army in 1988 when I realised that I was no longer enjoying myself. I had no idea what path my career would take, but I had come to the conclusion that I could not stay in an environment where I would not give of my best. There was nothing wrong with the environment; I had simply outgrown it. This was a brave choice, because I had no clue as to how I would earn a living and support my young family.

This outlook has remained with me all my life. I have already talked about my experience with my uncle's construction company in India. I watched in amazement while substandard work was approved and paid for. My uncle suggested I play golf and simply look after the cash to be disbursed on site. But I did not leave an honourable life in the army to now lead a dishonourable one. I did not leave to play golf and sign off on poor-quality work.

How does all of this connect with entrepreneurship? The traits that I exhibited from an early age were like dots in a picture, and as I started connecting the dots my destiny began to take shape. Over the years, the dots have all centred on an honour code of propriety.

We all build our lives around a few basic values that are dear to us. For me, my fundamental value was doing what was right and honouring my word. I have stuck to this principle all my life. I was perhaps influenced by the honour code in the army, where when you gave your word you honoured it. Save for a few instances, where other people changed the parameters of a relationship or attempted to deceive me, I have never gone back on my word. This kind of consistency builds credibility, which in turn builds the most important element of a relationship: trust. As an entrepreneur, you give your word to investors, bankers and vendors, to your own people and to all stakeholders connected to your business. You keep your commitments to all of them before you look out for yourself. My father resolutely stood by one value all his life: protect your name. He ingrained in us that the only thing that lives on after we are gone is our name. Your entire life, irrespective of what you do, must be spent protecting your reputation. Once your personal credibility is lost, you have absolutely no standing.

When I moved to Dubai in 1989, I met many smart people – bankers, lawyers, private equity managers, all highly skilled and competent professionals. They always had great advice for everyone and seemed to have all the answers. They should all have been entrepreneurs. The reality was that while most of them excelled in their professions, few of them ventured to do anything on their own. It would be logical for someone deploying capital to make superior returns, or for a professional manager making money to be able to do the same working for him- or herself. Unfortunately, this is often not the case. The difference lies in the ability to take risks and cope with the change in lifestyle that comes from a high degree of personal sacrifice. Once an idea has been developed operationally, a combination of risk-taking ability and management capability make or break an aspiring entrepreneur.

I had not figured out what I wanted to do until I travelled to

Russia in 1991. Being in an emerging economy, meeting new people and venturing into opportunities bottom-up was extremely appealing. The single greatest advantage was that I had entered a market where not having business experience was not a disadvantage if you came from a foreign country, particularly India. In fact, it was perceived as an advantage. At least I knew what chequing and savings accounts were, which comparatively speaking made me an "economics major". The Russians at that time did not even understand basic banking transactions. It was reminiscent of the 1960s, when the mail carrier was the sole source of news from the outside world. Change was welcomed with open arms; in a world of state TV, PABX phone lines and telex machines, my visits were like music to some of my business partners' ears. My early success in Russia was largely dependent on information arbitrage. The locals did not know much about anything; therefore everything I took to them was better than what they had. I was mapping the demand from one market onto the supply chain of another. I was capitalising on an opportunity.

During all my travels in Russia, I found opportunities with just about everyone I met. I relentlessly made deals and closed almost all of them. I priced myself right, kept my commitments and never let anyone down. It was small scale, simple, straightforward and profitable. What I could not do, however, was scale up. I had neither the experience nor the knowledge of corporate finance. The banking world encouraged a "fear of the unknown". The bankers were the guys in black suits who asked unnecessary questions and looked at me as though I was from a different planet. My first opinion of bankers was that they were snobbish and supercilious, judging everyone, all the time. Over the years, as I made some good friends, my opinion of bankers changed at a personal level, but not at the professional level. Like many people, I believe that most banks will give you an umbrella when it is not raining, but one whiff of rain, and they demand the umbrella back.

Initially, I struggled for capital. I could see all the opportunities around me and loved what I was doing. I had built relationships to secure licences and had the ability to execute, but despite all the passion and effort, I was unable to secure finance to build a large business in Russia. The main reason was that in 1991 I did not have either personal credibility or the single most important currency to raise money: a track record of successful and sustainable businesses. The expiry date on trading through information arbitrage was rapidly approaching and to stay in the game I had to constantly provide different value-added services to clients who were becoming increasingly demanding. I had to either establish manufacturing facilities or warehousing in Russia, or invest in a long-term business that would create local value for clients. In the absence of these options, I had to finally abandon my plans and withdraw from Russia in 1994.

Taking a step back to reassess the situation is never a bad thing. It puts into perspective where you are going and whether it is in sync with what you truly want. I recognised my entrepreneurial spirit during my time in Russia and knew that it was the direction I would eventually take. The gap in my training was finance and the time I spent with CEA was the best period of my life from a learning perspective. Learning and self-improvement are necessary components of the journey towards excellence and you can never study or learn enough. Life teaches you lessons every day, but a true assessment of your shortcomings comes from introspection. If you find a gap in your knowledge or skills that puts you at a disadvantage, it is imperative that you study and bridge that gap. I studied and read a lot in my formative years. I was fond of light reading until I joined the army and became the official librarian for the officers' mess in my regiment. Once I embarked on the path of building my life, my reading material changed significantly. Serious books on leadership and management replaced novels, and I learnt a lot from the biographies of great business leaders like Jack Welch.

Between 1994 and 2002, I worked relentlessly and travelled extensively. Most of the work was highly structured and the world of asset management, consulting and finance was perhaps my greatest classroom. The experience in Russia taught me about the need for capital; indeed, that access to sources of capital was a prerequisite for fulfilling my dreams. I saw first-hand the adverse consequences to your dreams of not having, or not having access to, capital. During my time with CEA, I came to understand that building a successful investment banking business from scratch was by no means a simple task. It required long hours and extended periods away from home. This sacrifice, from a personal perspective, was a matter of great concern, particularly because I had a young family and was not able to devote sufficient time to them. This was hard on my wife and children, but I was a man on a mission and determined to prove to myself that I could achieve my vision.

During this phase, I survived two economic cycles that rocked the world: the Asian financial crisis in 1997 and the dot-com bust in 2001. Once again, these dips taught me a great deal and I decided not to bank my future on the world of finance and asset management. I wanted to find the passion I had experienced setting up projects in Russia and building businesses bottom-up. Carsten Philipson and I discussed the possibility of setting up contact centres and document-management businesses, an industry that had come to the fore in the mid- to late 1990s. The team had a good laugh when I talked about it, but I nevertheless remained firm in my conviction that there were opportunities in this line of business. As previously discussed, my first foray into the industry was with my friend Rajiv Podar.

* * *

The business model that I carved out was to take global brands to emerging markets. I was ready in every way for each of the ventures that I started after 2002. I had built personal credibility; had experience in emerging markets; had worked with global brands; had the ability to prepare comprehensive feasibility studies that could be banked; had built relationships with financial institutions; and had a proven track record of success. These attributes and/or qualities cannot be bought or transferred. They are accumulated over years of experience and self-development.

My personal relationships with some of the financial institutions was so strong that for both the media vertical and our education business we got complete commitment within a few weeks of submitting the business plans. One of our traditional investors even asked to see every business plan I prepared before I took it to market. This was confirmation of my success. It took me a few years to build our relationship with the IDC before they finally invested in CNBC Africa in 2007. Despite all the ups and downs over the last nine years, they have never hesitated in stepping up whenever we needed their support. One of their senior executives told me that they are "backing the jockey" and have no doubt that, as long as the founders are visible and involved, the business will achieve its goals. While these acknowledgements are great from a personal perspective, it is also an indication of the satisfaction that our shareholders have found in the work that our teams are doing.

"Backing the jockey" is an explicit metaphor. Investors back an entrepreneur who has a vision they are convinced he or she can bring to fruition. To have vision you must have the ability to dream, and to dream big. No one wants to back small businesses that have no room for growth. Every investor believes his or her next project will be a gold mine or a home run. If you put yourself in the shoes of an investor, what type of venture would you back?

In October 2007, soon after we launched CNBC Africa, I brought the whole company in for a workshop, and rolled out my vision for our growth. As previously mentioned, in 2014, Sidharth, who was overseeing our MIS function, looked at the company and compared it to the presentation from that workshop. I was proud to see that we had set up each of the projected new businesses and had rolled out all our plans as per the initial vision. We had built the verticals, grown our content and grown geographically to be the most influential business media conglomerate on the African continent.

It was the same in the education business. In 2009, I held a strategy workshop with my senior team and rolled out a plan to launch a new flagship campus in Africa with a view to eventually set up ten universities across the continent. In 2012, we partnered with Lancaster University in Ghana and established our first campus in Accra in October 2013. As an entrepreneur, you have to have the ability to dream and think big, but, more importantly, you have to have the ability, drive and perseverance to implement your vision despite all the vicissitudes.

Shareholder satisfaction is a key deliverable for any entrepreneur. If the core requirement for any business is access to finance, then it is imperative to keep your commitment to your shareholders. Things may go wrong at some point in your journey, but it is critical to keep your shareholders engaged and fully informed of all aspects of the business. If they are part of the process, they will accept contingencies. No one likes surprises, particularly bad news. Investors expect timely, accurate, focused and concise information regarding the performance of their investment. I established strong reporting systems, so that there was always a steady flow of information to the board and shareholders. This ensured that we tracked our performance accurately on the one hand and provided periodic updates to shareholders on the other.

Another principle that I have stuck with is always ensuring that I have sufficient skin in any project, particularly when relatively large investments are involved. This is a great comfort for investors. During the 2008 financial crisis, Zafar and I matched our investors dollar for dollar in our media and education projects. We also stepped up and bailed out our Kuwaiti shareholders when they wanted to exit the business, something that very few entrepreneurs would ordinarily do, particularly when a business is bleeding. It was our way of showing good faith towards our shareholders. Acts like these provide comfort to shareholders and set a precedent: they know they can count on your support if and when needed. Stick to these principles and your credibility is assured.

Shareholders aside, the other key ingredient to a successful enterprise is surrounding yourself with good people. As the business grows, it is important for the entrepreneur to evolve his or her role. This requires delegation to the next tier of management, so that you build depth within management structures. Depending on one individual to deliver results and continuity is risky in any business, and a potential red flag for investors. To mitigate this, you have to develop several tiers of management expertise within the business. Your senior team members are not traditional employees; they are your partners in development and growth. You need to be able to trust them implicitly to carry forward your vision whether you are there or not. After the first few years, I delegated complete operational responsibility to my senior team members. The delegation is now complete to the extent that, other than signing off on the audited financial reports, I do not need to sign a single piece of paper in any of the companies. All the businesses are run with complete autonomy and accountability.

Most entrepreneurs hesitate to give up control, which is a big mistake. As long as you are a shareholder and committed to your business, delegating will only complement your efforts. The entrepreneur has the dream and vision. If you stay entrenched in the day-to-day activities, then there will be no one focused on strategy, innovation, competitiveness and growth. The business will reach a plateau and eventually decline. Just as you find the best people for certain responsibilities, you need to make sure that you assign yourself tasks that you are best suited to perform.

Delegation leads to yet another imperative for an entrepreneur: succession planning. As my businesses matured and I delegated all day-to-day responsibilities to my senior management, to the extent that they did not need me for anything except dealing with shareholder matters and cash flow, I began to focus on building strategic relationships and growth opportunities, and on making sure that the companies remained solvent. When I turned fifty, I began to worry about the possibility of something happening to me. This issue required serious thought, as it is not the same as delegating executive responsibilities. It is about finding the best person in each business and involving them in planning for the future. It also entails transferring all your relationships to the designated person/s. Over the last six years, I have consciously worked with my senior team to make sure that there is a succession plan at each level of management, so that the risk of discontinuity is minimised. To enforce the point, I stopped chairing meetings and stopped sitting at the head of the table during meetings, including in the boardroom. This signalling of transition of power is important and can only be implemented top-down. It is only when people at the top make room through their own repositioning that people below them will feel empowered to take on additional responsibility.

In finding and mentoring a successor, it is important to seek out some basic qualities. It is a given that senior people on my "A" team are highly motivated, skilled and loyal to the organisation and its vision. In addition, I look for four other qualities in individuals: the ability to remain calm in a crisis; highly developed intuition, including a strong instinct or gut feeling; the ability to get to the crux of any issue; and a complete lack of ego.

The fourth is the hardest for professional managers to overcome, but, as an entrepreneur, if there is anything you should lose on the day you start your business, it is your ego. To safeguard your business, you have to make personal sacrifices that include subordinating your very existence for the sake of the business. I have swallowed my pride repeatedly to ensure that my business received its due, continued to play on a level playing field, was not put at any disadvantage that I could prevent, and remained insulated from any threat. It is not only your pride that must remain in check; from time to time you may be faced with incompetent people in positions of authority (particularly in government) who you would like to put in their place, but you have to control yourself and take the higher ground of humility, for the sake of the business. The mantle of succession should therefore only be placed in the hands of people who have the ability to put the business before their own pride. Humility is one of the essential traits of a great leader.

*   *   *

The last three decades have had their share of extreme volatility caused by various events: the breakup of the Soviet Union, the Gulf wars, the Asian financial crisis, the dot-com bust, the 2008 global financial meltdown, and the collapse of oil prices and other commodities in 2014/15. Each time a crisis hit, I was embarking on something new. I survived by training my mind to always remain calm. Panic is the worst quality a leader can possess. It pains me to see people getting worked up and consequently escalating issues that could otherwise be handled calmly and quietly. Every problem that exists has a solution. This is God's gift to every human being; it is important to recognise and appreciate this gift.

Another gift from God is our instinct, or gut feeling. More often than not, my first gut reaction has turned out to be the right one. With very few exceptions, each time that I have gone against my instincts I have made a mistake. It is therefore important to reflect on decisions in a calm, logical manner. If the findings are overwhelming in any one direction, then follow the obvious path. However, if the gap is narrow, then follow your instincts. When I pose a question to my senior team, my first touch point is to get their instinctive response to the question or situation. I then map that with the results. People who consistently get it right will be able to protect the business instinctively.

Related to these qualities is the ability to "cut to the chase". You will often find people getting bogged down in long-winded discussions, going round and round in circles and not dealing with the issue at hand. Effective leaders go for the jugular every time. There is no point beating about the bush. When there is a problem, get to the cause, not the symptoms. Clinically and effectively deal with the core issues. If something is not working, find another way to fix it. When you are making a sale, ask the client if he is going to give you the business or not. If someone is not performing, ask that person to leave. Delaying the inevitable is inefficient, makes you look ineffective, and will harm your reputation as a leader.

These qualities aside, I believe there is one unpredictable element that plays a very important role in the life of an entrepreneur: "Lady Luck". Why is it that some people consistently come through crises unscathed, while others get bruised and bloodied? Think about the businessman who favourably exchanged currency yesterday, while you're facing huge losses today as a result of overnight currency devaluation. There was no early warning; banks and traders share the same data with everyone. It was just luck, pure and simple. And some people seem to have more luck than others. How do you mitigate something as intangible as bad luck? If you were one of the kids in school who was caught out for even the most minor infringements, or who never won raffles or prizes at bingo, Lady Luck is probably not on your side. And it is unlikely that things will ever change. Recognise and remain aware of this gap. Alternatively, and on a lighter note, make sure that you either marry someone with better luck or select partners who have nine lives, as Lady Luck will bail you out more than you can ever imagine; unscientific, but true!

I am often asked about the work–life balance of an entrepreneur. The reality is that, for an entrepreneur, there is no work–life balance. Starting a project is like raising a child. You are never off duty when you have children, even once they are adults and well settled.

When you set out on your own, you have to manage your business and take all the associated financial risks. You are also responsible for your staff and making sure that they are paid on time; their families depend on you and your business. Therefore, you face significant risk if you take your mind off the business for a single minute, particularly when you are starting out. Having the responsibility of both financial risk and organisational development is not easy, and it will suck the life out of you, especially if you've set out to do something significant.

For me my journey as an entrepreneur has become even more rigorous over the years because the business is now spread over three verticals in twenty-two countries. I seldom get to spend more than a week in any one city during the year. This nomadic lifestyle is extremely taxing. However, having the heart of a true entrepreneur, I believe that I have just started and there is so much more to build and do. I can only see the pressure of work continuing to increase, not decrease. But this is the lifestyle that I have chosen.

Having said that, I do believe that we all eventually find balance, either when circumstances force us or when we achieve our ultimate goals. But first there is the painstaking journey of extreme commitment.

The best you can do is make sure that you bring some sanity into your lifestyle. I manage my stress through sport. I have always been athletic and excelled at almost every sport when I was young. I especially loved playing bridge and golf from an early age and continued these activities when I was in the army. At CME I was runner-up in the club bridge championship. The problem is that both golf and bridge are extremely time-consuming and can be a strain on your marriage. I therefore encouraged Saloni to start playing both immediately after we got married in 1985. But I soon realised that having your wife as your bridge partner can be just as detrimental to your marriage. We came to a compromise in 1986: I would give up bridge and she would work hard on her golf. She soon became a worthy opponent on the golf course. We eventually replaced bridge with Scrabble, which brought harmony to our personal life as well as offered a respite from work.

In 1994, I injured my knee and back playing squash. From then on, I stuck with jogging, yoga and golf, activities that I continue to enjoy to this day. I make sure that I engage in my daily yoga session despite my brutal travel schedule. As far as my children are concerned, I have always ensured that we spend one holiday together each year and, without exception, I have spent every New Year's Eve with them from the time they were born.

Entrepreneurship is a way of life. You make a choice to engage in a business activity from scratch with your heart, soul and all your resources. It is your unique creation from conception to implementation. It is up to you to ensure its credibility, profitability and health, and to incorporate sufficient measures for succession and immortality. As an entrepreneur there are no half measures; you have to be "all in". Be fearless like a lion. Take bold decisions in the face of adversity and stand by them and by your people, irrespective of the odds.

6

CHILDREN IN BUSINESS

I deliberately chose to keep the entire discussion around my children in a separate chapter. Children are undoubtedly God's greatest gift. Saloni and I were blessed with our son, Sidharth (Sid), in 1988 while I was still in the army. I put in my papers two weeks after he was born, so he was five months old when I left the army. Our daughter, Shweta, was born three years later when we had moved to the Middle East. Dr Indira Kohli delivered both our children at the same private nursing home in Delhi. We had a great deal of confidence in Dr Kohli because she had also delivered the previous generation of Saloni's family.

Sid was born straight off the golf course. I was playing golf with my father at the Delhi Golf Club and Saloni had accompanied us for her morning walk. As we went into the clubhouse for breakfast after the ninth hole, Saloni started showing signs of discomfort. As a good soldier, I did not want to upset the four ball without completing the full round, so I asked her to continue walking. As we got to our second shots on the fairway, it was evident to all that Saloni was unwell. One look from my father was enough to know that there was a storm coming my way. We rushed home and then to the hospital. Saloni wanted to see only one face, that of her mother. I believe this was a blessing, as I was clueless. I was out of my depth and was happy to play second fiddle.

My parents visited that evening and my father, who was extremely busy in those days, reminded us that he had to travel the next morning, but he would stop by between 7 and 7.30 a.m., on his way to the airport. Much to my father's delight, Sid was born at precisely 7:13 that morning. As he blessed Sid on his way out, my father said, "This boy will always respect time." Sid was born on 13 April, which in Punjab is the auspicious day of harvest, Baisakhi. My troops, 40 per cent of whom were Sikhs, gave him the nickname "Baisakha Singh".

Two and a half years later, we were living in Dubai and the first Gulf War had started. My business was struggling and Saloni was pregnant again. Because she could not travel after the seventh month, she moved back to Delhi in December 1990. I went home a few times, but as we could not accurately predict the due date, I remained mostly in Dubai, hard at work. Shweta was born in the early hours of 27 January 1991, the day after India's Republic Day. Once again, my father had taken Saloni for a walk at the Delhi Golf Club, and from there they'd gone straight to the nursing home. I had immediately booked my flight for the next morning, but unfortunately missed the birth. I have always regretted not being present for Shweta's birth, something she jokingly reminds me about from time to time.

Holding your newborn child in your arms is perhaps the greatest feeling for any human being. No one will ever truly understand the meaning of the word responsibility until they have had their own children. It is not the same thing as helping your mother with a much younger sibling, or looking after a niece or nephew. Those are equally fulfilling experiences, but the responsibility is totally different. The complete dependence of a newborn on its mother is heart-wrenching.

Spending time with and bringing up our children has been the most fulfilling experience of my life.

We have always been indulgent parents and have given the children every possible opportunity to try whatever they wanted. I whole-heartedly believe that a broad base of knowledge, along with the experience of travel in your early years, enables you to establish what appeals to you and what you truly enjoy doing.

Sid went off to my old boarding school, Doon School, in 2000. He turned out to be an excellent sportsman and distinguished himself as captain of the cross-country team. He was an all-rounder and did exceedingly well in both academics and sports.

Sid was always fond of technology, and right from when he was young, he was the most sought-after kid with all our friends, as he would go from one house to another setting up computers or help-ing with internet connectivity – these were the good old days when Internet Protocol was loaded via floppy disks. We were on holiday in London when he was ten years old and offered him a chance to buy anything he wanted. He picked up a voluminous book on HTML, which he finished before we got home to Dubai. His ability to assemble computers and network them by the time he was eleven confirmed that he had exceptional technology-related aptitude and skills. Through my conversations with him, he started taking some interest in economics and business, but technology was his only love. It was not surprising when he was appointed boy-in-charge of the Technology Centre and then won his school colours at Doon. We had many discussions about his choice of courses for university and he finally agreed that a combination of technology and business would be something in which he would be most interested. He decided on the Schulich School of Business, at York University in Toronto, Canada. While there, he continued his self-study of technological developments – his real passion in life.

Sid was busy with his undergraduate programme when CNBC

Africa launched in June 2007. He did an internship at the network and enjoyed the environment thoroughly. In his summer holidays in 2009, he asked to do an internship with a private equity business and I spoke with a good friend, Rajiv Nakani, at Eastgate Capital, who happily took him on for a few months. The stint at Eastgate completely changed Sid's orientation towards business. When he finished university in 2010, he was keen to work for a private equity business on Wall Street, but unfortunately Wall Street was still in a tailspin after the bloodbath of 2008. It was then that I asked him to seriously consider coming to work for the family business. He had taken an interest in some of the projects in which we had been involved, but getting him to commit to media as a career was something of a hard sell. My argument was simple. I told him that it would help him get some valuable experience, after which he could go back to Canada to do his MBA, which would set him up better for life on Wall Street. After due consideration he finally agreed to move to Johannesburg as part of the media business. In 2015, he acknowledged that this was the best decision he ever made. The learning curve was steep and in many ways he had already earned his MBA in the workplace.

* * *

Shweta has always been artistic; a gift she obviously inherited from her mother. As a young girl, she was fond of reading, music, painting, debating and fashion. She started taking piano lessons at the age of eight and continued right through school, earning a distinction from Trinity College in the UK. She came first at her school in Dubai in all the elocution contests and participated in all the school plays. When she completed Grade 7, we considered sending her to Welham Girls' School, the sister school of Doon in Dehradun. Unfortunately, Welham did not offer piano lessons and so, despite her being accepted as one of two girls into Grade 8, we decided not to send her, as playing the piano was close to her heart and we did not want to take that joy away from her. Like her brother, Shweta finished school with top honours. She went on to major in fine art at York University in Toronto, and in her own time studied at George Brown College, enrolling in fashion-related courses that she could not take as electives at York. During her holidays, she took courses in fashion at the prestigious Central Saint Martins in the UK and started designing clothes, which she then showcased at fashion shows in Canada. In 2012, she was the youngest designer at the Ottawa Fashion Week and by the age of twenty-two had participated in over twenty-five fashion shows around the world.

Her passion was evidently incompatible with the businesses I had set up. I therefore completely understood when she said that she did not want to join the family business, but wanted to establish her own fashion label instead. I discussed the pros and cons with her, but she was determined and I respectfully accepted her decision. I did explain to her that she had a fallback position should she ever decide otherwise. However, I did not dwell too long on this, as she had to put her heart and soul into pursuing her own dream and I did not want to give her options, but rather the comfort that both her mother and I would always be there for her if she needed us. I have watched her over the last few years and admire her commitment to her work. She single-handedly designs, produces and delivers her creations to retail stores. I know, without any doubt, that she has the makings of a successful entrepreneur and will one day build a great name for herself.

In 2008, Shweta began using social media to market her own brand to extraordinary effect. She seemed to have developed a successful formula for reaching out to her customers and gaining their long-term loyalty and respect for her brand. Several retail brands noted her success and approached her to help them with their social media strategy. Since the age group of her customer base was similar to that of our university in Dubai, I asked her whether she would take us on as a client. I was overjoyed when she met with Bidisha Sen, our HR manager, and started working part time for the university as a social media consultant. In just a few months, she proved herself to be a vital asset in the marketing department and I could see that she was enjoying being on campus with students. Although she was part time, she would often work until the early hours of the morning on her social media campaigns. Through her humility, hard work and competence, she earned the respect of her peers and I was told that the senior members of the team had started engaging her in conversations around a more wholesome position at the university.

I was not too keen for Shweta to get involved full time as she was getting married in December 2015 and I wanted this decision to be made after she had consulted her husband, Vishesh, and his parents. A few months after her wedding and with blessings from her new family, she engaged with HR and joined our marketing team in a full-time role. In addition to her daily responsibilities, I encouraged Shweta to spend time with executive members to get an understanding of the business as a whole. To give her experience in governance, I also asked her to attend board meetings as an observer. At the end of our first quarterly board meeting in 2016, I asked her if she had followed everything. She told me honestly that she understood everything except the financial aspects. She also cheekily asked when she would qualify to receive the white envelopes that contained the board sitting fees.

Shweta's journey into the corporate world has only just begun, but with her strong values, work ethic and commitment, I am sure she will excel in whatever role she takes on.

* * *

It was difficult for me to understand what was going through my children's minds when I had discussions with them about joining the business. Although they never said anything to me, I am sure they must have feared being treated differently at work and perhaps losing their identity while working so closely with their father. Not having had any experience of working with my own father, I had to follow my instincts and rely on feedback from Saloni. Sid and Shweta have never told me if they've been uncomfortable with a decision I've made. This perhaps stems from the institution of fatherhood. Mothers seem to be the de facto barometers of their children's relationships with their father. If my kids have ever been unhappy with any of my decisions, the "not so subtle" messenger has always been Saloni.

When Sid joined the business in 2010, he entered in an MIS and internal audit role, a position that reported to the managing director. To my mind, this was the best way to get him into the company, as it gave him the opportunity to get to know every aspect of the business and the roles and responsibilities of every member of the team. I needed Sid to have a wholesome experience at work, as I wanted him to continue building what I had started, but on his own terms. There was the inevitable feeling that this was "daddy's boy" and people were obviously uncertain of what to expect. The first few months had their awkward moments, as all parties took their measure. Some things – like respect – cannot be inherited. My son often shared his frustrations with me at dinner, and I always affirmed that we had fantastic people working for us, and that he just needed to be patient in forming his own relationships with each of them.

Sid took to the MIS portfolio like a duck to water. He completely changed the format of the presentations and made the reports more efficient. He had the ability to look at global best practices and adapt our models accordingly. By benchmarking against world standards, there was a noticeable difference in the quality of our monthly reports and the board complimented him on the presentations he put together. This was a great learning phase for him, as he was able to gain a better understanding of every aspect of the business and see how the complex jigsaw came together. More than anything else, it gave him a detailed understanding of the people in the business: what they did and where we had gaps, either in skills or in coordination.

In an exhaustive risk report, Sid laid out all the risks the business faced and prioritised them. I asked him to update this document, incorporating individual departmental analyses, in conjunction with all heads of department and business units. He was able to do this efficiently and worked closely with the board's subcommittee on risk management to keep the register updated and relevant.

One of the major risks that we identified was the possibility of the existing infrastructure of studios and connectivity at CNBC Africa's headquarters in Sandton being compromised by fire or any other natural calamity. I asked Sid to work closely with Jean Landsberg, head of broadcast operations, to come up with a disaster recovery plan. While this was largely Jean's baby, I got a lot of feedback on the robustness of the plan from Sid, who by now had developed a tremendous amount of respect for Jean.

The first major test for Sid came when we were struggling with reconciling our sales contracts, play lists and transmission lists. Unlike most businesses where set relationships exist between invoices, item numbers, discounts and deliverables, in television, there are far too many variables and no two contracts are similar. Therefore, while many television software companies claim they have perfected software that integrates the various variables, the reality is that staff in the various television stations have to customise the software to make it work for them. Sid noticed that some of our people were duplicating effort by using Excel spreadsheets to ensure that they were not making mistakes. In addition, our auditors were having to manually prepare reconciliations each year, which was time-consuming and expensive. In desperation, I asked several international vendors to quote for a comprehensive application. The one that we felt was the best in terms of price and quality cost £250 000 plus an annual licence fee of £50 000.

I asked Sid to be part of the team reviewing the proposal. After going over the proposal he came to my office and requested permission to develop the software in-house. In fairness, he asked for five working days to review the terms of reference to determine whether he could do it or not. True to his word, he was back in my office within the week with a detailed spreadsheet on the terms of reference and work-flows. In short, he said he could do it. Later that afternoon, I asked him to present to all the stakeholders in the company to explain what he planned to do. It took Sid six weeks to have the first cut of the product ready, which he tested with the finance team. A week later, he tested it with the audit team. In eight weeks, he delivered a product that he had prepared in-house and that had cost us nothing. Sid trained the entire team on the product and we have not done any of our reconciliation work manually since.

This was a classic demonstration of his ability to combine his exceptional blend of IT, business and finance knowledge. During that two-month period, I did not see Sid at work or at home. He was at the office until the early hours of the morning as well as on weekends. He had taken on a responsibility and he wanted to prove that he could do it. By the time he finished the assignment, he had proved beyond doubt that he brought value to the team. His value was recognised by some of the senior staff in the sales and finance departments, but not by everyone. It was still early days and a lot more needed to be done.

During this period, Sid proved a few things to me, too: he was able to take instructions and follow them; he could assimilate things very fast; he worked hard and efficiently; and he was gifted with a superior sense when it came to integrating technology with any business process. At work, I saw that he had started building close personal relation-ships, particularly with people in his own age group. What I also noted, however, was his impatience with resolving issues and his lack of acceptance of weakness in others – all symptoms of eagerness and youth. I was exactly the same as a young man. Fundamentally, they were good traits that simply needed tempering with time. He came up against some expected closed-mindedness from a few people at work who were not making it any easier for him to settle in, but it was nothing that time would not resolve in his favour. Despite anything he may have felt, he recognised that he had to remain respectful towards everyone on the team at all times. He embraced this value from the first day, and it made me very proud of him.

As previously discussed, in mid-2010 I restarted our conversations with Forbes Inc. to launch an African version of the magazine. New projects always came under MIS, as it was important to have a good analyst on the team from the very beginning. Sid's first task was to complete the business plan and the financial model for the project. Once again, it required long hours of hard work, particularly the distribution plan, where we faced several challenges. He took over the entire project, including the negotiations and later, with Roberta Naidoo, the legal agreement with Forbes. All was completed by October 2010, when he was tasked with the financial closure and making presentations on the project to shareholders. Other than the IDC, all our shareholders agreed to participate in the project; it was a sign of great support at a time when there was a slump in the media industry in general and the print business in particular.

We then appointed Sid project director and tasked him with its implementation. At that time we were facing severe challenges with CNBC Africa, so I assured him that neither Roberta nor I would need to look into the details of the project. The only caveat was that he would keep us periodically updated on everything and would touch base before pulling the trigger on any major decision. As an incentive, we gave Sid and other members of the management team sweat equity so that he would understand the practical side of owning part of a business. Sid came into his own during this period. From the start until the launch of *Forbes Africa* in October 2011, I did not have to do anything and was gratified to see the outcome. Sid had delivered a fantastic product, on target and on budget. I could see he was thrilled with the results when he made his first public speech at the launch. My parents flew down from Delhi to be part of the event and were delighted with his progress. Saloni and I were very proud parents that day.

*   *   *

For years at each of our strategy workshops I had been drawing everyone's attention to the need for us to implement a digital strategy. We started taking baby steps to this end when Andrew Herd joined us in April 2008. ABN Digital was established in 2009 when Andrew put together a top-line business plan that we started rolling out in a phased manner. It included, among other things, uploading our videos to YouTube. What we now needed was to convert this into a proper real-time, online video-streamed channel. I spent a lot of time chatting to Andrew about this and, with his agreement, asked Sid to start compiling a request for proposals to get a vendor to put together the back-end required for the venture. When the proposals came in, we realised that we did not have the cash to implement another project under CNBC Africa because the business was still struggling to break even.

I then tasked Sid with putting together a detailed business plan for ABN Digital, which we could take to the board. Once again, he developed a detailed model and simulations that showed his absolute mastery of every aspect of the business including content, systems needed and the financial imperatives. These are rare skills. He made an excellent presentation to the executive team and later to the board, stressing the importance of evolving our business model. The board immediately recognised the need to implement the project in order to remain relevant and competitive. However, for cash we had to go back to the shareholders. Once again, the IDC declined to participate but did not have any objection to us setting it up as a stand-alone business. And once again, the other shareholders, including Zafar, Sam and me, agreed to fund the project. We asked Sid to implement this new venture and appointed him project director and CEO of ABN Digital. I took this decision with a lot of trepidation, as I was fearful that Andrew would think it remiss and seek another opportunity elsewhere. This would have been my greatest loss, and perhaps failure, as I needed them both. However, for the project to work, there could only be one person leading it. Thankfully Andrew embraced the decision without hesitation, exhibiting, to my mind, one of the greatest qualities of leadership and loyalty to the organisation and to me personally. To be able to put aside personal ego is one of the essential traits of a good leader.

The project encountered many glitches, mainly owing to the choice of vendor, who was simply not geared up to deal with the project and had outsourced all its deliverables to smaller companies, including a few in Europe. Sid went through his own trials and tribulations during this period, as he fought hard to make it work. He kept me posted with his frustrations and I saw the long hours that he was putting in. I did not intervene, however, as it was up to him to call for back-up when he needed it. One day he came to my office completely exasperated by the vendor's actions. He told me what had happened and indicated that, while he believed he could do it by himself, he needed advice on how to deal with the vendor. It was time for the old man to get involved. We held a series of meetings and finally came up with a settlement agreement that enabled the vendor to exit gracefully.

While the project was important, it was not mission critical from a time perspective. The delay therefore was a chance for Sid to learn some important lessons about dealing with contractors. I asked him to reassess the situation and to expedite the implementation and stay on budget. Sid came back with a revised implementation strategy and, after moving around some variables, he was able to come through with a plan that did not require additional funding, but would delay the planned launch by a few months. Sid kept his word and ABN Digital was launched in October 2013.

By the time this task was completed, Sid had truly grown up. He had seen his dream slipping through his grasp and had worked hard to bring it back on track. The project forced him to interact with all the senior team members and I could see that he had won their esteem. He had also strengthened his relationship with Andrew, for whom he had gained a lot of respect. Soon after launch, Sid recommended that Andrew be appointed general manager of ABN Digital, with complete responsibility for its operations and profit and loss. In 2014, Sid also appointed Andrew general manager of *Forbes Africa*. By now they had formed a true bond.

Perhaps one of the major exercises in self-discovery for Sid was our hike up Mount Kilimanjaro in 2013. On our return I organised an evening with the families of the team members to show them the documentary of our expedition. I asked each member of the team to say a few words about their experience. Sid said he learnt the true meaning of humility and the importance of having the support of a team. As his father and his friend, I was delighted by this acknowledgement, as he would never have made it to the top without the support of his team members, principally Quinton Scholes, the expedition leader.

Back at work, Sid's interaction with the team was no longer limited to the office. He and several others went running and hiking, played soccer and foosball, and partied together. During this time, his sense of loyalty to them became evident, as he stopped discussing everything with me. I think after a while he realised that as I was a father figure to most staff members, they did not want me to know some personal aspects of their lives. Sid respected that and began sharing things with me on a need-to-know basis. Winning their trust was as important as winning their respect. I knew from the comfortable atmosphere in team meetings that he was finally part of an effective group.

* * *

Before Sid joined the business, my nephew Raghav Lal came on board in the education vertical. Raghav is my older sister Sunanda's son. He was raised in Dubai and followed in the family tradition by going to the Doon School in India. His father, Rajeev, is also an alumnus of Doon. Raghav went on to graduate from Bentley College, Waltham, Massachusetts, and during his final year I requested Rick Michaels to arrange an internship for him with CEA in their New York office. Soon after his graduation, Raghav moved to Chicago in 2005 to work for a consulting business. It was over Christmas 2006, when he was visiting Dubai, that we got talking and I asked him if he wanted to come back to Dubai and join me. I was working on setting up CNBC Africa at that time, and had also put together some of the building blocks of our education vertical, including the partnership agreement with Murdoch University, Australia. After giving it some thought, Raghav joined me in April 2007 as project executive to set up the university in Dubai. By then we had completed the financial closure, but the legal paperwork and regulatory approvals for the university still had to be finalised.

We completed the legal and regulatory paperwork in the third quarter of 2007 and then took temporary space in the Knowledge Village, a part of Dubai Media City. We hired a core team of HR, finance and marketing professionals to start implementing the project. I think this was a good opportunity for Raghav to learn about a medium-sized investment. He worked diligently with the other team members to get the infrastructure rolled out on time and below budget. We launched the university on schedule in September 2008. At this point I moved Raghav to look after the MIS function of the business. It became evident to me during this period that his core strength lay in the customer-facing side and not so much in analytics, or in putting together presentations and financial models. While he gained some experience in this role, I could see that he was spending a lot more of his time on business development and marketing.

When the opportunity arose to map his strengths onto the business, I asked him to lead the business development and marketing portfolio. He excelled in this role. Historically, we had a lot of churn in this portfolio, but Raghav established continuity. He was also able to ramp up activities with external agencies and organise events that helped position the university favourably. During this period, Dubai was going through the worst recession and yet, along with some other senior team members, particularly Dr John Grainger, we were able to stabilise the business and break even.

Raghav experienced a similar learning curve to Sid in terms of gaining acceptance from the rest of the staff and vice versa. Being a start-up with staff from different parts of the world, there were many teething issues, most as a result of minor misunderstandings over relatively small issues. I asked Raghav to patiently work throughout this period with the entire team, as impatience was easily misinter-preted as disrespect. I knew that everyone was acting in the best interests of the business, so the challenge was to address the way in which staff members were communicating with each other. After several mentoring sessions with the entire staff, these initial issues were largely resolved, although some undercurrents continued to linger. I let the status quo remain, particularly since professional courtesy was being extended by all sides and I understood that time is a great healer when it comes to solving personal differences. On the flip side, Raghav had formed excellent relationships with the support staff, government administration, franchise partners and other external stakeholders that were valuable for the business.

As Raghav gained experience, he began representing the business at various international forums, workshops and conferences. These were all vital platforms for relationship building for the long term. Additionally, he was able to complete his MBA at Murdoch University Dubai, a useful addition to his personal development and to his overall growth in the organisation.

My vision for the education business was to roll it out in other parts of the world. We considered Malaysia, India and Africa. Raghav was part of the team looking at the expansion plans in these countries and travelled with John to evaluate some opportunities. Finally, after a lot of deliberation, we decided not to proceed with Malaysia and India. As previously mentioned, in 2012 I had travelled to the UK to meet with potential partners for Africa and we struck a great chord with Lancaster University. I took the entire team, including John Grainger, Chris Pilgrim and Raghav, to Lancaster to meet their senior team. By this time Chris had taken over as senior vice president for new projects and had prepared an excellent business plan and feasibility study for presentation to Lancaster. By the third quarter of 2012, we had concluded our agreement with Lancaster University and began positioning staff for executing the project in Ghana. John accepted the role of president of TNE and provost of Lancaster University Ghana. We now needed a strong team around him to establish an international branch campus, a business model completely new to Ghana.

In February 2013, I appointed Raghav project director for Ghana and he moved there to begin implementation. To give him long-term security, Zafar and I gave him significant sweat equity in the new project, so he could align his interests with those of the company in the long term. The set-up in Ghana was by no means easy, as the country lacked many amenities we took for granted in Dubai. However, with his resourcefulness and extrovert personality, Raghav was able to put together all the necessary building blocks and vendors to complete the infrastructure within budget and on time. There were several shortcomings with service providers, including poor internet connectivity, and a lack of basic services like water and electricity. Raghav adapted to these circumstances and toiled with the team to get things up and running as efficiently as possible. In October 2013, the Ghana campus was launched on schedule and continues to grow from strength to strength. Sunanda was at the launch and I could see her beaming with pride as Raghav gave the opening address. It was a proud and defining moment for all of us.

Perhaps my earlier experience with Raghav enabled me to correct many things with Sid. For one, I made Sid report to Roberta from the first day. In retrospect, I should have done this with Raghav from the onset too, as it would have set the right expectations. Sid's performance appraisals were thus far more objective than Raghav's, as you are always mindful of sensitivities particularly when dealing with family. That being said, I do not believe for a moment that either Raghav or Sid ever felt that I was being partial in any way. Through the family grapevine, I always heard that I was unduly strict. This is probably correct, as I tend to be more patient and forgiving towards other staff members than towards my own children. I remember separate incidents with Raghav and Sid in the boardroom. When I caught them using their mobile phones in the boardroom I asked them to throw the phones in the rubbish bin. That swiftly put an end to cellphone usage, not just by the boys but also by other members of staff when they were in meetings with me. Over time, of course, I realised that hand-held devices are also used for note-taking by the younger generation and I had to eventually change my own way of thinking.

* * *

No matter where you are in the world or how big your business, the most consistent question you will face as your children grow up is what role they will play in the future of your business. There are two roles that are fundamentally expected. The first is that of shareholder. In the case of my two children, it is fair to assume that they will one day inherit ownership rights in all our assets. The second role is that of managing the business and taking it forward on its path to immortality – in other words, building on the legacy. For them to be successful in this role, they need to be assured that they will be judged no differently than professional managers and senior executives, and they will need to compete with them for a place at the table. They must be as competent, capable and committed to building the organisation as everyone else on the team. It is easy to come in to the office and think that you can give instructions to people just because you are a shareholder; it is more difficult to work hard and make them willingly follow you to achieve group goals. For this, you need to earn their respect; and respect cannot be earned in a day. It is a journey.

This journey is not easy; only those who have walked this path understand how difficult it can be. Children in business are judged by the people around them; few will be forgiving when they make mistakes and credit will not easily be given when they do well. There is, therefore, simply no latitude for mistakes. For them to undertake this responsibility is in itself a big decision. Many children do not settle down into the businesses established by their parents, choosing rather to follow their own path. The onus of this also lies with parents. I had to work hard to sell my ideas to my children. I had to woo them as I would any other person who I wanted to hire.

Along the way, I made many mistakes in dealing with my children. One of them was taking them for granted. Another was placing expectations on them far in excess of what I placed on any other member of the team. If my son was not at work on time, I would be unnecessarily harsh on him. If he landed in Johannesburg after a long journey, I would expect him back at work within the hour. More often than not, I would not give him enough time for tasks and then expect him to be at the office late, and even on weekends. At times like this, Saloni, being a fiercely protective mother, would step in to realign my expectations and put things in perspective, at times not very pleasantly.

There was some advice I reiterated while the children were growing up. The first was respect for their elders and the experience that they brought to the business. The second was that the decision-making process had to be inclusive, but the decision had to be taken by the team leader to ensure inherent accountability. I ingrained in them the values of LIACC: loyalty, integrity, attitude, competence and commitment. I encouraged them to innovate and look at our processes and try to improve them through better technology and ideas. I asked them to participate in global conferences and events to build relationships, open their eyes to the latest trends, and observe how people were coping with change, and how this change could influence our future. More than anything else, I spent days emphasising the value of relationships with people. These, among many other lessons, should stand them in good stead along their path to self-discovery and excellence.

When they each came on board, I told Raghav, Sid and Shweta that they must follow their own dreams. If they ever outgrew the business or felt stifled, all they had to do was move on and try something else. This was an option that I had extended to all other members of my team and there was no reason not to offer my family the same latitude. There is undoubtedly a lot of pressure on children when they undertake to become part of a family business, and yet they must do it, for legacy's sake. I consider myself blessed that my son, daughter and nephew have seen their own dreams realised as part of the journey they started with me. It is my prayer that they see beyond what I do and carry the flag forward to build their own dreams and legacies.

7

CORPORATE CULTURE

Corporate culture is defined in a variety of ways, but this is how I summarise it: it is how a company's staff thinks, feels and acts, and encompasses their values and behaviour, which together constitute the unique style and policies of the company. The outcome of corporate culture is seen in the professional atmosphere within the organisation and in its attitude towards all external stakeholders, including clients. It affects the morale, behaviour and eventually the performance of the organisation as a whole.

While analysing this subject, I added the word "religion" to the mix. Dictionary.com defines religion as "a set of beliefs concerning the cause, nature, and purpose of the universe, especially when considered as the creation of a superhuman agency or agencies, usually involving devotional and ritual observances, and often containing a moral code governing the conduct of human affairs".

Irrespective of your faith, the basis of all religion is the same. Religion teaches you to be a good human being and being a good human being is the code of conduct by which you should live. This code of conduct may have different interpretations, but it embodies the basic value of righteousness. Corporate culture could be described as the religion of an organisation.

So how is this culture formed, how do people willingly adhere to this culture and to what extent do leadership and staff play a role in building corporate culture? Finally, what external factors influence the culture of an organisation? These are all complex questions, and over the last three decades I have tried to analyse them and build organisations with a distinct culture that I believe has made us unique in many ways.

At the outset, I want to make a distinction between the culture that exists in well-established, profit-making organisations and that of start-up businesses. While there is merit in the argument that well-established businesses were all start-ups once, their corporate cultures are now so entrenched that change can be almost impossible. For instance, a chief executive of a start-up business can influence its culture a lot more than a CEO who comes to the helm of a mature, old, listed company. Similarly, the fact that a well-established company has greater capacity and more resources to give material benefits to staff does not necessarily make it a happier place in which to work. When people accept the status quo as a compromise, it does not mean they accept the culture. A telltale sign of a complacent culture is the phrase "this is how things are done here".

Corporate culture does not come in a neatly packaged box. It can't be installed or reset to factory settings when things are not going well. Corporate culture is built over time and must be nurtured by both management and staff every single day. Your people have to live the culture in letter and in spirit. When things are going wrong, they need to fix them; and when things are going well, they need to improve them. It is a journey towards excellence.

Start-ups have a unique way of evolving and no two are the same. Each start-up's culture depends on circumstances, leadership and what it prioritises. In all the organisations I have built, I have focused a lot of my time on human resources and finance. These lie at the heart of any business, and if you get them right, the organisation will have a higher probability of success, provided, of course, that you have chosen the right product and market and are not undercapitalised.

Operating in the media, IT and education sectors, I have been blessed in being able to build organisations that require highly educated and skilled workforces. I have been privileged to have direct oversight for media and education, and while these are intrinsically different industries, they share some similarities. Both deal with the integrity of intellectual assets. The custodians of these assets, whether journalists or teachers, see themselves as working in a different quadrant to the rest of the business. It is therefore extremely interesting building a corporate culture that encompasses fundamentally fragmented groups of people. I will discuss each of these in a bit more detail.

MEDIA

When I started hiring staff in October 2006 for CNBC Africa, I received an overwhelming response from people eager to take up positions. It took us about six months, until March 2007, to hire all the staff we needed. All recruitment activities for the company took place in the executive lounge at the Park Hyatt in Rosebank, Johannesburg. I did not have an office to show my prospective employees. I was essentially selling them a dream, a dream that at that point was, at best, a very good business case on paper. At that stage, even our prospective shareholders had not yet fully committed.

The people who joined in the first phase were those looking for change, wanting better monetary benefits, attracted to the international brand, or simply unemployed. As a foreigner in a completely new market, I had to start looking at nuances that I had never dealt with before. For one, I was faced with the unexpected reality that because of BEE, the race and not the skills of an individual made a difference to the credentials of the company.

The entire recruitment process was a steep learning curve, as we had to determine people's skill levels against the assigned responsibilities. From a talent-pool perspective, there was a scarcity of financial journalists – there was a handful already employed by an existing business TV station, while the rest came from production houses and the state broadcaster. We would have to build capacity from the bottom up.

When we launched in June 2007, we had a lot of diversity in the team, both from a skills and an ethnic perspective. At the first staff workshop, held a few months after launch, I could see the divide in the group. We were all strangers. I was totally at a loss when our South African colleagues just upped and left a staff workshop or function at will, without asking permission or offering apologies. In most other countries, such "disrespect" would be grounds for immediate dismissal. Thankfully, I realised that I had a great deal to learn in a short space of time. I had not yet grasped the work culture and ethic in South Africa. One thing, however, was very clear to me: South Africa had a unique work environment and it was going to take a lot of introspection and patience to get things right.

I have always believed that as a foreigner you cannot export culture into the company from the outside. You also can't bring in Anglo-Saxons or Asians to run an African business. In the medium to long term it simply won't work. You can provide guidelines, policies and basic values, but the culture eventually is a reflection of the people in the organisation and their value systems. Corporate culture is thus a median of the beliefs and values of the people in the organisation. Getting to a median takes time.

For a start-up, it is even more difficult as there is considerable churn in the initial years. People join from different backgrounds and bring lessons that they have learnt from different employers. It takes a bit of time for the rubber to hit the road and the mismatch in expectations to surface. The commitment required from the staff of a start-up is totally different from that needed in a well-established or government-owned business. People who have never worked in start-ups do not understand this and often have mismatched expectations based on their experiences in well-established organisations. In the first three years we saw a lot of churn: some left because they did not get what they had envisaged, while others we had to let go because their skills and attitudes did not meet our expectations. The 2008 recession did not help, and we had to go through a retrenchment exercise to consolidate the operation. While the process was extremely tedious, we were finally left with a team with which we could work to build our vision and mission.

In South Africa, I adapted the operating guidelines used by our CNBC partners in the Middle East, and the editorial guidelines from CNBC International, but left everything else to evolve on its own. It was like giving people a blank canvas and an invitation to start painting. The difficulty in doing this is that everyone loves to splash paint but no one wants to take ownership of the painting. So everyone wanted to be part of popular decisions, but whenever anything difficult had to be communicated, it was never delivered in first person. While people may not have believed in the decisions, or were just too scared to hurt their colleagues, they were ready to hurt the company by accepting mediocrity. No organisation has ever achieved greatness through mediocrity and weeding out this malady is a laborious but essential exercise.

The greatest transition in an organisation happens when people stop talking about "this company" and start referring to "our company".

As long as people continue to say "this company", they have no emotional attachment to your organisation. This attachment needs to be felt across the board, starting with senior management and percolating down to the people with the most basic administrative responsibilities. It is a painstaking process that starts by talking about taking responsibility at every departmental, company or strategy workshop. You can encourage it by leading from the front and showing people how to do things.

Culture starts with basic things like greeting one another when the day begins, attending to a visitor even if she or he has not come to see you, and picking up waste that someone may have inadvertently left behind. It involves communicating effectively and letting people know where you are going or with whom you are meeting. Even if you have to leave the office to attend to a personal matter, you should feel comfortable to truthfully let someone know your whereabouts. We found that people were reluctant to document details of client meetings, something that is critical for follow-ups. This stems from personal insecurities, but is counterproductive for an organisation. Changing this behaviour required a great deal of mentorship to build an environment of trust between the staff and the organisation.

When two people don't spontaneously greet each other, it shows that there is no emotional link between them. People often forget that a workplace is no different from a family environment and I would be hard pressed to believe that people don't greet their family members at home. Rather than talk about it, I make it a point to walk to every office on the way to my own and say hello to everyone from the senior-most members to the cleaning staff. And I never enter my office unless I have personally greeted my assistant every morning. This sets a precedent for others. First and foremost, it breaks down barriers, as at times people may not know how to react to you or your position. If you show them that you are accessible, they will let down their guard as well.

I have asked that we keep an open-door policy in the company. It's widely known and accepted that people can just walk into my office and pick up something to munch from my comfort-food stash, or share a quick word and then move on to whatever they need to do. Sometimes it disturbs my routine, but the downside of not having people walk in and share their emotions is far greater than the loss in continuity of thought. I often do the same. I walk to people's stations and share their food or participate in their conversations, as I would with my family. This goes a long way to getting to know each other informally and helps break down barriers.

Over the years, I have introduced a culture of sports into the company. Initially, the focus was on soccer and rugby but I gradually encouraged staff to start playing golf. We bought a few golf sets and organised training clinics run by Kudzai Kanyangarara and later Andrew Herd. Golf may be considered an elitist sport, but it is growing in popularity in South Africa. We gave golf-club memberships to a number of senior executives, so that they could play with clients and build their contacts and expand their social circles. In addition, we started hiking and cycling clubs, and laid the foundation for a cricket club. We encourage staff to participate in marathons and cycle races. We arrange movie nights in theatres for staff and their families, as well as an annual cookout. For team activities, we encourage members from different departments to form teams. These extracurricular activities build cohesion, friendship and bonds between people, and raise staff morale.

Another aspect of culture is the way in which we speak to one another and deal with mistakes. It is very easy to assign blame and disrespect people, especially in our industry, where we are dealing with the egos of television and media personalities. I always ask staff to speak to others the way they would like to be spoken to, and I make sure to lead by example. Losing patience with people will not help when dealing with a crisis. I try to make my staff understand that most people have the right intentions, and thus mistakes should be corrected through mentorship. Having said that, I do not tolerate the repetition of mistakes; this is a clear symptom of negligence. Nevertheless, the manner in which you speak to people must remain consistent and respectful. If a person is deemed unfit, then he or she must be politely asked to leave.

A crucial aspect of company culture is getting people to take responsibility. This was a big challenge for us. The only person who showed an aptitude for this was Roberta Naidoo. She took no prisoners in her search for perfection and was given various nicknames by her colleagues, but they eventually grew to understand and respect her, and even emulate her example. This took years of sustained patience to accomplish. After nine years, I finally saw people in middle management take ownership of their actions and make decisions in the best interests of the organisation.

Another imperative is being able to respond to suggestions proactively and institute change if needed. Whenever an issue arose in a group meeting, a private meeting or in my reverse-mentorship meetings with middle management, I got the senior staff into the boardroom, where we analysed the feedback to understand where we were going wrong. Through brainstorming, we were able to make some important decisions and action them immediately. As an organisation, you must be prepared to change in pursuit of excellence. When people see that they can effect change that they believe is in the best interests of the organisation, they will take ownership of the decisions and ensure that the changes are implemented.

When I attended our various staff workshops in 2015, I could see that all the values that I had set out to instil were becoming visible in people's actions. There was collective responsibility from all senior members of the team, so much so that at first I thought some people were forming a trade union! In reality, the team had simply taken charge and put their own stamp on everything that the company stood for. It had been a painstaking journey, but the smile on my face said it all.

EDUCATION

The culture in universities is completely different from that in other commercial enterprises. In many countries, the education sector is dominated by not-for-profit organisations or government. Staff in these organisations have a totally different mindset to those involved in private education.

When we launched Murdoch University Dubai, two distinct groups formed within the business: academic and non-academic. Part of the reason for this was that legislation in Dubai makes a distinction between academic and all other responsibilities. The legislation was introduced to place accountability for academic matters on the university and not the operating partner. So, for example, the academic head was accountable only to the university. The operating partner was responsible for everything non-academic, but, as the investor, also carried all the financial risk. While the intention of the legislation was understandable, in reality it created an inefficient system with inherent contradictions that made it difficult to operate as a cohesive organisation. It inadvertently created significant conflict.

Dubai has grown into one of the most progressive cities in the world. One of the impediments has been the transient nature of the workforce. The local population is extremely small and largely dependent on the government for employment. Almost 85 per cent of the population comprises expatriates from over 150 countries. The workforce therefore is extremely multicultural and multi-ethnic. Since visas are issued for three years, there are no assurances that people will not move at the end of their visa period. The talent pool being small and transient creates significant churn. A number of families with young children move to Australia and Canada, countries that provide a lot more facilities for bringing up children.

We launched the university in September 2008, at the beginning of the recession. The Dubai economy, which had overheated because of the real-estate boom, suddenly came to a grinding halt. People were losing their jobs and companies were shutting down. As anticipated, as soon as people lost their jobs, they lost right of residence and had to leave the country. Those expatriates who expected problems repaying debts in the face of unemployment simply fled the country. The shrinking of the economy and the ensuing demographic changes created uncertainty for employers and employees alike. Against this tumultuous backdrop, I had to build an education business.

For the first year we continued with the structure dictated by legislation and operated two centres of power within the organisation. However, this state of affairs was creating inefficiencies and was extremely bad for morale. In 2009, recognising that we would never be able to build consistency, I merged organisational responsibilities and placed Dr John Grainger in charge of both groups. Besides teaching long hours, he had to meet with the business development and marketing teams to build the organisation's reputation. This was a big responsibility for him, as he had to ensure that all his actions were, at all times, in the interests of the Dubai campus and that he did not promote the interests of one partner over the other.

Bringing the two groups together was perhaps the biggest challenge that John faced. There were absolutely no points of convergence between the academics and the rest of the organisation. I have never experienced such polarisation. As an academic, John had to lead the way for all the other academics on campus. Most followed his example and began contributing to the operational side of the business. It is my belief that, over time, people realised that their futures were intrinsically linked to the commercial success of the organisation and that teams could not exist in silos. The same values were carried forward by Dan Adkins after he took charge in 2013.

Once again, rather than putting in place policies, I allowed the teams to build their own equations in interpersonal relationships. In three years, we ended up with staff from over thirty countries, the bulk from Asia. Since senior management was made up entirely of Western expatriates, communications and their interpretation had to be carefully managed. There was a dire need for empathy so as not to create perceptions of unintended racism. I mentored the senior teams using a management style that blended accountability with empathy, and urged the use of kid gloves when dealing with staff.

To make this work we placed a very strong emphasis on internal communications. John chaired the internal executive committee meetings, which included all department heads, and these meetings were documented through minutes for accuracy. This worked exceedingly well as the minutes provided clarity on what was discussed and nothing was left to the ambiguities of interpretation.

As a start-up business in a period of recession, we had to allow people to be entrepreneurial and take decisions that would be bold and different. This called for a lot of discipline, from both the staff and the shareholders. You cannot ask people to be bold if they are punished for making wrong choices. A strong internal audit system was set up from the beginning to work closely with management to ensure that no individual actions brought the business to its knees, whether financial or reputational. I encouraged people to try different things and this resulted in a culture of entrepreneurship and paid huge dividends. We became one of the few universities to not only survive the recession, but also break even in five years. Many of our competitors either consolidated or shut down.

We also tried to make a difference to our people's lives by showing empathy for their problems during the recession. Most staff had over-extended their resources during the boom period and started getting into trouble as the debt trap caught up with them. Since we were a start-up, banks were hesitant to give loans to our staff. We looked at staff requests for help judiciously and over the last nine years many staff members have received financial assistance from the company to tide them over difficult times. Our concern for our people gave them confidence in the company and its willingness to stand by them in their hour of need. This in turn made the staff more productive. Although we have a five-day week in Dubai, many staff members regularly come into the office six days a week or during holidays if they are needed.

We also encouraged staff to be open with us regarding their personal plans. As a small business, we recognised that some people would eventually seek opportunities elsewhere. Rather than surprise us, we built a culture where people could speak openly to HR about their plans. This allowed us to draw up succession plans if and when staff decided to move on. Over the years I reached an understanding with certain good people that they could always come back to the business if they ever felt that they were not meeting the goals for which they left. A classic example was Sanjay Rodrigues, who left us when he was head of finance to join his family business in Goa. From there he got a green card to go to the US. He became very disillusioned with the US, however, and wrote to me in December 2013, saying that he wished to come back, even if it meant joining at a lower position. We immediately created a position for him, as he had consistently been a star employee in the initial years of the business.

When we established Lancaster University in Ghana we were faced with some unique challenges. In Dubai we relied 100 per cent on an expatriate workforce, but in Ghana we had to employ mainly locals, as there are limited expats in the country. To bring consistency in policy, I made sure that the senior team came from our business in Dubai. In the education business, the real differentiator between institutions is the quality of teachers, and it is expected that international universities have expatriate teachers.

While legislation in Ghana also required strong academic oversight and quality assurances from the home campus, the regulator put more emphasis on outcomes than form. This allowed us to have a more unified working arrangement, with an umbrella management committee overseeing operations on behalf of both partners.

*   *   *

What, then, makes us different from other companies?

First and foremost is the emphasis we place on retaining the right people. You have to identify your crown jewels early and then mentor them into leading the organisation to glory. However, that in itself is not adequate. It is equally important to align their personal goals with those of the company. In all our businesses, we have provided equity to our senior management so that they have dual responsibility, one as management and the other as owners. They must reap rewards for their hard work, and owning equity ensures that their interests are economically aligned with the company.

Delegation of responsibility is another major value that I have worked hard to instil over the years. True delegation requires a lot of discipline from the person giving away the responsibility. The system needs to build in a balance between responsibility and accountability that allows people to grow in their roles and take decisions without feeling stifled. People will make mistakes and the organisation must accept that this will happen from time to time. People must be encouraged to learn from mistakes and move on.

Building trust in the organisation is important both internally with staff and externally with stakeholders. Trust takes time and is built through consistency. An integral part of trust is communication. Over the years, we have learnt that being transparent and honest no matter the circumstances is more rewarding than withholding information. People respect openness irrespective of the situation.

As previously discussed, I mentor my teams on the "rule of 51". A 51 per cent positive result from a person or task is far better than a 49 per cent positive outcome. You can improve on 51. Nothing and no one is perfect. We are all products of our imperfections and need a lot of work to improve. If you actively strive to create a culture of complementary development, the organisation will prosper over time.

Our approach to local legislation also sets us apart. As already mentioned, dealing with BEE in South Africa was a personal challenge. Coming from India, which has a similar history, I could empathise. However, pushing unqualified people into senior positions is, to my mind, counterproductive. Not only can it destroy an organisation, it can destroy the confidence of the people placed in such compromising positions. We thus approached BEE differently and worked with it bottom-up. We trained people through a strong internship policy and ensured that everyone at the ABN Group had the requisite skills. In six years we had achieved all our employment-equity criteria, but using a path that built value and allowed us to be an employer that did not use race as a means of making decisions.

Another important value that we have brought into our environment is that of transparency. Without diluting the principles of "need to know", I have encouraged staff to spend time with one another and to discuss matters openly. There is a need for open communications between all stakeholders in an organisation; the more respectful and candid you are in your dealings, the more people, external or internal, appreciate the interaction.

What I have developed organisationally over the years is a family culture in which there is a strong interdependence between the company and its staff. We cannot provide everything to everyone, but we have improved what we can do year on year. I have tried to be open to change and to learn from people. Your intention should be to create a culture in which people understand organisational goals, and willingly and happily devote their complete resources to achieve these goals.

Organisational culture expert Colin Browne interviewed me for his book *How to Build a Happy Sandpit*. He was looking for the views of a wide cross-section of business leaders who had been the architects of organisational culture. The aim of any business is to build a reputation of being a leader in best practices that makes it a pleasure for people to be associated with the business. Good leaders cultivate a healthy and happy environment, where people come to work not just because they have a job, but because they have a responsibility and feel that they are making a difference to the success of the organisation. I believe that every organisation has a distinct DNA that is its religion, and the greatest contributing factors to this DNA are the beliefs and ambitions of the people who work there.

8

TEAM BUILDING THROUGH ADVENTURE

We have all dreamt of doing the extraordinary, whether bungee jumping, white-water rafting, skydiving, mountaineering, deep-sea diving or anything else unconventional and adventurous. Other than the obvious exhilaration and fun, putting yourself through this sort of physical and mental hardship teaches you a lot about yourself. More often than not, you will be surprised by the amount of physical punishment you can take, particularly when the odds are against you. When you are in physical danger, your survival instinct kicks in and your alter-ego animal personality comes to the fore. Insight into your physical resilience is extremely important for self-assessment. Mental strength, however, is quite different. People react differently to adversity, and while everyone overcomes the hardship at the end of the day, their journeys will have all been unique. When you are part of a team faced with a challenge, your attitude to your team members is crucial. This is perhaps the one attribute that separates leaders from the rest.

As officers in the military, we were expected to cope with extreme physical hardship and take rational decisions on the battlefield. This was not something the army left to chance. In addition to the intense physical and psychological stress tests that we had to take when being recruited to the NDA, the camps during training were brutal. There was Camp Greenhorn in the second semester, Camp Rover in the fourth semester and Camp Torna in the sixth. Our training continued at the Indian Military Academy in Dehradun, and ended with the mother of all camps, Camp Chindits. Chindits involved seven nights of marches through the Siwalik mountains and a final assault with live ammunition. The nightly physical test was combined with tactics lessons and mission planning by day, as well as ambushes and raids that left little time for rest or sleep. These camps were designed not only to test physical and mental capabilities, but also to give officers an understanding of what to expect in different kinds of terrain.

During camps and training exercises, the directing staff had a single mission: to break you. They would use every possible means to accomplish this: screaming and hurling abusive language at you, constantly changing campsites, and forcing you to dig endless trenches and snake pits. It was a form of sadism that was difficult to understand at the time. Nevertheless, when we finished our four years of rigorous preparation and joined our regiments, the outcomes were evident. We had learnt the value of teamwork and the importance of the team for your own survival. Without the team, you are nothing. Beyond that, our training gave us the mental robustness to think rationally and positively, even when all physical faculties are exhausted and your body has almost entirely given up from fatigue. Leaders must be able to do everything that their troops are required to do; they must make sure their troops are comfortable and safe; and they must deal with the added personal responsibility as officers to make sure that the mission is accomplished.

These tenets also apply when you move to the corporate world.

The preparation and training requirements may change from a national cause to a corporate one, where profitability is a core objective, but the means, values and tactics remain the same. As does your dependence on motivated and good people. In many organisations, senior management get so caught up in their day-to-day needs that sometimes they neglect succession planning and team building. Succession planning is about building layers of leadership for immortality, while team building is about making sure that staff work together as a cohesive workforce. Both these activities are necessary for cultivating good leaders.

The best way to test people and build morale or *esprit de corps* is through physical team-building activities. Morale is a feeling of loyalty, enthusiasm and devotion to an institution or goal, particularly in the face of opposition or hardship. I am a great believer in team building and have initiated several group activities, including workshops, treks, picnics, treasure hunts and sports events. I have always tried to be at these events, in order to participate and guide the activities, and to meet the families of our staff members.

I have been fortunate to undertake several major adventure trips during my career. I will focus on three: a trip to the Antarctic as part of India's 7th Scientific Expedition in 1987–8; a trek to the top of Mount Kilimanjaro in 2013 with middle management; and an attempt to reach Everest Base Camp in 2015 with senior management, but which had to be abandoned when we got stranded in Nepal's worst earthquake. While they were all very different experiences, they had similar objectives and outcomes.

ANTARCTICA

My fascination with the Antarctic started in school. I read about the continent in my geography lessons and later was enthralled by expeditions led by explorers like Roald Amundsen, Sir Ernest Shackleton, Robert Falcon Scott and Admiral Richard E. Byrd. I was intrigued by the mystery surrounding the frozen continent. My opportunity to travel to Antarctica came just after I finished my engineering degree at the CME, when there was a call for volunteers to go on the Indian Antarctic Programme's 7th Scientific Expedition. The expedition would include a mix of scientists and members of the armed forces. The scientists were selected by the National Centre for Antarctic and Ocean Research (under the Department of Ocean Development) and had a mandate from the Indian government to carry out research, including climate, geological and other ocean research. The bulk of the contingent, however, came from the armed forces. The navy and air force contributed helicopters, pilots and crew, while the army provided engineers and communications experts. The mission for the army team was to help with logistics at Dakshin Gangotri, India's first permanent base station in Antarctica, and establish Maitri, India's second base camp, situated at approximately seventy degrees south and eleven degrees east in the Schirmacher Oasis, close to the Wohlthat Mountains.

The expedition comprised two groups. The first and larger "summer party" – which I joined – would spend a total of five months on the expedition, including sailing time. A second, smaller group would accompany the summer party but only return with the next year's summer party, having spent approximately sixteen months on the continent. The summer party would normally land in December and leave the Antarctic by the second week of March, so as to avoid getting stuck in the freezing Southern Ocean.

As part of the selection process, we had to undergo several medical and psychological tests. These were even more stringent for the fourteen-man team that would stay behind for the winter months. Living in a closed environment and sharing a confined cabin for an extended period requires high mental and emotional stability. There had been isolated examples of disciplinary issues during previous expeditions and the army could not afford conflicts under such stressful conditions. Those selected had to be team players, capable of carrying their own load and not blinded by rank.

Expeditions and living in close proximity create familiarity, which in the context of the military is not healthy. Finding a balance was critical and that's where the well-structured tests came in. When I looked at the final list, I could see that the process had worked well and we had an excellent blend of people with the requisite experience and skills.

Once my selection was completed and my commanding officer, Colonel Gandotra, agreed to release me from the regiment, my wife gave me the news that she was pregnant. My immediate reaction was to back out of the expedition, but when I conveyed this to Saloni, she once again surprised me. She encouraged me to go, saying, "I know what this means to you and I understand I will have to go through this pregnancy alone, but I don't want you to have regrets later about missing something so important." Defying Ayn Rand, Saloni proved that personal sacrifices go far beyond your own needs. I was stunned but thrilled. She jokingly even promised that she would not deliver until I got back, and indeed kept her word, giving birth to Sid shortly after I returned.

The army was meticulous in its training regime. We were all packed off to the High Altitude Warfare School (HAWS) in Gulmarg, Kashmir. At HAWS we did rock climbing and walked on the glacier for acclimatisation. While the terrain in the Antarctic is flat and thus different from the high altitude at HAWS, the simulation of the cold weather was useful. The period at HAWS was beneficial mainly because the whole team could meet, get to know one another and train together. Overall it was a great experience. Once the training was over, we were all dispatched back to our regiments to hand over our responsibilities and take leave to be with our families.

As part of my reassignment, I was posted, on deputation, to Army Headquarters in Delhi under the Engineer-in-Chief's Branch for a few months. It meant that I could be close to my wife until we left. Our expedition leader, Colonel Ganeshan, joined soon after and as I was the first to join, he assigned me most of the administrative tasks, including getting all the provisions properly packed. I also made a quick dash to our ordnance factory in Jabalpur to get the uniforms and other ordnance equipment for the army team.

Watched by our families, we set sail from Goa on MV *Thuleland* on 25 November 1987 and reached the Antarctic around Christmas, after a short stopover in Mauritius. Leased by the Indian government, the *Thuleland* was a 31900-ton icebreaker sailing under the Swedish flag and carrying a Swedish crew. Our team of ninety-two included twenty-five scientists, sixty-four defence personnel, one photographer and two members from the Department of Ocean Development. One of the scientists, Sudhakar Rao, was appointed the first honorary postmaster of the Indian Antarctic Post Office.

The journey of just over three weeks was relatively easy and we continued our physical training each day on deck. The ship had been modified to support the expedition but did not have any luxuries like gyms, so we had to make do with aerobics, stretching and yoga. Some of the scientists, particularly Dr Tariq Kureishy, surprised us with their fitness. The scientists and army personnel developed a healthy banter, but the civilians were firmly at the receiving end of a lot of the jokes. Besides training, we busied ourselves with preparations for the landing. We also played sports and celebrated festivals like Diwali and Christmas. Bridge became the main pastime in the officers' gallery; the teams got together in the evenings to watch movies or play board games, but the bridge continued regardless. Major Hem Lohumi became the resident expert, local champion and, might I add, a bit wealthier on the nominal wager that was accepted in the officers' mess.

During the entire expedition, the only contact we had with home was via satellite phone from the bridge of the ship. We were each authorised three minutes a month, which was really inadequate, but we looked forward to these calls. The only issue in those days was that you needed specialised transmitters and receivers for satellite calls. Saloni had to make her way to the communications centre at the Department of Ocean Development in Delhi once a month to speak to me and keep me updated on her health, something that I was anxious about. Most of the officers and scientists on board used their call allowance, but it was not easy for the other ranks as a lot of them came from villages and had absolutely no way to contact home. In acts of selflessness and with no personal motivation, we happily bartered their airtime for alcohol, for which I am sure they were most grateful.

Crossing the equator, where it is tradition to ask Poseidon, god of the sea, to approve one's passage, was a memorable and fun experience. A little while later, as we got to the Roaring Forties and Furious Fifties, we experienced the full fury of the sea, as the 31 900-ton *Thuleland* was tossed around like a matchbox. It was like being on a rollercoaster for a few days, and everyone except the well-seasoned crew preferred to stay in bed. Surprisingly, my body handled the ordeal well, and although the galley was closed because no one was in a condition to eat, I stole down there on a few occasions to raid the ice-cream store. I had read about the perils of the sea, and had finally experienced them first-hand.

As we neared latitude sixty degrees south, we could see the frozen ocean before us and the chunks of ice that had broken away from the continental shelf. The icebergs were huge and some had seals lazing on them. The ship slowed down considerably, as it was difficult to navigate through the frozen water, and for the last twenty-four hours of our journey the naval helicopters guided us. When we finally berthed on the continental shelf, we were welcomed by the penguin colonies, which seemed to be quite accustomed to visitors. It was immediately apparent that we were going to enjoy our stay in Antarctica.

For the first few days, we were assigned to Dakshin Gangotri to stock supplies and help the team prepare for the winter. I shared a porta-cabin outside the main station with Captains Kurup and Patole. Both men had been with me at CME and were ex-NDA. Being peers and of the same rank, we developed camaraderie. Being the senior captain, I got to choose my bed, but that was the only quarter given to me by the other two.

We got our first taste of a real blizzard within the first few days. We were living in an external shelter because the main station housed the team that would remain for winter. When we stepped out at about 7 a.m. one morning, we were met by a howling blizzard that made it impossible to stand. It was a complete whiteout, zero visibility. Five of us formed a human chain and started towards the main station at about 8 a.m. It took us over three hours to cover the 200 metres. In the meantime, the station commander was worried as they had lost contact with us, so he sent out a rescue mission. The rescue team passed us at a distance of ten metres. Because we were "downwind", we could hear them clearly and shouted to them, but they could not hear us over the whistling wind. It was straight out of a Hollywood movie. When we got to the base, the doors were covered with snow and we had to send one of the team to climb the roof to get in via the escape hatch. Incidents like this renew your respect for Mother Nature. For the first time, we all realised that we stood absolutely no chance against the elements and needed to take proper precautions, both for our safety and for the success of the mission. It was a lesson that I have carried with me throughout my life.

One night, after we had gone to bed, the porta-cabin caught fire when a backlash of wind swept through the heating furnace. In our longjohns and bare feet we bolted out onto the blue Antarctic ice. In photographs, the ice looks inviting and soft. In reality, it is rock solid with razor-sharp edges created by katabatic, or downslope, winds. If you stepped wrong, these ice shards could slice through your feet.

The porta-cabin finally exploded when some jet fuel stored nearby ignited. The three of us lost most of our valuables, but we were lucky that we had not yet fallen asleep. The result could have been catastrophic. Unbeknown to anyone, over the years gasoline had leaked from the heater and formed a layer of fuel along the base of the entire cabin, creating a time bomb just waiting to explode.

A few days later, we moved to Maitri, where we stayed in temporary shelters and began the mammoth task of shifting 200 tons of steel girders from the ship to a point about seventy-five kilometres inland. Maitri is an oasis, which in the context of the Antarctic is terrain where ground or rock is visible through the ice. It is located close to the Russian station Novolazarevskaya, which at that time housed an airstrip capable of landing the large Ilyushin Il-76 aircraft for three to four months of the year. The real lifelines and true workhorses, however, were the Mi-8 helicopters that flew sorties, day in and day out, to move the construction equipment to the new base camp. Approximately 50 per cent of the days we were there were suitable for work; the rest were impaired by blizzards and whiteouts. We therefore needed to maximise our work on the days when we had good weather. The fact that we had over twenty hours of daylight was very helpful, as we could work long hours without experiencing any issues with visibility.

The greatest challenge we faced was transporting a 250-kVA generator from the ship to Maitri as underslung cargo on a Mi-8 helicopter. I was on the aircraft that day and the anxiety was plain to see, particularly on the faces of the Indian Air Force pilots, who knew only too well the negative impact of any adverse wind conditions on the way. Luckily, the transportation was carried out without a glitch and we were able to put the generator into the designated housing constructed by our team. There was a fair amount of jubilation after this manoeuvre, as we all realised the importance of having accomplished this task successfully: we finally had electricity on the campsite.

The Maitri station was built on stilts, so as to minimise the impact of ice on the structure. Over time, Dakshin Gangotri had become completely submerged in ice and the integrity of the structure had been compromised, resulting in a decision to decommission it. Maitri was to be its replacement. We spent the next month surveying the terrain and completing the foundation up to the floor beams. The next team would build the station's superstructure.

Antarctica is a continent of great mysteries. The thickness of the ice averages 1.5 kilometres; in some parts it is over 4.5 kilometres thick, making the continent the world's largest refrigerator. In August 2010, scientists measured the coldest temperature ever recorded on earth in Antarctica's eastern highlands: about minus ninety-three degrees Celsius. That's colder than dry ice. Bacteria cannot survive in the Antarctic, so not one of us fell ill or suffered any serious ailment during our time there. The air that we breathed was completely fresh and unpolluted.

In between working, we did get some time out to visit a penguin rookery, as well as view the seals on the continental shelf. While the scientists did their experiments, we also managed to collect krill samples that we took back with us. I sent my samples to the biology laboratory at my alma mater, Doon.

We left Antarctica at the beginning of March 1988, to avoid getting caught in the freezing Southern Ocean. Colonel Ganeshan and thirteen other members of the team stayed behind to man the station through the treacherous winter months: eleven from the armed forces and three scientists. The summer party had completed its mission. The scientists had carried out systematic studies of the ozone hole, an airborne magnetic survey of over 12 000 square kilometres, and studies for long-term weather forecasting. The army had completed the maintenance of Dakshin Gangotri and laid the foundation for Maitri.

This was undoubtedly one of the greatest experiences of my life.

Despite the odds, namely adverse weather and relative isolation, we completed our mission as a team and formed lifelong friendships. Gunilla Slatis, our stewardess on the ship, knitted woollen socks and caps for my son when he was born. Dr Tariq Kureishy left the Department of Ocean Development and moved to Qatar, and we have stayed in touch ever since. Other than the close relationships with team members, the trip gave me a lot of time to think about what I wanted from life. Walking after work on the glacier, or sitting by the lake at Maitri, I realised that there was a lot more to life than my army career. When I packed my bags at Maitri, I knew that I was going to resign my commission and re-examine my purpose in life. The trip to Antarctica was indeed the turning point in my life.

We landed back in Goa on 26 March 1988. My son was born on 13 April, and two weeks later, to everyone's dismay and displeasure, I resigned my commission. My papers circulated over a variety of desks for four months, and on 28 September 1988 I was released from the Indian Army. An important part of my journey was over.

MOUNT KILIMANJARO

I had been planning a team-building exercise for my middle management at the ABN Group in Africa and for a few members from Murdoch University Dubai. After some discussions with friends and Sid, I decided to take the team up Mount Kilimanjaro. The main objective of the expedition was team building and to watch the middle management in action as leaders. Kilimanjaro is not an easy climb. It is the tallest freestanding mountain in the world at 5895 metres, and only 41 per cent of those who attempt the climb actually make it to the top. More people have died climbing Kilimanjaro than Mount Everest. Our head guide confirmed that of the 150 teams he had taken up the mountain in the last ten years, only nine had a 100 per cent success rate. We took it as our challenge to become the tenth successful team.

In mid-2012, I sent out a circular to the entire company asking for volunteers. The response was overwhelming from all departments and age groups. I set some criteria filters and selected twelve members from CNBC Africa and two from Murdoch University Dubai to accompany me. I was the oldest member of the team at fifty-four and Sid was the youngest at twenty-five. After consulting the hike operators, we decided on 11–17 March 2013, as this was the period just before the rains. I knew that if we missed this window, it was unlikely we would be able to go later in the year, due to work schedules and the general busyness of the second half of the year.

The expedition required a lot of coordination. I appointed Alexander Leibner, then group head of marketing, as the team coordinator for planning and logistics. Alex worked meticulously, arranging group meetings, budgeting, planning and implementing every tiny logistical detail from flights to personal equipment, so that we could execute the operation like clockwork.

I got the team to go on practice hikes, starting with trails in Johannesburg and culminating in an ascent of Sentinel Peak in the KwaZulu-Natal Drakensberg, which we did as an overnight trip. During these hikes, I rotated people in the marching order, to assess their strengths and weaknesses. I made the team stop every forty minutes and got them to eat, do breathing exercises and get into a routine. The average age of the team was well under thirty and they could not understand why I was asking them to take it slow. It was tough to hold back people in that age group, as they were all physically fit and raring to go.

On the last hike to Sentinel Peak, I asked the team members to bring their partners along for the overnight trip so that they could meet everyone. I also wanted to spend time with family members and give them comfort that their partners would be safe and well looked after.

Just before we set off for Kilimanjaro, I called the team to the boardroom for a review meeting to discuss the order-of-march and to assign responsibilities. Quinton Scholes, group head of sales at thirty-five and physically the fittest, was the obvious choice to lead the team. For her calmness and mental strength, I appointed Natascha Jacobsz as deputy team leader. I called Quinton to one side and gave him one clear objective: all fifteen people, without exception, had to make it to the top.

What followed was one of the most exhilarating experiences of self-discovery for each and every one of us. We flew to Moshi, Tanzania, on 10 March. After a group briefing, where we were introduced to our seven guides and team of forty-six porters and cooks, we set out on 11 March on the Rongai route. I had approved this route because it was a day longer than others and would give the team more time to acclimatise.

The routine for the first five days was quite consistent. The team had been split into "buddy pairs" to ensure that each person had someone looking out for them at all times. We progressed steadily through 2.4 KM on day one, 3.45 KM on day two, 3.68 KM on day three, 4.3 KM on day four and 4.73 KM on day five. Each day we would acclimatise by walking higher than the campsite by about 200 metres, according to the principle of "walk high and sleep low". We discovered, to our delight, that CNBC Africa anchor Samantha Loring was a yoga instructor, and so she took responsibility for making the team stretch and do breathing exercises that appeared frivolous when we started out, but became our lifeline as we climbed above 4 000 metres. The build-up for the first five days was gradual and it was heartening to see that most of the team managed to get by with little or no discomfort.

As had happened on the practice hikes, the team showed impatience with the slow pace and wanted to split up on summit night and each go at their own pace. I could see that there was some dissension in the team and that it would spell disaster. I got Quinton and some of the other team members together and reinforced the need for staying together in formation and for allowing everyone to take their time. "We are going to wait for every member and will not leave anyone on the wayside with the hope that they will catch up," I told them. I knew that we would be tested on summit night and that changing our plan would be catastrophic.

The final assault on Kilimanjaro normally starts at midnight from Kibo Hut at 4700 metres so that trekkers can view the breathtaking sunrise from the top. We started our ascent of Uhuru Peak, the highest point on Kilimanjaro, at midnight on 15/16 March, with our head-lamps providing much-needed beacons of hope as we progressed slowly but surely up the seventy-degree gradient. The temperature dipped to approximately minus seventeen degrees Celsius and the wind picked up as we crossed 5000 metres. The journey to Gilman's Point at 5700 metres took us about seven hours. We periodically stopped for comfort breaks, but we stayed together and the whole team made it to this first milestone.

At Gilman's Point, I faced perhaps the greatest test of my life. Sid had become badly affected by high-altitude pulmonary edema. He was shivering, had turned blue in the face and could not go any further. I asked the guides to check his physical parameters. They were all fine, but altitude sickness had got the better of him. I was now torn between taking the team up and turning back with my son, who was at this point extremely sick. Sid asked me to continue with the team, as there was not much I could do to help him. What he needed was to get warm and get down, fast. With a lot of uncertainty and apprehension, I took the decision to send Sid back with one of the guides and continued summiting with the team.

What I endured as a father for the next hour or so was indes-cribable. For the first time in my life I was really scared. The 195-metre journey to Uhuru Peak from Gilman's Point took approximately ninety minutes. We summited at 9:15 a.m. on 16 March. We had barely caught our breath when one of the team members shouted that Sid was coming up. I could not believe my eyes. Sid had descended with the guide, recuperated and then gathered his inner strength to turn back and start climbing again. It was my proudest moment. My son and I had both been pushed to our limits. He had been able to overcome his fatigue and sickness and put the group goal ahead of everything else, at great personal cost. For me, it had been a major decision to continue the journey and overlook my own personal need to stay with my son. In the end, it all worked out well, but I will carry with me until my dying day the emotions that I experienced that day.

At the summit, as we all wept tears of joy, it was clear that everyone in the team had achieved a personal milestone. We had all overcome fatigue in bitterly cold conditions and made it to the top. We had proved that we could do it and in doing so we had achieved a group goal. I was simply astounded at the courage and character that each member of my team had shown. The person who impressed me the most with her resilience was Svetlana Doneva, as she managed the climb without any help. After a short break at the summit, the team made its way back to Kibo Hut in three hours. It took another day and a half to reach our hotel in Moshi. The ABN team had conquered Mount Kilimanjaro and become our guides' tenth team with a 100 per cent success rate.

I was extremely gratified to see the outcomes of this effort. First and foremost, fifteen individuals went up the mountain but one family of fifteen came down. The team had not only successfully accomplished the mission, but had also formed priceless and enduring bonds of friendship, and established a deep sense of belonging, trust and renewed respect for one another's abilities. All inhibitions and apprehensions that they may have had about one another had been left behind on the mountain. Everyone had learnt that no goal is too great to accomplish if you work systematically as a team. Some of our

Kilimanjaro team members have since moved on to other careers, but I am sure that the bonds we formed on the expedition will endure forever.

EVEREST BASE CAMP AND THE NEPAL TRAGEDY

Soon after our return from Kilimanjaro, I started thinking about another adventure. Lars Jeppesen suggested a hike to Everest Base Camp and I decided to make this my next challenge. For this trip, I wanted to take sixteen people and asked for volunteers from the ABN Group and our educational vertical, TNE. Unfortunately, from a timing perspective, we just could not make it work for the ABN Group executives, so the final team was made up of nine members from TNE, including three students.

I entrusted the planning of this trip to Chris Pilgrim. As he had been on the Kilimanjaro trip in 2013, he was familiar with the planning needs. Chris is one of the most diligent and analytical people I know and spared no detail in putting together a perfect plan. He travelled to Kathmandu, Nepal, in November 2014 to meet with Mountain Monarch, the tour agency organising our logistics, and painstakingly went through the entire plan with them.

We started our preparations for the trip in January 2015, and apart from the personal-training requirements given to the individual team members to do in their own time, we organised several group treks to get to know one another and assess everyone's strengths. I accompanied the team on two practice treks in Ras al-Khaimah, which is an emirate in the UAE, located among the foothills of the Hajar Mountains. The first was to Jabal Jais, the highest point in the UAE, and the second was to Wadi Shah. Chris made the trip to Wadi Shah rather interesting. As our navigator, he took us on a wild goose chase that brought us all to the end of our endurance. We made a pledge that day to keep Chris away from navigation. These practice treks were compulsory and I had to drop two members from the final team, one for health reasons and the other for missing a training trek.

A week before we left for our Everest expedition, Chris organised a barbecue at his home for the team members and their families. It was an opportunity for everyone to meet and raise any queries they may have had, particularly around contact people and communications. The information session was useful and some of the points discussed stood us in good stead as we dealt with contingencies during the trip.

Our hike to Everest Base Camp was scheduled to start on 26 April 2015. The team travelled on different flights from Sharjah and Dubai, and we all met in Kathmandu on Saturday 25 April. I flew in from Delhi and was the last to arrive, at 10:50 a.m. No sooner had we loaded our vehicles and prepared to leave the airport parking area than, at 11:56 Nepal Standard Time, an earthquake occurred. Our vehicles began rocking from side to side; it was almost like being on a choppy ocean. At first we didn't realise what was going on, but when the rocking didn't stop and we heard people screaming and saw them running from the airport building, we realised that it was a massive earthquake.

When the tremors eventually stopped, we assessed the situation. Kathmandu airport is at a vantage point and we could see black dust billowing from various places in the city below. Early reports from the officials around us suggested that the airport was going to be closed. At this point the intensity of the earthquake and the damage was not clear, so I asked our drivers to take us to our hotel.

The journey to the hotel was extremely eventful. By this time, residents had started moving onto the streets. Dharahara Tower, the tallest building in the city, had reportedly collapsed. People were uncertain and nervous. The tremors continued at frequent intervals and in the traffic frenzy our cars got separated.

The driver of my 4x4 was young and seemed to have lost his nerve. He took us into a built-up area, parked the car in an enclosed parking lot and, without saying a word, deserted us. We never saw him again. I was with Gary Fernandes and Biju Veetil, both senior members of the TNE management. By this time, the communications network was completely clogged and we were unable to contact Chris Pilgrim and the other members of the TNE team. We were, however, able to connect intermittently with our HR manager in Dubai, Bidisha Sen. My most important mission was to let everyone's families know that we were well, and that none of us was either hurt or in any danger. Bidisha became the de facto communications centre in Dubai and played a critical role in coordinating with everyone.

At 1 p.m., Sid, who was in Johannesburg, started providing me with status updates based on what he was able to pick up from the news networks and online reports. We were told that there was another very severe quake expected at 3 p.m. Since we were stranded, Gary, Biju and I decided to find an open area close to the water canal until the next wave of tremors had passed. When the tremors hit between 3:00 and 3:45 p.m. we were prepared. At 4 p.m. we asked one of the people in a nearby garage to drive us to our hotel. Reluctantly he agreed. The journey was stressful as fallen buildings and debris blocked most of the roads leading to our destination. Kathmandu is an old city and the streets are extremely narrow. Another problem was the old, low-hanging power cables that formed part of the city's very dilapidated grid. While most of Kathmandu had lost power, there were still some main cables that burst at the nodes as we drove past. By this time, all the inhabitants had evacuated their homes and congregated on the streets. It took us an hour, but by 5 p.m. we had regrouped with the rest of the team at our hotel.

We were booked into the Tibet Guest House, but by now it was a complete mess: no electricity, visible cracks in the walls and very few employees present to help. All the guests had moved down into the lobby and small courtyard. When it started getting a bit nippy, people hesitantly returned to their rooms to collect sleeping bags and blankets in preparation for the night ahead. I assembled the team and my first goal was to make sure that everyone was calm. I gave them my overall appreciation of the facts, as I knew them to be, and urged them to stay together, no matter what. I told them that the safety of our team was the most important consideration when making any decision going forward. The team unanimously agreed that we had to abandon the trek and plan an exit strategy.

As the airport was reportedly closed, our next best option was to get transport and make our way to the Indian border and cross over to Delhi, from where we could fly to Dubai. This required visas from the Indian embassy as we had four other nationalities (Canadian, Chinese, Filipino and Egyptian) in our group. Through my family, we managed to get the details of the embassy and planned to go there at 9 a.m. the following morning.

At 6 p.m. we were told that the Indian Air Force had been mobilised and that they were deploying C-130 Hercules transport aircraft to evacuate Indian nationals. The team agreed that we were not going to evacuate piecemeal until there was a proper plan in place for each member. By now it was clear to me that I would be the last to leave. I also realised that rather than listening to rumours, a physical recce of the airport was needed so that I could decide whether our exit was going to be by air or by road.

As the evening wore on, we gathered more information from social media and family members. The extent of the damage was still not clear, but by this time we knew about the avalanche at Everest Base Camp, the devastation at the epicentre of the earthquake, which measured 7.8 on the Richter scale, and the rising number of casualties in the country. We could hear ambulance sirens and see rescue workers moving around trying to help people trapped in the worst-affected areas.

When I looked around me, I saw a tired group of team members who were emotionally drained, but who never showed a moment of weakness or despair. I determined that we needed to find a place to eat. The city had shut down, and other than small grocery stores selling water and some basic comfort foods, there was nothing open. People had understandably left their places of work and returned home to care for their families. At 7:30 p.m. we found a small restaurant that was still open. Apart from beverages, the only dish they could serve was *chow mein*. That barely warm bowl of half-cooked stir-fried noodles was perhaps the tastiest chow we had ever eaten.

Soon after dinner, Chris and Biju went to find a taxi for me to go on a recce. They returned with an old, broken-down vintage taxi that Gary and I used to go to the airport. It had started drizzling and it was really heart-wrenching to see families, particularly children, sleeping on the streets. Some people were keeping vigil and making sure that their groups were safe. At the airport, we found queues of tourists and expatriates waiting to fly out. The only flights at that time were operated by the Indian Air Force, which gave me hope that commercial airlines would soon start flying in. This was the information I needed to have a proper plan for the next day.

Saloni, in the meantime, had been in touch with all the airlines flying out from the UAE and had made tentative bookings for us on Air Arabia. After the airport recce, I asked her to confirm our tickets. She made her way down to Sharjah airport with Shweta, our administrative assistant Shaghir and my assistant Amor. By 3 a.m. Sunday morning they had secured us seats on the 10:55 p.m. flight from Kathmandu to Sharjah.

On our return from our airport recce, Gary and I were told that landslides had impacted the roads to the Indian border from Kathmandu and that bridges in some areas were unstable. Evidently driving to the Indian border was no longer a viable option. I got the team together and told them that if commercial airlines started operations the next day, our plan A was to fly out on Air Arabia. Plan B would be to fly out on an Indian Air Force aircraft. By this time we had made contact with General V.K. Singh, the former chief of the Indian Army who was leading the Indian evacuation efforts from Nepal.

We had a sleepless night. Besides several aftershocks, including another severe one at 5 a.m. on the morning of 26 April, the earlier drizzle had turned to rain and it was freezing cold. We had to move into the dining area where all the guests were packed like sardines. People were edgy, and every time a chair moved they would dart to the open courtyard. Wilbert, the cameraman on our team, took responsibility for making sure that everyone had something to eat. Despite all the commotion, Wilbert and Ahmed, one of our students, diligently took videos and interviewed people around us.

At 7 a.m. we received a princely breakfast of tea, bread and jam. It was a blessing. Then Mountain Monarch surprised us with an unusual gesture. The owner arrived and informed Chris that, other than direct costs incurred prior to the 26th, they would refund all our money as soon as the banks opened. At 9 a.m. the hotel owner came to meet us and on learning our plan offered to take us to the airport in his van. The only problem was that the van could not accommodate both the team and its luggage. As we had over twelve hours before our expected departure, I asked him to take our baggage to a safe location near the airport, with our travel agent's assurance that he would be able to get it to the airport by 7 p.m. That being arranged, the team started its trek to the airport on foot.

We decided not to walk through any built-up areas, because many of the buildings were unstable. We found a city map and planned our route: we would travel approximately twenty kilometres along the perimeter water canal and then cross onto the wide main road leading to the airport. The walk was an eye-opener, as we saw first-hand the extent of the damage and the displacement of people. The open areas were completely packed and temporary shelters made from tarpaulin and plastic materials had been established to house people for what appeared to be an indefinite period. In some areas, we saw dead bodies being pulled from the wreckage. These sights filled us with remorse. It could easily have been any one of us. Walking in largely open areas we were finally able to use our satellite phone. I made sure that everyone had a chance to speak to their families to assure them that we were safe.

We finally made it to the airport after a six-hour march, during which another severe aftershock hit at around 1 p.m. At the airport, we joined the multitude of people waiting in line to board various commercial aircraft. The airport had been shut down again and we had no idea if we would be able to fly out. Saloni stayed in close contact with the airline and at 6:30 p.m. she told us that the flight to Kathmandu had taken off from Sharjah. Hope was once again revived. We checked in at 9 p.m. with our luggage, but it was clear from the chaos and the lack of any tracking and staff that the baggage was not going to be loaded. We boarded at 1 a.m. and took off an hour later to the cheers of exhausted passengers. For us, the ordeal was over. The sight of our families bearing hot coffee and muffins at the Sharjah airport in the early hours of the morning more than made up for our lost baggage. (Despite giving up all hope, our luggage miraculously turned up a few days later.)

The Nepal earthquake taught us many lessons, the first being man's total helplessness before nature. No government or emergency service can ever be prepared for such colossal damage and destruction. It becomes even more difficult when the country is poor and does not have the resources to react efficiently. Having one operational airfield is a major shortcoming and in Nepal it created a bottleneck, hampering relief efforts. Flights had to be diverted as they could not land and much-needed help could not get to the people in time. We learnt first-hand that the most important need in such emergencies is communications. In a crisis, it is imperative that the flow of information is accurate and continuous, so that rumour-mongering is prevented. We also learnt that humanitarian assistance at such times comes from your neighbours; the Indian government played a vital role in evacuation, provided supplies and helped save thousands of lives. As an Indian, I was proud of my native country's response. Other countries, too, were quick to support the Nepalese government and help out wherever they could.

The effects of the 2015 Nepal earthquake were catastrophic. Towns were razed to the ground and the final death toll was just short of 9 000. Over 22 000 people were injured and six million were displaced. The avalanche triggered on Mount Everest killed at least twenty-two people, making it the deadliest day on the mountain in history. In the immediate aftermath, there was no food, water, power, sanitation and basic hygiene. The likelihood of diseases spreading not only across Nepal but also into India was extremely high. Nepal relies largely on tourism; it is an important source of revenue and employs many people. The effects of the earthquake severely impacted this sector. The country required billions of dollars in aid.

For me personally this experience was a reality check. We often believe we are invincible; the truth is that we are not. I was just happy that I could bring all members of my team back safely. I would not have been able to live with myself if anything untoward had happened. Our team members in Dubai and our families stepped up to the plate and played a crucial role in boosting our morale. We went to Nepal on a team-building exercise; nothing could have prepared us for the real-life catastrophe that brought out the best in each of us and brought us together as a family. Our experience inspired us to contribute funds to relieve the suffering of the Nepali people. We were also amazed by the integrity of our tour company, Mountain Monarch, for willingly offering to refund all our money. While a refund was the last thing on our minds, the gesture left us with very positive feelings towards the people of that great country.

* * *

Adventures help put life in perspective, particularly if they are eventful. My three major expeditions taught me a lot. Whether it was the ordeal at sea in the Roaring Forties, the blizzard in Antarctica, the fire in our porta-cabin, summit night on Mount Kilimanjaro or the earthquake in Nepal, each experience brought me closer to the belief that we are all vulnerable to things that are beyond our control, and that the only way we can overcome adversity is through our interdependence with others. When the chips are down and you are faced with life-threatening challenges, it is the belief and support of the people around you that will see you through. I have been blessed to have the right people with me throughout my life, making my journey an absolute pleasure.

9

BUILDING A LEGACY

During the course of our lives, it is through our actions that we build our legacy. From great leaders like Mahatma Gandhi, Nelson Mandela and Abraham Lincoln to our own relatives, there are those people who leave a lasting impression on us. We remember them usually for their bravery, dedication, sacrifice and selfless devotion in the service of others. Seldom do we remember people for the money or material assets that they accumulated during their lifetime.

In the last few years, I have visited a number of institutions of learning in Europe, including Lancaster University in the UK, the University of Aberdeen in Scotland and Charles University in the Czech Republic. While Lancaster is still relatively young, Aberdeen dates back to 1495 and Charles University to 1348. These incredible institutions have endured because of the vision of their founders, who continue to touch the lives of students 600 years after their passing. Such institutions are beacons of knowledge and learning that attract the best minds from around the world, uniting and nurturing them so that they may continue carrying the baton of excellence for future generations. This is what legacy is all about.

Growing up, I drew lessons from people with whom I associated personally and professionally. Throughout this book, I have mentioned those who have been part of my universe and whose values have made an impression on me in some way. The legacy that affects us the most is that of our parents. Through their teachings, they lay the foundation for our character. My parents were my superstars; they always strove to do right and they were paragons of virtue. Cherish your relationship with your parents for as long as they are with you, because this will be the most meaningful bond in terms of defining who you are.

To my mind, the next most important connection you form is with your own family, starting with the partner you choose and extending to your children and grandchildren. You transcend to a different level of existence when you decide to share your life with someone and start making sacrifices and healthy compromises to accommodate each other. The journey with your partner will be a pleasure if she or he is also your most trusted friend. This is a goal worth working hard to achieve. The journey with the children you raise together is your greatest legacy. It is your children that make you immortal. The lessons you teach them and the values they embrace will determine how they will remember you. That is your true wealth.

It does not matter what vocation you choose. You do not have to be a successful businessperson to leave a legacy. You could be a piano or guitar teacher, or work for a non-profit organisation, and leave an equally meaningful legacy. You are not defined by what you accumulate for yourself, but by the impact you have on the lives of others. Make each interaction count. Create interdependence with other human beings and contribute to their lives as much as possible. Show genuine concern for those around you. Be honest in your dealings with people, and build trust and personal credibility. Make your word mean something.

If you become an entrepreneur or rise to great heights in your chosen profession, then learn to give back. Work hard and tirelessly to achieve your goals. Choose your teams well, and develop leaders around you, as there is no greater achievement for a leader than to cultivate future leaders who can build on his or her legacy. Make room below you for people to grow, so that they can achieve their own dreams. Once you have achieved your dreams, devote your energy to giving back to those less fortunate. Over the years, as a family we have been able to give back in small but meaningful ways and make a difference in the lives of others. You will only feel the satisfaction and joy of giving back when you see those who have benefited from your engagement rise and build legacies of their own. Even if you only make a material difference to one other person during your lifetime, you have done well and created a legacy for yourself.

I left the military in 1988 with the responsibility of a young family, armed with the foundation for a strong value system, and with 17 000 rupees in my bank account. I did not know where I was headed at the time, but I knew that hard work and patience were integral to success, and I never faltered in this belief. I did not shy away from trying new things, taking risks, doing things differently or looking for new opportunities. I ventured into new markets and embraced the idea that the world was collapsing into a unified economic zone, and that people, material and capital would become commodities chasing good ideas. More than anything else, I lived my life fearlessly. I never accepted the status quo or compromised my value system, sometimes to my own cost and discomfort. Instead I pursued a path that I believed to be right. The journey of the last twenty-eight years has been one of self-discovery and of creating interdependence with people I've met along the way.

Through my near-fatal accident in 1981, I learnt that we cannot take life for granted. Make each moment count. If you want to achieve something, then go out and achieve it fearlessly, but keep to the ethical standards for which you want to be remembered. Define the values that represent you and, like a lion, live by them. Do not negotiate or make compromises when it comes to those values that define your existence. You are not born thinking about your legacy. Your legacy is formed through a lifetime of consistent actions. People will remember you for the good you did and for the way in which you touched their lives.

My commitment has always been 100 per cent. Through the alignment of hard work, opportunity, good people around me, the support of my family and a lot of luck, I have built an organisation with a footprint in over twenty countries. I have traversed the army, trading, investment banking, private equity, media, IT and education. And my journey is far from over. If I could do it, then so too can you.

ACKNOWLEDGEMENTS

I would like to acknowledge and thank the following people without whose help I would not have been able to publish this book.

Writing *Be a Lion* was no easy task given my business and travel commitments. Writing an autobiography requires a lot of introspection when your goal is to convey your experiences in a meaningful manner. It took me three months over a period of three years to complete this task.

My gratitude first and foremost to my wife, Saloni. Knowing my need for solitude and cold weather, she selected the best venues for me to write undisturbed: Montreux on Lake Geneva, Switzerland, in December/January 2013/14; Edinburgh, Scotland, in December/January 2014/15; and finally Prague, Czech Republic, in December/January 2015/16. Each setting was truly inspirational. Saloni and I would take walks during which we would discuss events so that I did not miss anything important. She would then critique and ponder the various drafts to make sure that I got everything chronologically and factually correct.

My gratitude to my children, Sid and Shweta, for their patience as I encroached on their holiday time and forced them to comment on stories that they had heard a million times before. Sid's technological know-how was particularly invaluable in helping to prepare the book for electronic distribution, and Shweta's creative input when it came to designing the book's cover was priceless.

The first edit was done in 2015 by Professor Dilip Menon, director of the Centre for Indian Studies in Africa at the University of the Witwatersrand. Dr John Grainger, provost at Lancaster University Ghana, tackled the second in 2016. My gratitude to them both.

I would also like to thank my two assistants, Amor Roksa in Dubai and Celeste Meidecen in Johannesburg, for their priceless help with logistics and collating photographs.

And finally, my gratitude to Penguin Random House South Africa for publishing *Be a Lion*, with special thanks to commissioning editor Melt Myburg, senior editor Bronwen Maynier and designer Ryan Africa for their help in editing and compiling the book.

TESTIMONIALS

As I read through the draft of *Be a Lion*, I couldn't decide whether to haul up Rakesh Wahi for revealing the truth of my coarse behaviour or to be pleased that he considered me an influence on his life and for his magnanimous words on my qualities of leadership. True to his nature, he calls a spade a spade and is unsparing in crediting the positive contribution of others, be they his seniors, colleagues or juniors.

Be a Lion makes for interesting reading and one can't help admire a man who started life as a soldier and dared to venture into the mystifying worlds of trading, finance and education, and then made a success of all he delved into.

As a youngster he must have been bewildered on meeting his first company commander – me – a sand-covered, wild-eyed and bushy-moustachioed man ordering him to arrange the funeral of a soldier who had been killed. But he took it in his stride. Later, during the classified task, he was loved by the men for being in the front. Sub-alterns were to be seen, not heard – that was the golden maxim in the army. But Rakesh Wahi didn't hesitate to state politely his views on the methods used and suggest changes. Naturally this made me see red, but I had to agree with his suggestions, as they were sensible. His greatest quality was his courage in rejoining the task and requesting his old position after his near-death experience.

I followed him to Antarctica and could see the efforts put in by Rakesh and his team in the initial foundation work on the icy continent. It made it easier for me and my team to construct the Indian Antarctic station, Maitri, much against the scepticisms of the neighbouring Russian station Novolazarevskaya and the then East German station, Georg Forster.

This book will be a valuable read for all those who want to learn what true leadership is and what it is like daring to venture into the unknown.

I am proud of him and wish the Lion many more successes in his business and personal life.

COLONEL S. JAGANNATHAN (RETD)
NEW DELHI, INDIA, 2016

From the deserts of Rajasthan to the Indian base in Antarctica, Rakesh Wahi's life journey has led him on an incredible adventure. With the twists and turns of a thriller, *Be a Lion* invites the reader to accompany Rakesh on his path to becoming a highly successful international entrepreneur.

The strong values instilled in him by his parents in India, and a career in the Indian Army where he received one of India's highest military award, provided the foundations for his determination, perseverance and skills, which allowed him not only to survive, but also to thrive in a variety of challenging places and situations. His career has involved some hard lessons, ranging from the "wheeling and dealing" post–Soviet Union era to the frontier days in Dubai. He has learnt many valuable lessons, which are conveyed in this exciting book.

Rakesh's adventures and exploits are worthy of a page-turner. However, the most beneficial aspect of this book is his well-thought-out, systematically organised approach to imparting the valuable knowledge, insight and advice that every entrepreneur should know: the values of sacrifice, patience, determination and team building are all presented through meaningful stories.

Be a Lion is an exciting read that not only discusses the essentials of entrepreneurship, but also presents them in an entertaining way through the author's life and personal experiences, as well as his philosophy. Do not miss an opportunity to follow Rakesh through both success and failure, and the colourful stories and characters encountered along the way. From leading a team to the peak of Kilimanjaro to building Africa's most successful business news network, you will enjoy his story. I'm grateful to have been along for part of the ride.

RICK MICHAELS

TAMPA, FLORIDA, USA, 2016

I have known Rakesh Wahi for the better part of a quarter of a century, and since our first meeting on the Dubai waterfront in the early 1990s I have watched with deep admiration his amazing journey from a one-man trading business to developing and leading an international media and education conglomerate spanning two continents. Armed with an impeccable business instinct, raw intellect and a willingness to put in gruelling work hours, Rakesh is an inspiration to us all, and proof that the entrepreneurial dream is alive and achievable.

Be a Lion details the many twists and turns in Rakesh's remarkable career. His exploits in the Indian Army alone – from the extreme heat of the Rajasthan desert to the frozen continent of Antarctica; from being declared clinically dead following an accident to being awarded the Vishisht Seva Medal by the president of India – could fill a book, but this is merely the starting point. Rakesh's career only began when he left the army and *Be a Lion* takes the reader through his humble beginnings in Dubai and the "wild East" of post-Soviet Russia, to the emerging markets of Africa and Asia.

What makes *Be a Lion* particularly interesting is the perspective and lessons learnt that Rakesh draws on from his multifaceted career. The book demonstrates through examples how he skilfully applied each lesson or observation, as enlightening or as painful as it may have been, to the next set of challenges that he encountered. In the process, Rakesh articulates what it takes to be a successful entrepreneur, and which core values are required. Loyalty, focus, trust and perseverance are repeatedly illustrated with real-life examples. Whether drawn from his many successes or occasional failures, Rakesh's lessons, values and leadership philosophy are universally applicable and fundamental to becoming a good manager and entrepreneur in today's world.

I'm privileged to have had a front-row seat to much of Rakesh's remarkable career and I'm proud to call him my friend. I have no doubt that the past quarter of a century was merely a warm-up act to what he will achieve in the decades to come.

CARSTEN PHILIPSON
WASHINGTON, DC, USA, 2016